CALGARY PUBLIC LIBRARY

DEC — — 2011

*For Geoffrey, David, and Jane*

*with all my love*

# Contents

# Preface

This book was written for my sons. Because I owe them an explanation.

They were brought up as Christians. But in the spirit of this book, their upbringing was in the *doing* of religion more than in talking *about* the doing. Their religious education was in liturgy, music, choir practice, daily prayers, and weekly worship. Sometimes many times a week.

That is not a bad form of religious education. In fact, it may be the best. But it is not enough. At some point (as I will discuss in the Introduction), it becomes necessary to talk about the ideas and experience that lie behind religious practice.

Our family is the same as many others in the contemporary Western world. Perhaps reflecting the bias of our secular culture, we have not found it easy to talk about the adult meaning of our religious life. But I have been lucky enough to have such conversations with my sons, as they grew older. In fact, this book owes its origin, at least in part, to one such conversation over a lively dinner whose insights and affectionate spirit owed at least something (in the tradition of Plato's *Symposium*) to a good Bordeaux. "You know, Dad," my son concluded, perhaps finally eager to change the subject, "you should write a book."

I have chosen to regard his suggestion as an invitation I could not refuse. Because I owe it to him and to his brother to set down why they were raised in a religious tradition, and what that means, at least for their parents. This book is therefore partly in the nature of an *apologia*, explaining what is past, and why it occurred.

※

Although this book was written for my sons, now that it is finished (if books like this one can ever be "finished"; Northrop Frye rightly said – echoing Valéry – that books are never finished, they are merely abandoned) I realize that I have also been writing it all my life. The basis of its argument – especially the first chapters – was already set out forty years ago, and developed over the following decade.[1] The argument of chapter 12, for example, may seem present-minded but was already anticipated as long ago as 1974.[2]

Over such a long period I have acquired many debts. My first thanks must be to Tom Symons and Denis Smith. Tom's vision and Denis' leadership gave me my first opportunity to develop a writer's voice and to try out the ideas that are the starting point of this book. Later, David R. Cameron and John Wadland were editorial colleagues and friends. David's elegant prose has always offered a model for me to aim at. He read the initial draft of this book and gave friendly support for it.

Kenneth Windsor first put to me the questions that led to the ideas presented here. I have never stopped thinking about them over the more than forty-five intervening years, and I honour his memory. Alan Toff introduced me to the works of R.G. Collingwood in those years when I was learning how to think, and Ted Chamberlin did the same for Susanne Langer and Ernst Cassirer. By what he was as much as by what he said, Michael Treadwell helped me to consider that there might be virtues of reverence. He was a model of intellectual energy and integrity allied to manly grace and deep generosity of spirit. His early death was an inexpressible loss to many. The death of my dear friend Ian Chapman was another enormous loss. His life showed in deeds rather than words that, before it can become anything else, faith is something to do rather than to have. I miss him more than I can say.

I am grateful to the clergy and people of Christ Church Cathedral (Anglican) of Ottawa, which has been my spiritual home for forty years. I must especially acknowledge my debt to the Reverend Canon Peter J. Smith, former canon residentiary of the Cathedral, whose gifted preaching and spiritual example were deeply meaningful to me and to many other fortunate parishioners. I owe another special debt to the distinguished musicians who have served as organists and choir directors at the Cathedral during that time: Dr Godfrey Hewitt, Frances Macdonnell, Matthew Larkin, and Timothy Piper. Their inspired musical ministry has been at the centre of my spiritual life – and that of my family – through four decades.

Much earlier, Birnie Hodgetts helped me to encounter the spirit in nature, especially in the beauty of the Georgian Bay he taught so many to love. The west wind shaped the pine tree of my life, just as Birnie said it would.

Philip Cercone and the staff of McGill-Queen's University Press welcomed my book proposal and provided helpful support through the publication process. The readers' reports for the press were models of constructive peer review and helped save me from several serious errors of expression. Susan Glickman was a sensitive, discerning editor.

Heather and Jim Steele both read the first draft of this book. Heather gave it the benefit of her impeccable editorial eye, and Jim suggested several new sources. André Burelle, Barbara Campbell, Ramsay Derry, and Graham Fraser also read drafts and gave warm encouragement which was deeply appreciated. With André I have the honour to share a longstanding interest in the thought of Étienne Gilson. He also introduced me to the work of the estimable Father Geiger, the "master" to whom Gilson claimed to be only an "apprentice." From the perspective of a young adult reader, Mark Ruban gave the first draft one of its most thorough and searching readings. His honest criticism and suggestions for revision and restructuring were immensely valuable.

My fellow pilgrims, Tony Campbell and John Fraser, both read the first draft. John gave friendly encouragement – in the most sincere way: by quoting from the draft in his own work – and advice about potential avenues to publication. With his usual candour, Tony made many detailed comments and suggested several works I might otherwise have missed. I have cherished their companionship in spiritual dialogue for many years.

Stephen Bonnycastle has been another indispensable companion in dialogue and discovery for over fifty years. He it was who introduced me forty years ago, for example, to the prose of Samuel Taylor Coleridge. As I hope this book makes clear, I believe Coleridge merits even wider recognition not just as one of the greatest poets of the English language but as one of the greatest thinkers in any language. Stephen's mind and friendship are pole stars in my universe.

✳

I dedicate this book, informally, to my godchildren, both official and unofficial: Mary, Ryerson, and Jeffrey Symons; Jessie Fraser; Eric

Campbell; Nicholas Butler; Nora Fleury; and Jessica Wilson. I hope they will receive it in the spirit of friendship and in lieu of all the other things I may have left undone.

I also dedicate this book to the memory of my parents. It is uncertain whether they would have agreed with much in it. But their example – especially the example of their marriage – taught me most of what I have tried to say, much less eloquently, here.

This book is formally dedicated to my sons, Geoffrey and David, for whom it was written. May they find in it not just explanation and *apologia* but also a manifestation of their parents' love. The gift of their presence in our lives is precious to us beyond expression.

The book is also dedicated to their wonderful mother. She was the one who brought me to the Anglican tradition, and our shared spiritual journey has been one of the growing bonds of a lifelong friendship. Publication of this book happily coincides with the fortieth anniversary of our marriage. But she has been the centre of my existence for longer than that. Her sudden appearance in my life on a sunny August day in 1966 changed everything, including my understanding of what is possible in a life. It was an unexpected and undeserved miracle, a true epiphany. And I do not cease to give thanks for it.

Ralph Heintzman
Chenodin, Sans Souci
The Georgian Bay, Ontario
Thanksgiving, 2010

## REDISCOVERING REVERENCE

How got the Atheist his Idea of that God he denies?

Samuel Taylor Coleridge, *Notebooks*[3]

Construire une métaphysique sur la présence en nous de l'idée de Dieu demeure donc une entreprise toujours légitime, pourvu qu'elle ne se pose pas comme une déduction *a priori* à partir de Dieu, mais comme une induction *a posteriori* à partir du contenu de l'idée que nous avons de lui.

Étienne Gilson, *L'Esprit de la philosophie médiévale*[4]

"Funny," said Lancelot, "how the people who can't pray say that prayers are not answered, however much the people who can pray say they are."

T.H. White, *The Once and Future King*[5]

Virtue and honour will not be banished from the world, however many popular moralists and panicky journalists say so ... Nor do I think love as a high condition of honour will be lost; it is a pattern in the spirit, and people long to make the pattern a reality in their lives, whatever means they take to do so. In short, Davey, God is not dead. And I can assure you God is not mocked.

Robertson Davies, *The Manticore*[6]

# Introduction

This book aims to give a rational explanation of what the modern Western[1] world calls "religion." In doing so, I will call into question our evolving use of that word over the last five or six centuries. But I will also try to explain the ideas and experience that lie behind religious practice in words that might be meaningful to today's readers.

This is not meant to imply that the ideas are the inner reality, and the religious practice merely the outer form or shell of that reality. Quite the contrary, as this book will argue. But there comes a time to turn what we *do* in our religious life into rational concepts, if only to answer the question, "Why?"

For religious persons, the "why" question is normally answered, if at all, by religious life itself. If a religious life doesn't bring its own justification – if we could imagine living a full life other than as religious persons – then no amount of rationalization will help. But this is only true for adults who already live and know a life of sincere religious practice. There are others who stand on the threshold of faith. They may be young people who have been raised in a household of regular religious practice, but who hesitate to commit to such a life as they grow older. Or they may be adults dissatisfied by a life lived without nourishment for the spirit and hungry for something more, wanting to know whether it would be reasonable for them to explore a religious life once again, or for the first time. And, for them, a rational answer to the question "why" is important.

It's especially important in a secular age. In a secular culture like ours, intellectual and media opinion is overwhelmingly sceptical about religion in all its forms. This creates an initial barrier, even for enquiring minds or thirsty souls. A rational account of religion is needed to lower this barrier in an age that claims to worship only reason (though much of the evidence is to the contrary). That's the objective of this book: not to persuade those who have no wish to be persuaded, but to remove some obstacles for those who have already begun to search.

In any age, secular or not, offering a rational account of religious life is important even for persons of religious faith and practice, because religion, like anything else, must meet the test of reason. Not that reason stands higher in some kind of hierarchy and judges religious claims from a superior vantage point. If anything, it's the reverse. But regardless of their relative standing, reason, like religion, is one of the highest expressions of the human spirit. And nothing that is fully human can fail to meet the claims of both.[2]

Meeting the claims of reason is part of what it means to have an adult faith. A child's faith doesn't yet have to meet this test. And journeying over the treacherous mountain pass from childhood to adult faith means meeting and undergoing the trials of reason along the way. In our culture, most don't make it to the other side of the mountain.

*

In taking up this challenge, I'm conscious of several problems, or obstacles to success. The first is the inherent contradiction of attempting to give a rational account of something that, by definition, goes beyond the rational. Not something *irrational* but something that inhabits a larger space than human reason alone. Reason is necessary, as I just said, but it isn't sufficient for the fullest expression of the human spirit. This puts limits on what can be done. It means that the objective can't be fully accomplished. The so-called "proofs" of the existence of God, for example, convince no one except those who are already convinced.

No matter how hard we try, we can never give a purely rational account of religion: one that would be convincing to a disinterested bystander on rational grounds alone. There are at least two reasons for this. The first is the very fact of being disinterested. Religious life engages the heart and the will. It grows from experience and need; not, in the first instance, from logic and "objective" evidence – though there is plenty of that once you get going.[3] A life of religious practice is an answer to a question. If the question is not already a sincere one, and deeply felt, the answer, in a secular world, will be irrelevant at best, preposterous or even threatening at worst.

Another reason a fully rational account of religion cannot, in the end, be given is the very fact I just mentioned, that religious insight *includes* reason but also points beyond what can be known by reason alone. Religious practice is a human response to the profound mysteries that surround and inhabit human life: the mysteries of life and death, and suffering and evil, and meaning and, above all, existence itself. To these questions, philosophy, science, and human reason have not, historically, been able to provide fully satisfying answers, on their own, though they are precious allies. Religious life embraces and explores these mysteries of human life, drawing on them, as from a deep well, to illuminate and ennoble life, and to provide the foundation from which thought can do its best work. But since religion includes reason but goes beyond it, you cannot give a fully rational account of the first, any more than you can give a fully rational account of music or of art. If you could fully translate the one into the other, you would have no need of it in the first place. So there will always be a gulf of some kind between them. What can help to bridge or, rather, to leap over that gulf is one of the subjects of this book.

A second obstacle is the gap between the tools and the job. I want, as far as possible, to give an account of religious life in general, not of one religious tradition in particular. But my own experience, for what it's worth, is of Christianity. My knowledge of other religious traditions is necessarily more limited and obviously not first-hand. So I sometimes have to generalize from the particular. Many of my examples and illustrations will be drawn from Christian sources. But I hope you will find they serve to illustrate something more.

A third difficulty is the problem of language. In a discussion of religion, especially one that aims to give a rational account of it, language is a barrier at many levels. First of all, there's a specialized, technical language of thought itself, which is immensely useful to professional thinkers like academic philosophers, but can be a barrier for other people. Since my purpose has been to write a book for those other readers, especially young ones, I've tried as much as possible to avoid using philosophical words – words like *epistemology, ontology, transcendental* or *teleological* – splendid and invaluable though they are in other contexts. I have not entirely succeeded. But I've tried as far as possible to translate ideas into everyday language that can more easily be understood.

In a discussion of religion, the question of "translation" arises at an even deeper level, because religion has its own specialised language. In fact, at one level, and with some exaggeration, it might almost be said that religion *is* a form of language. It's a way of *talking* about the world and about life as they are really experienced, beyond the prejudices of the modern, secular world. This works fine from the inside. But the language of religion can be a barrier for those on the outside. One of the objectives of this book, therefore, has been to find a way to translate the insights and truths of religious experience into language that might be meaningful to people, especially young people, of today.

✳

One way to approach this book is in three parts.

The first six chapters introduce you to some of the realities behind words like "religion" and "faith." They do this by starting from everyday experiences and then moving gradually beyond them, step-by-step, to show how a religious life develops out of them, or is related to them. These chapters challenge some current assumptions about religion, and invite you to re-think them in the light of your own experience. Religion may not be what you think it is. It may turn out instead to be a developed form of something else you already know well.

Chapters 7 to 9 build on the groundwork of the first six chapters to explore some key issues and features of religious life in greater depth. These three chapters refer more frequently to some of history's major spiritual texts and thinkers. I've tried to do this in plain language so that you can follow the arguments without any special background or preparation. But if you're strongly allergic to abstract thinking, you could, if necessary, jump over these three chapters. However, I should warn you that they are in some ways the heart of the book, from which the first and third sections draw much of their fuel. So if you decide to skip over them, you may want to come back to them later, after you've finished the third part of the book.

Chapters 10 to 14 apply the insights and arguments of the first two sections to a series of current practical challenges. Chapters 11 to 13 are about today's world and problems like climate change, religious conflict, and the relationship between secular and religious outlooks. Chapters 10 and 14 are about you, and about your life. About the difficult transition from childhood to adult faith, and why so many people in the modern world don't make it. And about the big question we all face: how to live with dignity and fulfilment in a secular world.

These last five chapters are an important part of the book, because they're about our own lives. And that, as I said, is what religion is also about. If there's a key argument that runs through this book, it's simply that religion is neither an escape from life nor an abstract framework of beliefs that is arbitrarily imposed upon it. It's a way of living, something you *do* – and, to a degree, can't help doing – something that emerges from humankind's deepest and most authentic experience of life itself. An experience that extends back over thousands of years. But also an experience each one of us has, in our own life, if only we have the eyes to see it. Or ears to hear.

✳

Describing human experience the way I've tried to in this book, I may sometimes sound more certain than I really am. So it's important to state, right at the beginning, that everything in it is open to question, to doubt, and to correction, including by myself. In fact, as you will discover, doubt is an important feature of a true religious life.

Like any book, this one can only be an interim report on my experience and reflection so far, at this point in my own journey. It's where I've reached, in my own internal dialogue. Fortunately, it's also a report on the human journey and the wider dialogue that have been going on for the last three thousand years, so you don't have to rely on my understanding alone. And the journey continues, with more learning all the time, learning that normally occurs in the same kind of dialogue: a process of question and answer, an exchange between different points of view, or different insights, and different voices. We can call this kind of dialogue a conversation. And the best kinds of conversation are those that take place between friends, or between different perspectives that see how much they need each other – and therefore how much they need to listen carefully to each other – and how much the conversation itself changes them both, for the better. As we will see in chapter 1, this kind of conversation takes place in our families, in our communities and societies, but also (and perhaps most importantly) in our own minds and hearts.

So you're invited not to listen to a lecture or to a sermon, but to participate in a conversation: a conversation that began long ago, and will never end. A conversation in which you have your own part to play, and on which your own life may depend. A conversation that – if you listen carefully – has probably already begun, in your own heart.

# I

# The Human Paradox

Let's begin at the beginning. That is to say: where our own lives begin.

✳

Every human being has the experience of growing up in a community, usually in some kind of family. We don't choose our families, but the experience of growing up in them marks us for life.

Some of the ways are obvious. Language, for example. We learn our first language from our families, and it becomes the filter through which we learn about the world, shaping all our understandings. We can't understand or express things except in the ways our language will allow. In this sense, we don't control it. It controls us. As German philosopher Hans-Georg Gadamer (1900–2002) said, "it is literally more correct to say that language speaks us, rather than we speak it."[1]

Language is only one of the many ways in which our families shape the persons we will become. The Canadian novelist Hugh Hood (1928–2000) expresses some of the other ways our families mould us and our outlook, beginning long before the moment of our birth:

> Genetics and family inheritance – your mother's eyes, your father's sandy hair – don't explain, don't add up to you. There is a much wider matrix of memory and fantasy – the mere sense of being – which you bring with you to this world, even though you didn't witness it in your own flesh, but simply found around you in the world when you woke. Your present when you are an infant isn't simply what

happened since you saw the light. No! No! It is what your parents are feeling and thinking and talking about, what your family has been experiencing for an indefinite time past, what the people of your country have evolved as their national character and culture ... which is part of your presence as soon as you possess 'your experience.' It is a complex fate to be anybody.[2]

To deepen our understanding of this broader way in which we're shaped by our families and surrounding communities, let's consider the question of language a bit further, from the point of view suggested by Hood when he refers to the fact that we enter a world created by what our parents and families are "talking about." It's not just the fact that our families give us the language (i.e. the words) through which we come to understand and express the reality around us. It's that we *use* these words in our families and communities, and we develop our understanding of the world and of ourselves, both in childhood and beyond, through an ongoing process of *conversation*.

Remember the ways you first began to understand the world, sitting on your mother's lap, reading a picture book, or talking about the scene around you. Or playing with your first friends in the backyard. These conversations were essential steps to becoming the person you are today. A person deprived of such conversations wouldn't learn to be a person at all. Because they would never have been part of the ongoing human conversation.

This conversation is ongoing in more ways than one. It is ongoing throughout our own lives, of course. But as Hood suggests, the conversation was going on long before we were born and will continue long after we die. As children we enter into a conversation that has already started, and that's the context in which we develop our sense of ourselves and of the world. We join the conversation. And it is by joining the conversation that we become who we are.

Of course we eventually learn to carry on this process – the process of dialogue, of question and answer – in our own minds. That's what it means to be thoughtful adults. But we never grow beyond the need to be part of a wider conversation, in our families, communities, and professions. Someone who defiantly cut herself off from all conversation with a surrounding community would have no way of verifying whether her thoughts were connected with the real world, and would in all likelihood begin to exhibit some pathology that made her less than a fully adult human. A definition of sanity might well be the ability to participate effectively in the ongoing conversation of your family and community.[3]

✳

So when we begin to think about what it means to be human, we can't think about ourselves without also thinking about the family life and environment that made us who we are, even when we reject them or move beyond them. And as soon as we recognize this fact, it starts to draw our attention to something even deeper than the language, the habits, the culture, the prejudices, or even the religion our families gave us. The experience of family life points our attention to something deeper than these: something that not only shapes our human experience, but also reflects the fundamental structure of the world itself.

We begin to grasp this deeper reality as soon as we see there are at least *two* things to think about, not one. Not just the individuals we are, but also the wider family and communities in which we live, and grow, and find meaning. These two go together. They cannot be disentangled. You can't have individuals without family or community. You can't have family or community without individuals. They are inseparable.

But they're also often in conflict. If we know anything about families, we know that. The joys of living in our families are at least equally balanced by the pain and the frustration, the many ways in which our families seem to restrict or limit us, the way they often refuse to respond as we would wish to our deepest desires. We struggle and even fight with our families just as much as we love them, and the love and the conflict go together. Families are the sum of both.

This kind of basic contradiction you can't get rid of is called a *paradox*. In a paradox (or in philosophical language, a "dialectic"), two opposites are joined together in an unbreakable partnership. Though they seem to be in conflict, you can't have one without the other.

The paradox of family life is well reflected in many traditional sayings or proverbs that contradict each other. "Honour thy father and thy mother," for example, is a good precept (at least fathers and mothers think so!), but it is balanced and contradicted by other ancient sayings, such as that a man shall "leave his father and mother and cleave unto his wife."[4] Both may be good counsel, but they are in tension with each other, at the very least.

We could repeat this exercise over and over again: in fact, as long ago as 1605, the great English philosopher and statesman, Francis Bacon (1561–1626), did exactly that. In one of his books, he included an appendix which listed commonplace maxims arranged in contrasting pairs. For almost any proverb, he demonstrated, as many people have since, there is an equal and opposite saying of traditional wisdom that contradicts it. And, though they *contradict* each other, both are *true*.[5]

How can this be?

Part of the answer is that many of these contradictory truths reveal a tension or conflict at the very heart of human life. On the one hand, we are individuals who need to assert ourselves *against* our families and surrounding environment in order to grow and develop, and sometimes even to survive. But, at the same time, we are *part* of that wider environment, and can't escape it, no matter how hard we try. The assertive individuals we are have been created by our families and our communities, and we depend on them for many things, not only in our early years, but all through our lives. As the American political scientist James Q. Wilson (b. 1931) remarks, human beings "are not born into a state of nature. They are born into a social compact that has long preceded them and without which their survival would not have been possible."[6] We can only assert ourselves as autonomous individuals in the context of our *involvement* with the world around us. And this very process of self-assertion (or what some psychologists and philosophers call "individuation") usually leads, surprisingly, to new forms of involvement. This is true of biological life.[7] But it's equally true of human life. Think of a teenager, for example, who rebels against his family, only to fall into the even closer embrace of a peer group, or gang. Or the more positive example of a young person who leaves his or her family, only to found a family of their own.

A human being who did nothing but assert his or her own needs and wishes would be little better than a brute. What makes us most fully human – that is, what makes us most fully *ourselves* – turns out, paradoxically, to be what connects us to *others*, and to the wider universe.[8]

This contradictory or paradoxical character of human reality has been expressed by Irvin Yalom (b. 1931), an American psychotherapist, who notes that human life is defined by a necessary relationship (a "dialectic") between "two diametrically opposed responses to the human situation": "The human being either asserts autonomy by heroic self-assertion or seeks safety through fusing with a superior force: that is, one either emerges or merges, separates or embeds."[9] Marcel Gauchet (b. 1946), a French philosopher/historian, finds this same paradox throughout the history of humankind. Human history and culture are shaped, he argues, by two "founding dimensions" or "basic possibilities," a "primeval double-sidedness": either "submission to an order ... determined before and outside our wills" or assertion of "an order accepted as originating in the will of individuals."[10]

Actually, this paradox is built right into the basic structure of the universe. Everything, human or *non*-human, is the *individual* thing that it is, yet, at the same time, is connected to everything else, and can only be the thing that it is as part of this wider whole. The modern ecological and environmental movements have rediscovered this truth (something we'll come back to, later in this book), but it has fascinated philosophers as long as human beings have thought about the nature of reality. For the ancient Greek philosophers, especially Plato (429–347 BCE), the paradox of "the one and the many" was one of the central problems of human thought.[11] The German philosopher, G.W.F. Hegel (1770–1831), expressed the same paradox, in typically abstract language, when he said that "Life is the union of union and non-union."[12]

This is a very important insight we'll also come back to. But, for the moment, let's continue thinking about the way we experience this paradox in human life, in our families and communities.

✳

One side of the human paradox is very familiar to us. In fact it's the only side of the paradox our modern, Western world easily acknowledges, or knows how to talk about very well.

Since about the fifteenth century, and especially in the last three hundred years (as we will explore again in chapter 12), Western culture has increasingly celebrated the feelings and behaviours associated with the assertive side of our nature we just considered. In this book I am going to call them the virtues of self-assertion.[13] Virtues are habits of behaviour we approve of, that we consider good.[14] Virtues have two sides: an inside and an outside. The outside is a habit of behaviour; the inside is a habit of feeling that accompanies and is nourished by the behaviour.[15] The outward habits of behaviour are the visible expression of habits of inward feeling about the "good": habits of feeling which I will call "values."

In the modern world, the virtues of self-assertion occupy a very large part of our thinking and assumptions about the good life. They haven't entirely eliminated other virtues, not by any means, but they have marginalized them, or hidden them, or given them new names and a new slant. With a few important exceptions, one of which we'll consider in chapter 12, they represent the leading edge of the modern, Western world. "Now," remarks an important modern study of what I have called the human paradox, "we are all supposed to be conscious primarily of our assertive selves."[16] The virtues of self-assertion are what it *means* to be modern.

As a result, the "goods" associated with these virtues are very familiar to us. They are expressed by words like "liberty," "equality," and "the pursuit of happiness." Reflecting the fundamental impulse from which it proceeds, the language of self-assertion is the language of liberation, of freedom, autonomy, separation, independence, individualism, empowerment, self-development, self-expression, and self-realization. In the last fifty years or so, this language has come to occupy an overwhelming place in public, media, and intellectual discussion. As Canadian philosopher Charles Taylor (b. 1931) says: "What is universal in the modern world is the centrality of freedom as a good."[17] The moral vision underpinning this idea of the good is that of individuals associating together freely, to secure certain benefits for themselves. So the idea of freedom is also closely linked to a rational "cost-benefit" calculation, or, at best, to a calculation of "mutual benefit."[18]

In the first decades of the new millennium, you are likely to encounter the virtues of self-assertion in the public language of newspapers, magazines, television and the Internet in at least four typical ways.* One is the language of human rights. Almost all social claims must be expressed nowadays in terms of some kind of human (or even animal) "right," and unless you can express your ideas in this way – unless you can *assert* a right of some kind – you will have great difficulty in getting anyone to take you seriously. Some modern values rooted in more traditional

---

* Reason (especially in its post-Enlightenment rationalist mode) and modern science themselves are also largely expressions of the virtues of self-assertion, which enormously complicates "rational" exploration of the *other* side of human reality. The links between the virtues of self-assertion and both reason and science are explored again in chapters 4, 8, and 12.

virtues – benevolence or sympathy for the suffering of others, for example, a secularized version of an older virtue of "charity" – are often required to dress themselves up in the language of rights or freedoms, the language of self-assertion, because that's the way our modern world expresses what we owe to other people. The only forms of grievous harm our society spontaneously recognizes are allegations of unfairness, inequity, exclusion, abuse or harm, based on a denial of someone's fundamental rights.[19]

Another typical way the virtues of self-assertion are celebrated today is in the glorification of physical pleasure. Everything that pleases the body and the senses is given a very high value today, and vast industries cater to their gratification. French writer Alexis de Tocqueville (1805–1859) thought this passion for comfort and sensual pleasure was typically modern, and very worrisome for the future of democracy.[20] But Tocqueville could not foresee how far the virtues of self-assertion would take the pursuit of pleasure, especially sexual pleasure, in the twentieth century.

A third way the virtues of self-assertion are glorified today is in the importance and value we attach to competitive, market-based, economic self-assertion. Our culture attaches great value to entrepreneurship, to the acquisition of wealth and the ownership of things, to the virtues of consumerism, "conspicuous consumption," and what another Canadian philosopher, C.B. MacPherson (1911–1987), called "possessive individualism."[21]

In the last fifty years or so, this very consumer culture seems to have led to a fourth way the virtues of self-assertion express themselves today: in expression itself, especially a self-conscious and even self-indulgent expressiveness, sometimes called "expressivism," through which individuals celebrate, explore, fulfil and in some sense even create their own unique, individual self.[22] Consumerism, communication technology, mass media, advertising, music, fashion, the Internet, and many other influences combine, especially in North America, to create a mass culture of "narcissism,"[23] or "expressive individualism," perhaps summed up in the word "lifestyle." Expressive individualism "holds that each person has a unique core of feeling and intuition that should unfold or be expressed if individuality is to be realized."[24] It is often associated with a therapeutic outlook on modern life: it emphasizes personal feelings, and so is sometimes thought to balance or remedy the dehumanizing downsides of "possessive" individualism. Many people live in the third mode in their public and professional lives, but they often escape into the fourth in their personal and private lives: "A simplified expressivism infiltrates everywhere. Therapies multiply which promise to help you find yourself, realize yourself, release your true self, and so on."[25]

Unless you can frame an argument or a position in one of these four ways, or in some other form the virtues of self-assertion take today, you cannot expect – with only a few exceptions, one of which will be discussed in chapter 12 – to find much of an audience. In fact, it might almost be fair to say you cannot expect to be understood at all. Your argument will be incomprehensible at best, suspect or even taboo at worst.

*

The virtues of self-assertion are real virtues. They express real human goods. Nothing in this book should be interpreted as calling into question the good they embody, or the social progress their growing recognition over recent centuries has brought us. My reason for highlighting them here is simply to point out how they define our modern world – how they define what it means to *be* modern – and the resulting difficulty we now have in discussing, recognizing, *or even naming* other goods that are in tension or conflict with them.

Just because something is good doesn't mean it's the whole story. The virtues of self-assertion are real virtues, but they reflect only half of what I have called the human paradox. They are only one half of what it means to be fully human, the half that has to do with the pursuit of individual autonomy and self-realization. So if we are to give a full account of our humanity, we need to find a language to talk about the *other* half, that which reflects our necessary involvement in a greater whole we did not create and did not choose. Without this other half, we will not be able to give a full or plausible account even of the virtues of self-assertion themselves, since they are only one side of a larger whole. Rediscovering a language for this other side of human experience is also a necessary first step in understanding the role that religion plays in human life, and its contribution to the full expression of the human spirit.

# 2

# Reverence

In order to begin developing a vocabulary for the other side of the human paradox – so we can name it – let's think about some of the virtues we normally associate with family life, especially the life of a family we admire.

One word that comes to mind right away is "respect." That's what it means to "honour thy father and thy mother." But in a successful family, respect goes well beyond parent-child relationships. It's the way every member of the family treats all other members. For parents and older members of the family, respect will often be tinged with something more: with deference, for example, or an explicit acknowledgement of superiority, or authority, or primacy. In traditional cultures, and even in the West until the last few decades, this deference would be openly expressed by symbolic gestures such as calling older males "Sir," or by standing up when adults came into the room, or by holding the door or a chair for an older family member, and so on.[1*]

Another word that comes readily to mind is "commitment." Unlike other human attachments now governed largely by the virtues of

---

\* Respect (like several other virtues) is a virtue both of self-assertion *and* of the *other* side of human reality we will explore in this chapter, but it is seen from very different angles, in either case. As a virtue of self-assertion, it is seen from the point of view of the person to whom respect is shown, or by whom it is claimed. As another kind of virtue, the kind to be explored here, it is seen from the point of view of the person *showing* the respect, and the good that person experiences by showing it, quite apart from the merits or claims of the person (or persons) to whom it is shown.

self-assertion, families are not normally a matter of free choice. We are born into them, for better or for worse, and we are part of them, "committed" to them, for life. That's what makes a family a family. If we are fully human, we do not discard our parents or our children when they become infirm, inconvenient, tiresome, or burdensome. We go on shouldering their burdens, even when it goes entirely against our own self-interest to do so.

For this obvious reason, another word closely connected to commitment is "concern." In a genuine family, we can never remain emotionally and morally detached from the welfare of other family members. Their struggles and tribulations are, in some sense, ours too. As are their joys. We're concerned about them, and this concern frequently takes priority over our own needs. This willing commitment to the welfare of family members is what humans call "love," in its true and noblest sense (as distinct from erotic desire, which belongs, as we have already seen, to the virtues of self-assertion). Love, in this sense, is something you *do*, not something you *have*, or fall into, or that happens *to* you.

Another word that flows directly from commitment is "duty." Duty is the opposite of freedom. It's a conviction of absolute obligation "toward an other than yourself": an obligation that trumps any personal preference.[2] A sense of duty can sometimes be accompanied by an element of fear. We may fear the consequences of neglecting our duty, either the direct consequences (might my sister drown?) or the indirect consequences (what will my parents, or my brother, or my cousins, think? will they still respect and love me?).

For this reason, among others, duty can be a solemn virtue. But families aren't always or usually solemn. In fact, another word we spontaneously associate with family life is "celebration." We come together most often, as families, to celebrate something: a birthday, a graduation, a marriage, opening or closing the cottage, Thanksgiving, and so on. Celebrations are usually joyous. And, to express our shared joy, to give it recognizable form, we often have favourite family rituals and ceremonies (lighting and blowing out birthday candles, giving Uncle David the wishbone, parading from the kitchen to the living room and so on), often accompanied by music and singing ("Happy Birthday," "For He's A Jolly Good Fellow," carols, campfire songs).

Not all the ceremonies are joyous, however. For it's in the family, above all, that we experience the most profound mysteries of life, those rational thought is often helpless to explain, much less for which to offer us any real comfort: the mysteries of life and death – especially death. At funerals, wakes, and during shivas, we summon all the resources of custom, ceremony, and ritualized family behaviour to help us bear the burden of the greatest and most painful mystery of all.

✳

Let's pause here for a moment, to review some of the words we've already collected from our culture's experience of family life: respect, deference, commitment, concern, love, duty, fear, solemnity, joy, celebration, song, ritual, custom, ceremony, mystery. How can we sum up these virtues, feelings, and practices associated with the *other* side of the human paradox, the side that signifies not autonomy and freedom but rather our union with something like a family, something larger than our individual selves, something to which we belong, and to which we have obligations, even though it's not the result of our own free choice? It's a significant fact about our modern world that no word would come spontaneously to the minds of most readers to express this range of experiences and behaviours. But one English word that covers most of this territory is "reverence."[3]

Reverence conveys a human attitude of respect and deference for something larger or higher in priority than our own individual selves; something that commands our admiration and our loyalty, and may imply obligations or duties on our part. In a gesture of reverence, either physical or mental, we acknowledge superior worth, our relationship with it, and our potential obligations toward it. "Reverence results from humility," as a Jewish text puts it.[4]

In this book I propose to use the word "reverence" to name the family of virtues associated with the natural human impulse to attachment, to union with others and with the surrounding environment. These virtues stand in contrast to the virtues of self-assertion we discovered in the equally natural impulse to freedom, autonomy, and "non-union." The virtues of self-assertion and the virtues of reverence are the two sides of the human paradox described in chapter 1. They are the two necessary and complementary halves of the totality that is a full human being.[5] Whatever you do, both ways of being are always present in your action, even if you can't see it. Though they are in conflict, or at least in tension with each other, you can't have one without the other. And they have a natural order of priority in their relationship. But that's for later.

For now, let's continue exploring some of the further dimensions of reverence you experience in the wider community and world, beyond the simple experience of family life. Though it is the arena in which you first encounter reverence, the very intimacy of family life, your close familiarity with each other, may limit its full expression there. When you consider how you experience your connection to a wider community, or to your country, or to the world itself, reverence can take on more solemn, powerful, even scary overtones. If you were to meet the Queen, for example, or the Prime Minister, or the President of the United States, or a pop star, or a sports hero, you would likely feel even more than respect. You would probably also feel intimidated, very privileged, and a little overwhelmed. You'd probably say it was "awesome." And you would, in fact, almost certainly feel an emotion something like awe.

Awe is the emotion we feel when we encounter someone or something that transcends our normal life, and embodies qualities of excellence, or beauty, or some kind of power or authority that force our admiration, and to which, in some way or other, we submit ourselves, voluntarily or involuntarily. Awe is "an acknowledgement of the surpassing value" of something.[6] It is a natural component or source of reverence, and a very important human emotion because it is a critical source of human motivation. It often provides the drive that causes people to act: to devote themselves to something, to stand up for something, or to take a stand against something – or even, sometimes, just to go on living. Awe can overwhelm us, but it also motivates and empowers us.

Another way we may feel emotions akin to awe is when we have a vivid encounter with nature. Throughout history, human beings have been moved by the beauty and power of the natural world, and have felt emotions like wonder and admiration leading often to a feeling of oneness, communion, harmony, and peace. Much of English lyric poetry since the beginning of the nineteenth century expresses the feelings inspired by such encounters with nature.

Looking at a peaceful landscape can be a warm and fuzzy experience, but a stormy or vast one can stir up more fearful emotions by making us acutely aware of our fragile place in something immense. A first encounter with the Grand Canyon, or the Rockies, or the ocean, or even the Great Lakes, can fill an alert and sensitive mind with wonder tinged with anxiety or even dread.

Awe and wonder can become almost dizzying, when we begin to think seriously about our puny place in the universe.[7] When the discoveries of

Copernicus (1473–1543) and Galileo (1564–1642) began to reveal the nature of the solar system in the sixteenth and seventeenth centuries, the great French mystic and mathematician, Blaise Pascal (1623–1662), reacted with a shudder. "What is man in the perspective of infinity?" he asked. "The eternal silence of infinite space frightens me."[8] Since Pascal's time, modern astronomy has shown us that the universe is not made up of our own galaxy alone, but of an endless series of galaxies. Thinking about the infinitesimal place our own planet Earth occupies in this vast space can make your head spin, and fill you with anxiety – or even fear, similar to the vertigo you can feel looking down from a great height.[9]

The emotions associated with an attitude of reverence are evoked not just by thinking about your connection to the physical universe, or to *space*, but also by an awareness of your place in the whole, unending span of *time*. The way in which time never seems to stand still, and the puzzling connections between past, present, and future have fascinated and worried thinkers throughout history.

Time presents us with yet another paradox, the kind of paradox you will encounter fairly often in this book. The present is all we have. We can never live in the past or the future. But the present is also an illusion. We never seem to be really *in* it. It's gone as soon as it's here. We can never hang on to it long enough to actually feel or appreciate it. So we end up living, paradoxically, in a mixture of memory and hope: that is, in realms of time that don't actually "exist"! As the great English essayist, Samuel Johnson (1709–1784), observed, "almost all that we can be said to enjoy is past or future; the present is in perpetual motion, leaves us as soon as it arrives, ceases to be present before its presence is well perceived and is only known to have existed by the effects which it leaves behind."[10]

As human wisdom has struggled with this paradox of time, it has often concluded that the answer is to see ourselves as *connected* to the *whole* of time, to see the past and the future *in* the present. Dr Johnson was typical in arguing that "whatever makes the past, the distant, or the future predominate over the present, advances us in the dignity of thinking beings."[11] But this conclusion obviously runs counter to the virtues of self-assertion, whose natural impulse is to act *now*, without worrying about either past or future. A person in the grip of an overwhelming desire doesn't think about yesterday or tomorrow.

A conviction that past, present, and future are and should be *united in the present* proceeds from an ability to see and value the *connectedness* of things, one of the virtues of reverence. That's one of the reasons many traditional societies give so much reverence to elders and to dead ancestors: because the past is still alive in the present, and the present – as German philosopher G.W. Leibniz (1646–1716), put it – is already "pregnant" with the future.[12] "The organism is never located in a single instant," said another German philosopher, Ernst Cassirer (1874–1945). "In its life the three modes of time – the past, the present and the future – form a whole which cannot be split up into individual elements."[13] In fact, for some thinkers, this sense of the unity of time is the very essence of reverence. Alfred North Whitehead (1861–1947), a British mathematician and philosopher, argued that "the foundation of reverence is this perception that the present holds within itself the complete sum of existence, backwards and forwards, that whole amplitude of time, which is eternity."[14]

The fact that we can no longer spontaneously name this half of our human reality, and therefore cannot talk about it, does not mean it has fled from our world. That would be impossible, since we go on living in a world in which we are both connected and free, both one and many, both individuals and parts of a larger whole. Our modern sensibility has blinded us to it, and largely silenced us about it. But the world hasn't changed. And neither have we. So we go on living and cherishing the virtues of reverence without being aware of it. Some of the highest values held by people in the West today – values like compassion or honesty – are actually virtues of reverence.[15] But we don't recognize these virtues for what they are, and are hence unable consciously to cultivate them, as such.

Whenever you celebrate a family birthday or anniversary; whenever you comfort a friend; whenever you help a neighbour; whenever you willingly obey the laws; whenever you volunteer to help your community; whenever you vote; whenever you observe the code of sportsmanship; whenever you tell a truth inconvenient for yourself; whenever you mind your table manners or your language; whenever you behave like a "gentleman" or a "lady"; whenever you are civil in the face of rudeness; whenever you shake hands; whenever you get dressed up for a formal party; whenever you participate in a graduation ceremony; whenever you are genuinely concerned for the welfare of those you lead, or for whom you are responsible; whenever you commit yourself to the goals or welfare of an organization, a team, a college, a club, or a firm – in short, whenever you are self-*giving* rather than self-*seeking* – you are expressing and observing the virtues of reverence.[16]

In our modern world, the hunger for reverence sometimes expresses itself in surprising ways. Starved for other ways to express itself, reverence re-emerges in new forms that can risk flipping over into a caricature of the real thing. The rock concert, the mosh pit, and the rave, for example, are all expressions of a hungry search for connectedness and ritual that are not satisfied in other ways. So are big media events like the Olympics, the World Cup, Princess Diana's funeral, or a natural or human disaster that rivets millions to their TV screens for weeks on end. In all of these forms of activity, isolated citizens of Western countries seek to be gathered into the kind of communal, ritualized experience that our societies, on the whole, no longer afford. Sometimes this unsatisfied hunger goes beyond caricature to express itself in radically evil forms, as in the Nuremberg rallies of Nazi Germany in the 1930s.

As the American classical scholar, Paul Woodruff (b. 1943), remarks, what modern societies have lost is not reverence itself, but rather the *idea* of reverence.[17] That is to say, we go on practising the virtues of reverence, and craving the feelings associated with them. We could not do otherwise, because they furnish one half of a humanity we cannot shed. But our public language, the language of self-assertion, excludes any reference to the connecting thread that runs through them: the idea, or concept – or reality – of reverence itself. "As householders, housekeepers, parents we maintain allegiance to it in practice, possibly even in diffident principle," observed Lionel Trilling (1905–1975), an American literary critic. "But as ... participants in the conscious, formulating part of our life in society, we incline to the antagonistic position."[18] This makes it very hard for us consciously to nourish or develop the virtues of reverence, so essential to the kind of society any of us would want to live in. And it also makes it hard to understand the roots of some of the deepest, most persistent, and most *human* forms of expression, such as religious practice.

# 3

# Spirituality

The natural human instinct for reverence is the soil in which religious practice grows, beginning with human spirituality.[1]

Of course reverence can and should be expressed in purely – or almost purely – secular ways. Most of the ones we have mentioned so far – the necessary reverence of daily life in a family, or community, or organization – can be thought of, and practised, without any reference beyond secular realities. Some of the great traditions of reverence from the past, like the teachings of the ancient Chinese sage Confucius (551–479 BCE) or the classical tradition of the Stoic and Epicurean philosophers, can be seen as wholly, or at least largely, secular in character. Thinkers from Confucius and the ancient Greek philosopher Aristotle (384–322 BCE) to James Q. Wilson have argued that the virtues of reverence are largely the product of family upbringing, and "habituation" (the development of the *habits* of reverence) in the family, and in the community.[2] Therefore much can and, no doubt, *should* be done to develop the feelings and virtues of reverence, without stepping outside a secular frame of reference; outside, that is, the conscious, rational, "scientific" world of our modern, Western societies.

But reverence, like self-assertion, has a logic and an internal dynamic of its own. Once you start down one of these roads, it takes you to places you didn't expect to go. The human instinct for reverence almost necessarily points beyond a purely secular frame of reference. Confucius, for example, strove to remain within secular forms of reverence, modestly refusing to speculate on the ultimate realities toward which the practices of reverence he taught inevitably direct human attention. But in his *Analects*, one of his students is recorded as remarking "that even if I wanted to stop I could not do so. But having done all I can, [the goal] seems to rise sheer above me. I long to go after it but I cannot find the way." As Paul Woodruff comments, "however high you rise on your own ladder of advancement [in reverence], there is always something higher – Heaven or the Way – that draws you upward even though you cannot say what it is."[3] So it is at least debatable whether the secular virtues of reverence – reverent behaviour in the family and the community – can be easily or richly sustained without support from the *non-secular* forms toward which they draw us.[4]

There are many reasons why secular forms of reverence "reach out beyond" themselves, reasons that are inherent in some of the dimensions of reverence I already noted.[5] We can trace this natural human journey beyond the secular in two directions: outward and inward.[6]

✳

First, let's think about the outward journey.

Reverence and its virtues proceed from our connection, and our *sense* of connection, to something larger than ourselves: something we did not create, and over which we have little, if any, free choice. Our most intimate and familiar experience of reverence occurs in the family, but, by its very nature, it cannot stop there. Because reverence proceeds from the principle of unity or connectedness or attachment built into all human experience, it cannot, by its *own* dynamic, stop at the boundaries of the family (unless it is intercepted, as it so often is, by the virtues of self-assertion), but spreads outward to the surrounding tribe, community, culture, nation, and eventually to humanity as a whole. In our time, this last step has finally been accomplished. We are all universalists now, as Charles Taylor remarks; that is to say, the boundaries of our concern now necessarily extend to the whole human race.[7] This is because the innate sense of "loyalty to one's fellows," as Bernard Lonergan (1904–1984), another Canadian philosopher and theologian, observes, "reaches out through kinsmen, friends, acquaintances, through all the bonds – cultural, social, civil, economic, technological – of human cooperation to unite ever more members of the human race in the acceptance of a common lot, in sharing a burden to be borne by all, in the building of a common future for themselves and future generations."[8]

If it is unimpeded by the virtues of self-assertion, the impulse of reverence doesn't stop at the boundaries of humanity alone. It also seeks to connect us to the physical world we inhabit, starting with our own bodies. Through our bodies we experience a sense of connectedness, perhaps even vulnerability, to the specific natural setting in which we first find ourselves. And in this same way, the impulse of reverence continues its outward journey, reaching out to nature in general, and eventually to the universe as a whole.

As it moves outward, this widening sense of connectedness brings with it a growing sense of mystery, because every individual thing we can perceive or control is encompassed by a totality that remains elusively beyond our understanding.[9] No explanation could ever include everything, and the details of any explanation would always be influenced by what we have left out.[10] So the reverence that spawns an ever-widening sense of connectedness also brings a growing sense of dependency, power, and mystery; feelings human beings have always felt impelled to express in groups (consistent with the impulse to connection), in the characteristic forms of reverence I already noted, including ritual, ceremony, singing, dancing, and music. In the earliest cultures, these practices were probably intended to express not only group belonging but also to propitiate and to ward off powers little understood, and greatly feared. In more developed cultures, while retaining some of the initial elements of mystery, awe, and fear, they increasingly involved elements of celebration, joy, understanding, thankfulness, and identification with the external world.

In an important Chinese tradition, the goal of this outward journey is called the *Tao*. In the Hindu tradition of India it is called *Brahman*. The Tao and Brahman are both names for the ultimate destination of this outward journey of reverence.

But in the Hindu and all other authentic spiritual traditions, this outward movement is paralleled by an equally inevitable *inward* movement. The same instinct for connectedness that draws humans toward the external world also leads them into an encounter with the forces, emotions, instincts, and visions of their own *internal*, psychic landscape.[11]

I almost said "mind." But "mind" conveys to us something conscious and rational. One of the lessons we have learned from the modern sciences of psychology and psychiatry is that the conscious, rational mind is a relatively thin covering for a very deep well of feeling. Feeling serves as the bridge from the life of our physical bodies to the life of our rational minds.[12] Most of this realm of feeling is probably unknown to the conscious mind, and carries on its own, subterranean life, revealed to us only in forms such as dreams. In fact, even what we think of as "rational" intellect, as American philosopher Susanne Langer (1895–1985) points out, may well be nothing more than a very high form of feeling, "a specialized, intensive feeling about intuitions."[13]

These internal forces are powerful, and they are often at war with each other, threatening to tear the individual personality apart, or to make him or her an aggressive danger to others, or perhaps only to make him or her a fretful, unquiet, unhappy person. From ancient times, one of humanity's chief tasks has been to try to bring peace to this internal battleground.[14] The age-old impulse to harmonize and to unify these psychic forces – thus allowing the individual human personality to find inner peace and serenity – is both the expression and the source of the virtues of reverence turned inward, to identify, explore, and honour the ground of our being, the inner *spirit* that makes us who we are, and makes us whole.

This inward journey, and the forms it takes, are also shaped by the experience of reverence itself. If we are the least attentive, the habit of performing reverent actions – performing the small, daily actions of courtesy, concern, or generosity that contribute to a good family and community life – can't help drawing our attention to what they have in common, and to the spirit that underlies them and shapes each one of them: the feeling or *spirit* of reverence itself.

The more we pay attention to this inner feeling or spirit of reverence, the more we notice the sense of rightness or fulfilment that comes with it, and the way in which it seems to respond to some of our deepest needs. Paradoxically, we find we are most at home with ourselves when we are able, with dignity and conviction, to acknowledge our place in some kind of larger order we did not create and do not control. It becomes natural to cultivate and express this spirit for its own sake, and to follow where it leads, including to its own self. In other words, the inner journey leads us not only to the source or sources of our *own* spirit but also to *another* spirit we find inside ourselves but which seems to have a life of its own.

In the Chinese tradition of the Tao, the ultimate destination of this inward journey of reverence is called the "real" or "true" self, the "inner core," "innate nature," or the "Real Person." In the Hindu tradition, it is called simply *Atman*, or the Self.

But here there is a surprise. Where the inner journey ends up turns out to be exactly the same place as the outward journey. The Tao of our inner nature is not different from the Great Tao, the Perfect Tao of the universe. And Brahman and Atman turn out not to be the opposite poles they at first appear but rather *exactly the same thing*, in different manifestations, internal and external. A famous epigram in the *Chandogya Upanishad*, one of the Hindu scriptures, proclaims "Tat tvam asi": "*You* are that."[15] The true Self at the end of the inward journey of reverence turns out to be the same as the unchanging reality discovered by the outward journey.

The combination of these outward and inward journeys – the reverent impulse to connectedness with both the external and internal worlds – gives rise to what we now call human spirituality. The word "spirituality" is an old one, going back at least to the Latin Bible, the Vulgate of St Jerome (c. 347–420), in the fifth century, and appearing first in English around the fourteenth century. But its meaning has evolved considerably over the centuries, and its popular use to designate a broad area of human experience seems to be relatively recent, beginning first in French toward the end of the nineteenth century. In preceding centuries, this same area of human experience would have been called simply *religio*, or later (as that word became appropriated for a system of intellectual abstractions and beliefs), piety or mysticism. But whatever you call it, the area of authentic human experience the word spirituality now designates is as old as the human race.

Human spirituality is the domain of experience – and its expression – that arises from the discovery that there is much more to life than appears on its surface. Spirituality goes both broader and deeper than reason or "mind."[16] It engages all the human faculties and modes of being, and it engages them to their very core. "Man lives in the spirit," said the Jewish philosopher Martin Buber (1878–1965), "if he enters into relation with his whole being."[17] Because, as spiritual beings, we participate in situations with the *whole* of our being, spirituality has the quality of life or vitality which is absent from mind.[18] Spirituality goes all the way down. Mind does not.

Any close attention to life suggests that we are more than the rational, conscious, self-seeking, choice-making, autonomous creatures celebrated by the virtues of self-assertion. In fact, these virtues, by themselves, seem to leave us feeling, at the very least, unfulfilled, if not deeply unhappy, or even angry and aggressive in one direction, or depressed and suicidal in another. So, from the earliest civilizations, human beings have sought to explore the ground of their being in ways that can bring peace to their inner spirit, while recognizing and responding to their need for connection with the external world.

This quest can't be separated from the search for meaning and purpose. Because we are rational creatures, and because we are formed by an external and internal conversation of question and answer, we are impelled to seek answers to questions such as, "Why?" Or, "What for?" And answers to these questions can't be separated from other questions about the value of what we experience. As soon as we are active in this world, we necessarily make distinctions between things based on quality and value. A sharp knife is "better" than a dull one. An elder is more experienced, knows more about the world, and is "wiser" than I am. Or, to use two of Aristotle's examples, some eyes see better than others, and some horses run faster than others.[19]

It's not just that we are and seek to be connected to others. We also seek to be connected in ways that have value. So any answer to the "why" question requires other answers about the hierarchy of goods: what good things have *more* value than other good things? In the realm of the good, what's the order of priority?

These are questions that seem to be written indelibly into the human universe. Aristotle expressed this reality when he distinguished between four different kinds of "causes": "material" cause (the silver of a silver bowl, for example); "efficient" cause (the impact of something on something else, like the impact of two billiard balls, or a person who advises another); "formal" cause (the unfolding of the inner form or essence of something, like the growth of an oak tree from an acorn); and "final" cause (that for the sake of which something is done, the motivations that cause animals and humans to seek some purpose, goal or "end"). Aristotle's important insight was that the human world is shaped not just by "efficient" and "material" causes – the causes that *push* us, as it were (to use a spatial metaphor), from "behind" or from "below" – but, equally, by "formal" and "final" causes: the ideas, purposes, and aspirations that *pull* us human beings forward into the future, from "ahead" or "above," as it were.[20]

To our modern ears, Aristotle's use of the word "cause" in this context sounds odd, because efficient and material causes are the only ones recognized and studied – the only ones that *can* be studied – by the techniques of science. In fact, the modern scientific world was created, in the seventeenth and eighteenth centuries, largely by banishing final causes from explanations. The advantage of Aristotle's language, however, is that it puts both material causes and ideas (or values) on the same plane, with no hierarchy between them, and shows that our human world is shaped equally by both.

Since human beings are meaning-making creatures, the quest for harmony, peace, and fulfilment also involves a search for purpose or value, for what we sometimes call the "meaning of life." This quest is a spiritual one, and the characteristic mode of spirituality is the spirit of reverence. What distinguishes this quest from other, similar explorations (say, scientific ones) is the intimate, felt need that prompts it (the urgent, personal need for wholeness, healing, and meaning), and hence the characteristic virtues of reverence (concern, engagement, commitment, deference, ritual, ceremony) with which it is undertaken.

This spiritual hunger and its accompanying modes of expression are enduring features of all cultures. Some recent definitions of spirituality by scholars who study it include "the inner dimension of the person ... [where] ultimate reality is experienced," or "the constituent of human nature which seeks relations with the ground or purpose of existence."[21] These definitions are not very different from those given back in 1911 by the English writer, Evelyn Underhill (1875–1941). She called it "the expression of the innate tendency of the human spirit towards complete harmony with the transcendental order," or "the movement of the heart, seeking to transcend the limitations of the individual standpoint and to surrender itself to ultimate reality."[22]

As these definitions suggest, spirituality covers a broad range of experience and practices, from the body and its role in spiritual wholeness at one end of the spectrum, through to our conscious sense of meaning and ultimate value at the other end. Indeed it might be said that spirituality is an expression (and evidence) of the unquenchable human need to unite these extremes – and the vast domain of conscious and unconscious feeling in between – in a unified field of meaningful and purposeful harmony that responds to both our deepest physical and emotional needs and our highest mental and spiritual aspirations.[23]

✳

There can be secular forms of spirituality, just as there are many secular forms of reverence. In fact, as an integral part of our "expressivist" culture, there has been almost an explosion of secular or quasi-secular practices and disciplines of spirituality in the West over the past forty years. Store-front yoga practitioners can now be found on many streets and shopping centres in Western countries. Instruction in secular forms of meditation is widely available. Practices from Chinese spiritual traditions, including Tai Chi and Feng Shui, have become mainstream. Reflecting the inability of a rational, atomized, scientific culture to respond adequately to half of our human nature (or even to recognize it), our Western societies have spawned an enormous variety of secular spiritual industries the products of which can be found in our pharmacies, gift shops, music, and bookstores under titles such as "wellness," "new age," "self-help," and sometimes even "spirituality." Some of these, like "*self*-help," show the lengths to which the virtues of reverence must go – how they must often disguise themselves in the accepted contemporary language of self-assertion – in order to be respectable.

Some other forms in which the prevalent spiritual hunger is expressed are even more socially acceptable, especially to intellectual elites. Since the beginning of the nineteenth century – under the impulse of the Romantic movement – many people in the West have sought to quench their spiritual thirst in the productions of high art and culture. With the rise of the virtues of self-assertion, imagination "stands in for soul."[24] This new respect – even reverence – for artistic expression, for its own sake, is one of the characteristic marks of modernity. As Irish literary critic Terry Eagleton (b. 1943) remarks, the arts provide "an ersatz sort of transcendence in a world from which spiritual values have been largely banished."[25] For many educated people in our societies, richness of life and meaning are now to be found in the experience and enjoyment of classical music, painting, sculpture, theatre, dance and so on. In the consumption of cultural and artistic products, they seek to meet a need that "used to be assuaged more surely and more often by sacred objects and offices."[26] For others, popular culture, music and film play a similar role. Many people – members of the iPod and iPhone generations – can now be seen in public places wearing earphones to connect themselves to a private world of music at all times. Since the eighteenth century, we have evolved from a culture of religion to a religion of culture.[27]

It's not surprising that art and culture should fill part of the vacuum left by the decline of religious spirituality, because they are, and always have been, closely related. As Scottish psychologist Margaret Donaldson (b. 1926) has pointed out, they are both expressions of what she calls the "value-sensing" mode of the human "mind."[28] But whether, in the absence of any saving vision to express, this new religion of culture can have the same saving properties as the former ones, or whether it is, at best, distracting us from our deep anxieties and at worst, cultivating the very instincts true reverence seeks to tame, are questions of the greatest importance for people today.

Another socially acceptable way in which the spiritual quest of modern people disguises itself is by employing the language of science itself, especially the modern sciences of psychology, psychotherapy, and psychoanalysis. These sciences represent a perfect compromise between the modern ways of seeing the world and the reality of the human psyche, the spirit and its needs. They help enormously to explore that vast domain of conscious and unconscious feeling which, as I already noted, links the biological life of the body to the conscious life of the mind. But as the English poet, W.H. Auden (1907–1973), observed, psychoanalysis can tell you all the reasons why you are sick, but it cannot make you want to get well.[29] It can't give you a reason for living. Hence the famous story about the psychiatric patient who could give a full analysis of his psychological condition, as exhaustively and completely as any physician or professional analyst, but went out and hanged himself anyway. As the Polish philosopher, Leszek Kolakowski (1927–2009) remarked: "Let us suppose that I am an inveterate and uninhibited liar and that a benevolent and philanthropic philosopher succeeds in convincing me that "lying is wrong" is true in the same sense as [another scientific] principle: what reasons would I have to quit my deplorable habit provided I can indulge it with impunity, and what might prevent me from shrugging off this new scientific discovery by saying that I do not care?"[30]

These are some of the reasons why the best modern psychotherapists, beginning with the Swiss pioneer of psychoanalysis, C.G. Jung (1875–1961), have recognized that, in their therapeutic role, they are not so much scientists as spiritual practitioners, and that the roots of psychic healing lie not in psycho*analysis* (which only mires you deeper in the problem) but rather in the traditional spiritual and moral wisdom of humankind. Indeed, British psychotherapist David Smail (b. 1938) suggests that the healing power a psychotherapist has to offer is actually nothing more than the reality, or at least the appearance, of human love.[31]

✳

Like the secular forms of reverence, there is nothing wrong with secular forms of spirituality. They are needed, and they have their place, especially in our modern world. A great many people – possibly even the majority – exist today in what Charles Taylor calls a "middle space" of "undefined spirituality": "on the one hand drawn towards unbelief, while, on the other, feeling the solicitations of the spiritual."[32]

As this suggests, we can perhaps identify two kinds of spirituality which might be called "general" and "specific."[33] General spirituality is that which is lived by many if not most people whenever they are actively practicing the virtues of reverence not just with their minds but with the whole person – body, senses, feelings, emotions, intentions, aspirations, interiority, relationship – whenever vitality, intentionality, connectedness, and wholeness are joined.[34] Specific spirituality is the same thing within a specific religious framework or tradition. Specific spirituality is the real, lived experience or activity of a religious life. General spirituality is the ante-chamber, vestibule or corridor that leads to – or should lead to – a specific, religious spirituality.

Like reverence itself, secular or general spirituality points beyond itself, to something more, including by its own inherent limits and risks. The limits include the potential for superficiality, and even triviality. A resolutely secular spirituality can't take you very far on the spiritual journey, and therefore condemns itself to remain on the surface of things.

The risks are the potential to take your spiritual journey down the wrong or even a very dark path. Once you open up the domain of spirituality, almost anything may pop out, from the merely banal or mistaken to the profoundly evil. That's why, from earliest times, many spiritual traditions have warned against false prophets. Because the domain of spirituality deals with both the powerful depths of the human psyche and the deepest, most impenetrable mysteries of human life, it is ripe for exploitation by the naïve, the misguided, or the truly evil. In our own time we have seen the dreadful potential of cults and cult leaders, who offered spiritual poison to a parched and desperate flock. For these reasons, like the secular forms of reverence before it, secular spirituality points beyond itself to genuine religious practice.

# 4

# "Religions" and Religious Life

Religious life is a deeper form of human spirituality.

Just as spirituality is a deepened and more focused expression of the permanent and universal human instinct of reverence, religious practice is a deepened and more focused form of spirituality. A religion is a more organized, structured, disciplined, rigorous, historically rooted and tested form of spirituality.[1]*

And just as there are secular forms of reverence and spirituality, it could also be said, without too much distortion, that there are secular forms of "religion." The continuum leading from the secular to the religious can also be found within religion itself. When we are unsatisfied in our need for reverence and spirituality, we find other ways to express them, some of which are caricatures – sometimes grotesque caricatures – of the originals.

The Nazis, as I already noted, offered their adherents many quasi-religious elements, including ceremonies, ritual, utopian vision, commitment, and belonging. Indeed, writing in 1939, C.G. Jung said that the Nazi movement came "as near to being a religious movement as anything, since AD 622," the year of the prophet Muhammad's flight to Medina, and the birth of Islam.[2] Similarly Marxism – especially, but not

---

* In the Introduction, I already offered a first word of caution about the word "religion," which has caused great misunderstanding in the modern world. I will come back to this problem at the end of the chapter.

exclusively, in its Soviet and Chinese varieties – displayed many of the characteristic features of religious life, even though it proclaimed itself officially and dogmatically anti-religious. This is an excellent example of the fact – to be observed in many areas of life – that when you try to put some necessary feature of the human spirit out the front door, it slips in, while you aren't looking, through the back.

Nationalisms can also offer people a distant – and sometimes not so distant – imitation of some of the comforts and outward forms of religious life. In the late nineteenth and early twentieth centuries, nationalism gave many citizens of the British Empire a sense of meaning, purpose, and loyalty at least as powerful as their professed Christian religion. And non-American visitors to Washington and to such monuments as the Lincoln, Washington, and Jefferson Memorials cannot help but feel themselves to be standing in the temples of a powerful secular religion.

These examples help to confirm that the human hunger for religious practice cannot be banished simply by a Western intellectual fiat that God is dead. It is a pattern in the spirit that demands to be satisfied. It used to be thought and said, by many scholars in the West, that religion was simply a feature of pre-modern societies that would be eliminated by the inevitable processes of secularization brought about by modernity. By now, we should be able to recognize these "modernization" theories as the illusions they were. As Mircea Eliade (1907–1986), a Romanian scholar of comparative religion, remarked, the sacred "is an element in the *structure* of consciousness and not a *stage* in the history of consciousness."[3]

✳

So the inextinguishable human hunger for religious expression spawns many "false" religions. What about the authentic ones?

Broadly speaking, and overlooking many important qualifications, the great and authentic religious traditions of humankind fall into two categories. In this book I will only be talking about those religions which were shaped by what German philosopher Karl Jaspers (1883–1969) calls the "Axial" age: roughly 800–200 BCE.[4] So I have to pass over many aboriginal and pre-Axial spiritual traditions, though that would be a very interesting subject to pursue. It might show, for example, that they leave us with many unresolved issues, and also that human civilization and communal life, including language itself, have religious roots.⁵ That religion "isn't invented by man," as the American novelist Robert Pirsig (b. 1928) remarks. "Men are invented by religion."⁶

But, limiting ourselves, for the moment, to the major current world religions, the two broad categories in which they can be considered might be called "Eastern" and "Western." The Eastern religions – among which we can include the Buddhist traditions of India, China, and other Eastern countries, the Hindu and Jain traditions of India, the Chinese tradition of the Tao, and the Shinto tradition of Japan – are (again, very broadly speaking) religions of *interiority*. If the spiritual journey emerging from the virtues of reverence takes the two forms I already noted – inward and outward – the typical Eastern spiritual journey is predominantly (though not exclusively) inward. The result to modern, Western eyes is surprising, however.

This journey does not end, as you might expect, by emphasizing the individual "ego." It does not lead to individual self-assertion or to the "individuation" prized by Western philosophy and psychology. On the contrary, the inward spiritual journey (for which Eastern religions offer a wide variety of exercises, techniques, and practices) aims to overcome individual consciousness and to merge it with something larger, sometimes to the point that the individual ceases to exist as such.

The Buddhist tradition, for example, is founded upon the four "holy truths," the third of which is the state of *Nirvana*: extinction, or release from the suffering that is a necessary part of earthly life. The literal meaning of the Sanskrit word "Nirvana" is "blown out," like a candle that is blown out, expressing the final extinction of the individual ego and its merger with being or consciousness as a whole. When someone has seen that his whole physical and psychic being "is something that ought to be extinguished," the Buddha taught, "then he has the correct vision."⁷

Similarly, in the Hindu tradition, the practice of Kundalini yoga (the Sanskrit word "yoga" means to "yoke," or to connect) is based on six or seven "chakras" or "wheels," located in or associated with parts of the body, from the area between the anus and the genitals to the crown of the head. Through various physical and mental exercises that have become popularized by commercialized and secularized forms of yoga, the Hindu seeker aims to awaken the serpent (the meaning of the Sanskrit word "kundalini") of life that lies coiled below the genitals, causing it to rise up the spine through the various levels of the body (genitals, navel, heart, larynx, eyebrows), corresponding to different levels of human activity and consciousness, such as torpor or minimal consciousness,

sex, power, philosophy and art, purification, and the blissful vision of
ultimate reality. The seventh and final stage is, once again, the extinction
of the individual ego, and its merger with the ground of all being.[8]

The spiritual journey of Eastern religious life is a predominantly inward, mystical, and psychological one that leads not to the valuing or
enhancement of the individual – that is precisely what needs to be overcome to achieve spiritual fulfilment – but rather to the dissolving of individual consciousness and its blissful union with the source of life and
reality as a whole. But this broad generalization needs immediately to be
qualified, because there are important distinctions that should be made
within it, and within the various individual Eastern religious traditions.

On the whole the religious temper of India is more other-worldly
than that of the Far East, whose spiritual instincts tend to be more concerned with the here-and-now, and the everyday.[9] Chinese Confucianism,
for example, is a tradition of reverence that seems almost to be more
secular than religious, even though, as we saw in chapter 3, some of
Confucius' followers drew the conclusion that his teaching pointed beyond itself to spiritual realities, and did not make sense without them.

Another important Chinese spiritual tradition is that of the Tao. This
tradition can be contrasted to the emphasis in Confucianism on moral
rules. Taoism tries to recover the inner spirit of the rules, the inner spirit
of life itself. It teaches a way of human living, the "Way of Heaven" and
of "nature," based on opposed but connected principles – light and dark,
active and passive, heavenly and earthly, spirit and flesh, *yin* and *yang* – in
constant, permanent interaction. The Tao itself is the source of all these
dualities, the source of all being, from which come the power and unity
that sustain all things. It is wholeness, unity, the One. It is in all things
and around all things. "The power that makes things what they are
doesn't have the limitation that belongs to things … The Tao is the limit
of the unlimited, and the boundlessness of the unbounded."[10] The way
of the Tao teaches an ability to "make oneness your home," to live in the
power of this oneness: to live – and hence to "see" the world – with "in-
ner·reverence" and humility, developing freedom from attachment to
the individual things of the world, and thereby letting them (including
ourselves) grow in harmony with each other and with their own "innate
nature," their "true nature."[11] Through the "fasting of the heart," the
follower of the Tao develops an inner "emptiness" that opens the door
to a "transference of power": merely vital energy is surpassed, and the
Taoist sage taps into the "primal" or "quintessential" energy of the

universe.¹² Is the Tao a religion? Or simply a philosophy? Questions like these reveal Western confusion about the meaning of religion more than anything else. The Tao is a deeply spiritual tradition of reverence that calls into question our own notions about the borderline between the secular and the religious.

The continuum of secular and religious life can also be found within Buddhism, which contains several distinct spiritual traditions, especially the two traditions of the "Hinayana" or "lesser vehicle" – which is the predominant Buddhism of India, Sri Lanka, Burma, and Thailand – and the "Mahayana" or "big vehicle" which is the predominant Buddhism of Tibet, China, Korea, and Japan. The latter has become well known in the West since the 1960s, in a popularized form of its Japanese version, "Zen" Buddhism. The first is a more transcendental and strongly monastic tradition (for which the model was provided by the Buddha himself), and often involves renunciation and retirement from this world to practice various ascetic disciplines. The second is a more worldly tradition, in which the "awakening" at which Buddhism aims can be achieved in this world and in its daily tasks, a Buddhism more inclined to discover a Nirvana already here, if only the seeker can learn to see it, sometimes through sudden insight.

Zen Buddhism, as many people in the West know – in fact that is what has contributed to its popularity – has very few of the characteristics of what we in the West would associate with a religion. It involves no God or gods. It does not ascribe any supernatural role to the Buddha. In fact it might almost seem to exclude the supernatural altogether. "Zen" (a corruption of a Chinese word, itself a corruption of a Sanskrit word) means "contemplation." The mental exercises of Zen Buddhism – including meditation on deliberately absurd topics or aphorisms called "koan" – are intended to confound the mind so that it eventually gives up its striving to be rational and achieves non-rational insight into the unity of all reality.

The character of Zen Buddhism illustrates once again that the continuum of secular and religious life runs through religion itself. But it also illustrates, as I suggested at the beginning of this chapter, that religious life is simply a deeper, more structured form of human spirituality. From that point of view, Zen Buddhism, like the tradition of the Tao, deserves to be included in a survey of religious life, even if it does not – perhaps especially *because* it does not – conform to the expectations of a secular, Western mind about the nature of religion.

With these qualifications and distinctions, it remains a reasonable generalization to say that the great Eastern religious traditions focus mainly
(but not exclusively) on the *inward* spiritual journey, in which the exploration of the various levels of consciousness leads to a final union
with ultimate reality, a union whose objective is "detachment" from this
world and its cares, or even the obliteration of the individual, and his or
her absorption into a larger unity. In this sense, they might almost be
called religious traditions of pure reverence, or pure union: that is to
say, religions only relatively lightly marked (though somewhat more so
in their far Eastern forms) by the virtues of self-assertion.

The Eastern religious traditions could also be called traditions of "immanence." Immanence simply means the *in*dwelling of something, its
presence inside something else. It would be easy to exaggerate this feature of the Eastern traditions. It's a matter of emphasis rather than of
absolute difference from Western spirituality. The Buddhist, Hindu, and
Taoist traditions don't lack reference to Heaven, or even to God or
gods. But when they try to identify ultimate reality, the ground of all
being, the Eastern traditions seem to emphasize that it is found inside
the world, or inside each human being.

These assumptions are not absent from the great Western religious
traditions. But the latter emphasize something else, something that is,
paradoxically, both their greatest contribution to human culture *and*
their greatest handicap in a secular world.

*

The development of this spiritual emphasis is one of the most important
turning points in the history of the West.

This momentous process began in the Mesopotamian region (roughly
the region of present-day Iraq) somewhere between 3000 and 2000
BCE.[13] Joseph Campbell (1904–1987), an American scholar of world
mythology, calls it "mythic dissociation."[14] By this, he means that, for
the first time, a distinction began to be made between the king and the
god whom the king served. The king was no longer a "god-king," like
the Egyptian pharaoh, but was simply a "tenant-farmer," exercising
stewardship over a land that belonged to someone else. At about the
same time, new myths also began to appear in which men were created

by gods to serve them. The result of these new mythologies was a growing separation between this world and another one, a world *beyond* or outside this one. This separation had many profound implications for human beings' understanding of the world, and of themselves. In Joseph Campbell's words: "Man was no longer in any sense an incarnation of divine life, but of another nature entirely, an earthly mortal nature. And the earth was now clay. Matter and spirit had begun to separate."[15]

This was the world view within which all the later Western religious traditions developed, including the modern religions of Judaism, Christianity, and Islam. They were also religions of immanence, like the Eastern religions, but their emphasis was often on its opposite, or on what is called "transcendence." For them, ultimate reality was beyond or outside of this world, not just within it. And sometimes the vision of transcendence in these religions almost overwhelmed the element of immanence – the indwelling of the spirit – the Western traditions shared with the Eastern. To put this in my earlier language, the Western religions emphasized the outward spiritual journey, seeking to connect the individual not only with an internal world, but with the external world. If the essence or aim of the Eastern religions was *identity* with the ground of being to be found *within*, the guiding spirit of the Western religions was a search for *relationship* with something *other*.[16]

The results of this spiritual shift were surprising, the opposite of what you might expect. Whereas the inward spiritual journey of the Eastern religions has the unexpected effect of obliterating the individual in an undifferentiated unity, the outward spiritual journey of the Western religions allowed both nature and the human individual, paradoxically, to appear on the world stage. This was not completely new, but what occurred in the West went beyond even the Chinese traditions. Because religious practice was now based on *relationship* rather than *identity* with the "other," the human individual (who is, after all, *half* of the relationship) could now step forth, in his or her own right. Human beings now had an existence of their own, a new "freedom."[17]

And because God or the gods were not just *in* the world but also *outside* it, the natural world was no longer simply the clothing of the divine but assumed a separate life of its own. Nature became an *object*, not a *subject*, an object that could be studied, objectively. And, confronted for the first time by an "objective" nature, human beings came face to face with their *own* otherness, both as individual *subjects*, and as potential natural *objects* of study.[18]

These two important developments go together, and must be understood together. The individual ego confronts and "creates" (i.e. perceives the otherness of) an objective nature. An objective nature confronts and creates (i.e. causes human beings to feel the reality – or illusion – of their own) individual egos. The virtues of self-assertion and the emergence of an objective natural world go hand in hand, for better and for worse.[19]

The gradual turn to naturalism that resulted from the turning point of "mythic dissociation" became especially evident in ancient Greek society and culture. The legendary Greek poet known as Homer, from whose works much of Greek (and therefore Roman) culture developed, was both influential and typical in this process. In his great epic poem, the *Iliad*, the primary focus is no longer on the gods but on men. In Homer's writing, a revolution has occurred: "there has been a transvaluation of all values in warfare and in life, a substitution of human ideals for the divine ideals that had previously been conventional."[20]

In ancient Greece, even the gods were cut down to the size and image of human beings, with foibles and weaknesses as great or greater than those of any human. This made the gods more approachable, less fearsome, but also less awesome, less spiritually profound. This helped open the door to the first flourishing of humanistic thought: the philosophy of Socrates, Plato, and Aristotle, the literary flowering represented by Homer, Aeschylus, Sophocles, and Aristophanes, the beginnings of science and mathematics represented by Pythagoras, Euclid, Archimedes, Hippocrates, and so on. Absorbed and combined with Roman culture, with its own distinct genius for law and organization, this new humanistic culture furnished much of the basis for Western civilization.

But precisely because this new culture was based on a separation between the human and the sacred, between matter and spirit, its own specifically *spiritual* contribution was relatively minor. Plato and Aristotle themselves retained a real awareness of the open-ended mystery of life, and the necessary role of reverence. Philosophy was still regarded as a kind of spirituality, "a transformative way of life rather than a purely theoretical system," as it would become in the modern world.[21] Aristotle said the highest form of human flourishing was "too high" to be attained by something purely human: the person who sought this kind of fulfilment could not do so just "as a human being but in virtue of something divine within him."[22] Plato was shocked by Homer's frivolous depiction of the Gods, and argued that in a "well governed" city, such descriptions should not be allowed, especially in the presence of impressionable young people: God or the gods (Plato uses both expressions) should only be identified with the "good."[23] For Plato, reverence should be present even in human love.[24] But some ancient Greek and Roman thinkers such as Epicurus (341–270 BCE) and Lucretius (c.99–c.50 BCE) became atheists, initiating yet another tradition that has flowered in our own time.[25] Thus the specifically religious future of the West lay not with Greece and Rome but with the great and closely-linked, monotheistic religions of Judaism, Christianity, and Islam. The culture of the West was shaped by the dialogue between these three traditions and the humanistic heritage of Greece and Rome.

Histories of Western spirituality usually assign an important role to the historical/mythical figure of Zoroaster (or Zarathustra) who lived, somewhere between 1000 and 600 BCE, either in the steppes of southern Russia or in the eastern part of present-day Iran, where his teachings finally took root, significantly, almost the exact geographical dividing line between Eastern and Western spiritual traditions.[26] In addition to proclaiming one transcendent God, Zoroastrianism introduced a number of features that would be developed in the three main Western religions, including a new ethical orientation in which an essentially corrupt or imperfect world was to be reformed by human action. Thus human experience, for the first time, has a direction, a purpose, a history. And humans have a role to play – through their relationship, even their partnership, with God, and through the use of their free will and the virtues of self-assertion – in bringing about the purposes of a transcendent God for the world.

The three enduring Western religions each worked out the many potential implications of these and other spiritual insights in their own ways, and continue to do so today.

For the people of Israel, as for many ancient peoples, God was originally a jealous, national God whose concern was the welfare and advancement of the Israelites themselves. But gradually their understanding of this God deepened. A reading of the Torah and the other books of the Tanakh (the Jewish Bible, the Old Testament of the Christian Bible) tells a rather simple story with two intersecting plot lines. The first is a story about God. It is a story of unrequited love in which God seeks, unendingly, to establish a relationship with a faithless and unreliable people whom he is repeatedly obliged to forgive and restore as his still beloved people, despite their own waywardness. The second, more subterranean plot line is a story about the Israelites themselves. It is a story about

learning, the learning they do as they gradually alter their initial assumptions about their God, learning to see him less and less as a fierce,
bloodthirsty, primitive God of their initial conception, and more and
more like the force of love and being behind the universe. A critical moment in what was to become the religion of Judaism is the encounters
between God and Moses on Mount Sinai when He gives His people not
only His law, but even His name, "I AM THAT I AM."

This revelation is carried forward in the two other great religions that
sprang from the religion of the Israelites: Christianity and Islam. Of
these three, Islam is perhaps the most "Western" of them all. If the hall-
mark of Western religion is "mythic dissociation" between God and this
world, between God and man, between earth and heaven, between matter and spirit, Islam represents this new ideal in its purest form. It is
certainly the most starkly and uncompromisingly monotheistic.

Almost the whole of Islamic theology is contained in the simple profession of faith, known as the *shahadah*, one of the five Pillars of Islam:
"There is no God but God, and Muhammad is his Prophet." This declaration implies much more than a simple statement about Islamic mono-
theism. It expresses the fundamental Islamic teaching "that God is
Oneness. God is Unity: wholly indivisible, entirely unique, and utterly
indefinable. God resembles nothing in either essence or attributes."[27]
Reflecting "mythic dissociation" in its fullest form, God is wholly "other," and Islam's greatest sin is to infringe, impugn, dilute, or in any way
confuse God's absolute uniqueness, otherness, and absolute unity. One
of the prophet Muhammad's first (and most symbolic) actions, when he
and his followers assumed control of Mecca in 630 CE, was to purify
the Ka'aba, the traditional holy site of all the religions of the Arabian
peninsula, by removing and destroying all idols or images of gods.
Nothing was henceforth to stand between humans and the absolute
otherness and "transcendence" of the one true God.

Compared to Islam, Christianity looks like an attempt to compromise, or to seek a reconciliation between Eastern and Western spiritual
traditions, an attempt to reconnect heaven and earth, matter and spirit.
This is true of the different forms Christianity took both before *and*
after the decisive Councils of Nicea (325 CE), Constantinople (381) and
Chalcedon (451) at which most (but not all) of the churches officially
adopted the doctrine of the Trinity. Prior to Nicea, many of the non-
canonical gospels then circulating but not incorporated subsequently
into the Christian Bible – the so-called Gnostic Gospels, especially the

"Gospel of Thomas" – seem very close to the Eastern forms of spirituality we have already examined. For them, God and the human person are, in some sense, one: they proclaim the *identity* of the individual and the ultimate reality to be found *within* each human person. Even after Nicea, the ideas made finally official in the doctrine of the Trinity – that Jesus was both man *and* God[28] and that God is present in the world in the form of the Holy Spirit – these "Trinitarian" ideas seem like yet another effort to knit up the Western breach between heaven and earth, man and God, body and soul, spirit and matter.

This initial, very brief survey of the world's great religious traditions suggests at least two things. Each of them is unique, with its own specific insights and forms of expression. Yet all of them are the same, or part of the same whole, and all are complementary. Each one reflects some significant, distinctive aspect of the spiritual experience of humankind. And together they seem to tell the complete story about the life and testimony of the spirit.

The Eastern traditions reflect predominantly the inevitable "inward" spiritual journey we observed in chapter 3. The Western traditions reflect predominantly the "outward" journey. The Eastern mind sees ultimate reality as *inner*. The Western mind sees it as *other*. The one fosters religions of *immanence*, the other of *transcendence*. For Eastern spirituality the essence of spiritual life is found in *identity* with the ground of all being. Western spirituality seeks it in *relationship* with a transcendent God, reigning outside the world as well as in it.

The Eastern outlook seeks to "extinguish" individuality; the Western outlook creates and values the individual, and gives him or her important social responsibilities, to promote God's purposes on earth. For the first, history has no direction, if such a thing as "history" makes sense in this kind of cultural context at all. For the second, history has a direction, and a moral, which is the working out of God's providential plan for His people.

Each of these spiritual outlooks has its weaknesses and its strengths. Or to put it another way, each of them has the weaknesses of its strengths, and the strengths of its weaknesses. It is not always easy to have one without the other. Many in the West today are attracted by Eastern religions because they seem to allow their followers to connect in a direct way with their interior life, without some of what now appear to be the obstacles and intellectual baggage that come with the Western traditions. It would be premature to consider here what some of those are. I will have more to say about that in the next chapter. But it's not perhaps premature to note that giving up the weaknesses of a tradition can also mean giving up its strengths.

✳

So far, in this chapter, I've been tracing some of the key features of the major spiritual traditions we call "religions." But thinking about these traditions as if they were religions can be very misleading. It can be a way of trading the substance for the shadow, the spirit for the letter.

The problem is that when we talk in this way about religions, we almost necessarily do so from *outside*, and from an analytic, theoretical, or objective point of view. Yet this is not what religious life is like at all. And it most certainly is not how it appears to those who live it. For this reason, to get at the reality of religious life, we must find a way to shake off the misleading notion of a religion as something like an intellectual "school" or "world view" to which one belongs or adheres. We need to think of religious life as just that: a *life that is lived*, and how that life *feels*, not from the outside but from the *inside*.

Remember what I said at the beginning of this chapter: religious life is simply a deeper form of human spirituality. And true spirituality is merely a deepened and focused expression of the necessary human virtues of reverence. According to Augustine of Hippo (354–430), the great thinker who laid the foundations of Christian thought and civilization in the late Roman empire, the Latin word "religio" (from which our word "religion" comes) originally expressed the virtues of reverence, respect, and piety displayed "in the family and between friends," and was later adopted to express, by analogy, "the worship we hold to be due only to him who is the true God."[29] The Islamic "bible," the *Quran,* also suggests that religious practice is simply a deepening of the practice of reverence originally encountered in the family: "remember God," it says, "as you remember your forefathers, or *with deeper reverence.*"[30] So religious life is a further development of the practices of reverence we learn first in our families and communities.[31] It supports and nourishes them, and takes us in the direction to which they all point. But that means it must be something that is experienced, that is practised, that is *lived*, not by an institution, but by real people.

A "religion," even a church, is not a "real" spiritual entity, apart from the people who compose it.[32] A religion is made up of persons, all of whom are on some kind of a spiritual journey, who are leading a religious – that is to say, a spiritual – *life* (both individual and collective). As Wilfred Cantwell Smith (1916–2000), a Canadian scholar of comparative religion, remarked: "The most important single matter to remember in all this is that ultimately we have not to do with *religions* but with religious *persons*."[33]

Unless you can get inside the minds of these religious people, and understand a bit better how they live, and how that life appears to them, you will not be able to understand what they do, or why they do it. Nor will you be able to consider, seriously, whether such a life is for you. Among other things, that means gaining a better insight into the true nature of religious life, or what, in the Western world, we call faith.

# 5

# Faith and Belief

Faith and belief are *not* the same thing.

This may come as a surprise to you. Many people assume that the essence of religion is belief. Isn't that what you do, in a "religion": believe something? Isn't this *something* the thing that makes a religion a religion, and makes it the religion that it is?[1]

Those who take this view assume that one decides to lead a religious life somewhat as if one were joining a political party or taking sides in an academic or philosophical debate: you check out the statement of beliefs, or the creed, and if you agree, you sign up. Or don't, which is more likely, from their point of view. Indeed, much facile criticism is directed at what appear (at first) to be implausible belief systems or creeds, which the critic takes to be the heart of religious faith.

To be fair, much of this confusion has been created in the West by one of its leading religions, Christianity, and by its later opponents.[2] The alliance between Christianity and Greco-Roman culture in the first centuries of the common era is one of the glories of the cultural history of humankind, and has furnished the basis of Western civilization in ways we can scarcely number today. In fact, even many of the aggressively non-religious or anti-religious schools of thought today are, without recognizing it, secularized versions of Christian thought.

But this alliance came at a price. Perhaps partly because of the political circumstances surrounding the adoption of Christianity as the official religion of the late Roman Empire, but, even more, in the long run, because of the brilliant marriage between Greek and Christian thought accomplished in those centuries by the Greek and Latin Fathers of the

Church, many Christians (and their later rationalist opponents) came to assume that the essence of Christianity (and therefore of religion in general) was to be found *in the mind*: in catechisms or creeds, like the Nicene Creed, or in "dogma," theology, or some intellectual or abstract statement of beliefs.[3]

Wilfred Cantwell Smith has suggested that this confusion is also the result of the limitations of Western languages, and of Latin in particular. They offered only a single verb – *credo*, "I believe" – to describe two quite distinct activities. This one verb had to serve "both for intellectual belief (belief *that*) and religious belief (belief *in*) – though men of faith have insisted that the two things are different."[4]

Because of the heritage from the early Greek and Latin Fathers, this emphasis on "beliefs" was already strong in medieval Christianity, especially among the higher clergy and laity. But by the late fourteenth century it was becoming dominant, as theology and spirituality began to split apart – the latter gradually banished to a marginal and eccentric sphere of piety or mysticism – and religion became associated more and more with theology; that is, with the mind.[5] This trend was heightened even more, after 1400, by the Protestant and Catholic Reformations, and by the new humanism of the Renaissance. Despite the more nuanced views of many leaders, these three movements had the over-all effect of emphasizing the doctrinal aspect of religion while downplaying religious practice or action.

Charles Taylor uses the very expressive word "excarnation" – disembodiment – to describe this process: "the transfer of our religious life out of bodily forms of ritual, worship, practice, so that it comes more and more to reside 'in the head'."[6] Some Protestant traditions rejected images and symbols, and almost eliminated liturgy altogether, focussing everything on preaching, scripture, and theology.[7] The pulpit replaced the altar as the focus of worship in many churches, especially those influenced by John Calvin (actually a Frenchman, Jean Cauvin or Calvin (1509–1564), one of the leaders of the Protestant Reformation).[8] Calvin himself seems to have defined faith as a kind of "knowledge."[9] The growing rivalry between the Calvinist and Lutheran branches of Protestantism in the sixteenth century led to a "quest for differences" found in increasingly "explicit and extensive doctrinal formulations."[10] The late sixteenth century witnessed an avalanche of new "confessions" and formalized statements of belief, "a vast pile of catechisms" as one historian has described it: "true doctrine was now at a premium."[11] The rich tradition of living Christian spirituality was reduced to "doctrinal concepts ... preached as objective truth."[12]

By the seventeenth century, in the period leading to the European Enlightenment, the word "religion" had already begun to be used in the way we normally use it today: to designate no longer *religio*, the practice and experience of religious piety referred to by Augustine, but rather an intellectual construct, a rational system of ideas and beliefs, often viewed *from the outside*. It was in this fertile soil that "natural religion," deism, and, inevitably, atheism grew. It was no coincidence that cities like Geneva and Edinburgh which had been strong centres of Calvinism in the sixteenth century became equally strong centres of rationalism only two centuries later.[13] After all, if religion was just a matter of "beliefs," why not develop them in other, more "rational" ways?[14] Though the concept of "religion," in this new sense, was often used first by reformers, critics, or opponents, it was also picked up, as so often happens in such debates, by the mainstream. By the mid-eighteenth century, it was more or less assumed, by those on all sides of the debate, that a "religion" is something "that one believes or does not believe, something whose propositions are true or are not true, something whose *locus* is in the realm of the intelligible, is up for inspection before the speculative mind."[15]

This view was never unanimous. It was challenged at the time by devotional or "Pietist" movements that wanted to restore emphasis on the virtues of reverence (or "piety"). And again, at the beginning of the nineteenth century, by thinkers such as the German philosopher, Friedrich Schleiermacher (1768–1834), who argued, contrary to the eighteenth-century consensus, that "religious principles and ideas" are *not* the essence of religion: they are only the "scientific treatment of religion, knowledge about it, and not religion itself."[16] But, on the whole, these general assumptions about the nature of religion have prevailed, at least in the popular mind, to this day.[17]

For most people in the West today – both religious and non-religious – this is still assumed to be the right way to understand a religion. The concept of faith "has lost its genuine meaning and has received the connotation of 'belief in something unbelievable.'"[18] The essence of being a religious person, in this view, is to give assent to some statements, propositions, or ideas.[19] The way to understand a religion is to study these statements. And the way to criticize a religion is to demolish them.

Now the intellectual or rational formulations that any religion develops (as the life of faith embraces the life of reason) are not unimportant. Indeed, they are sometimes to be numbered among the glories of that religious tradition. In the case of Christianity, for example, the thought of Augustine, based largely on that of Plato and neo-Platonism (but going beyond them), or of Thomas Aquinas (1225–1274), based largely on that of Aristotle (but also going beyond it), are among the highest · achievements of the human intellect.

But the very brilliance of these achievements helps to obscure the role that these kinds of intellectual formulations play and the place they occupy in authentic religious life. While they are important, they are not the heart of the matter. Being the product of reason, they are in many ways the weakest or most vulnerable part of any religious tradition, the one most subject to debate, and so to change and variation, as ideas evolve. Genius though he was, many of Augustine's assertions now seem to us unconvincing. So religious "ideas" or doctrines are not the core of religious life, not its living heart. Not the essence that makes it what it is.

✳

If faith isn't the same thing as belief, what is it?

We can begin to see how faith differs from belief – in the rationalist sense assumed even by many Christians today – by looking at cases where the issue of faith arises in the Christian scriptures themselves. One of the many biblical stories where the nature of faith is on display is that of a "sinful" woman (probably a prostitute) who pushes her way into a house where Jesus is dining, to wash, kiss, and anoint his feet. Rather than being annoyed, as his host was, Jesus tells the woman her sins are forgiven: "Your faith has saved you," he says; "go in peace."[20] Another woman, suffering from menstrual haemorrhages, steals up behind Jesus in a crowd and touches him. Immediately Jesus turns to confront the woman and tells her, "Your faith has made you well."[21] Similarly, a blind man named Bartimaeus calls out to Jesus to be healed, and Jesus makes the same response.[22]

Now obviously Jesus (or the writers of the Gospels) didn't mean these people were saved by subscribing to the Nicene Creed, or the Apostles' Creed, or the Catechism, or to the doctrines of the Trinity or of Justification, or the Augsburg Confession, or the Thirty-Nine Articles of the Church of England, or anything of this kind. What is it then that

Jesus recognized, and that the Christian scriptures call "faith"? These stories seem to suggest it is something altogether different.

What are the elements of faith we can see in these stories? First of all, both the women and the blind man decide to *act*. A decision is required, because none of them can get to Jesus or get his attention without effort, because he is in a strange house or surrounded by a big crowd. This decision to act is not based on knowledge or certainty, but on simple human need. They are desperate for something to save their lives. They not only make a decision to act, but they also act on their decision. (The first is a lot easier than the second: how many times have you made decisions – New Year's resolutions, for example – but then failed to act on your good intentions?) And finally, the way they act is also important: they act on their decisions with a naive trust, a simple confidence and hope, that what they are seeking can in fact be accomplished, despite all the evidence to the contrary in their lives so far.

So, based on these examples, we could start by saying that faith seems to involve at least three things: a decision based not on certainty or knowledge but on need and hope; an action or actions that follow from the decision; and a spirit of trust and confidence, as well as hope, in which the actions are carried out.

We can test this initial cluster of potential characteristics of faith by looking at some other examples. In another story from the Christian scriptures, Jesus and his friends are in a boat at night when a storm comes up. His followers wake him in terror, complaining that he doesn't seem to care about them. He responds to them, rather sternly: "Why are you afraid? Have you still no faith?"[23] This is a counter-example to the previous three. Jesus' own followers displayed the absence rather than the presence of faith. But our initial check-list holds up. The absence of faith seems to be the failure to act in a certain way, or a failure to carry through on previous decisions. And also a failure to act in the right way, with trust and hope. In fact, Jesus' friends are scared to death.

But we don't need to confine ourselves to the Christian scriptures. Abraham occupies a special place in the three main Western religions. In fact, in all three, God is the "God of Abraham." Abraham is presented in the Jewish, Christian, and Islamic traditions as the spiritual archetype, emblematic of the deepest form of righteousness and faith all three uphold. This is somewhat surprising because the behaviour attributed to him, on some occasions, can seem to modern eyes less than perfectly honourable. The American political philosopher Thomas

Pangle (b. 1944) explains why he is, nonetheless, so important. "Abram [the original name of Abraham] is not given a clue as to how this nigh-incredible promise [that, even though he is an old man, he will have descendants without number, who will inherit the whole land of Canaan[24]] might be fulfilled. His trust in the promise is accordingly of the utmost merit; it is a manifestation, Scripture says, of his justice. By 'justice' in this context, Scripture would seem to mean, most simply, the willingness to give God his due, and what is due to God is *trust, even or especially in the absence of earthly plausibility or evidence.*"[25]

Similarly, the *Quran* asks: "Who but a foolish man would renounce the faith of Abraham?" and explains that what makes Abraham such a "good example" is that he and those who followed him said, "Lord, in You we have put our *trust.*"[26] In speaking of Abraham, this is what the letter to the Hebrews calls the "righteousness of faith."[27] The letter reviews the whole history of the people of Israel, from Abel to Samuel and David, and declares that all its great figures, including Abraham, accomplished what they did "by faith." It clearly doesn't mean they subscribed to a certain set of ideas or "beliefs" (much less Christian beliefs), but rather that they *acted*, and acted in a certain way, above all with perseverance, confidence, and trust. This review helps to illustrate, by concrete example, Hebrews' great definition of faith, which emphasizes the crucial element of hope, and its necessary triumph over uncertainty: "faith is the substance of things *hoped for*, the *evidence* of things *not seen.*"[28] Faith is only faith, as Augustine remarked, "when what is not yet seen in reality is awaited in hope."[29]

So faith, like love, is something you *do*, not something you have. Before it can become something you might be said to have, it must instead be a form of *action* or *activity.*[30]

"Religion is neither a theological nor an intellectual virtue," said Thomas Aquinas, himself a supreme intellectual. It is a "moral virtue ... not tested by emotion but by the fairness of the *actions* we offer to God."[31] In his eagerness to disentangle religious faith again from the simple equation with "belief" to which the seventeenth and eighteenth centuries had consigned it, Friedrich Schleiermacher identified faith instead with certain states of "feeling." This reaction, which reflected the Romantic assumptions of his era, did not sufficiently recognize that (as

Schleiermacher himself said – and as we will consider again in chapter 9) an "exercise of feeling" is itself a form of "action."[32]

The *acts* (including acts of feeling) that constitute a life of faith are forms of action carried out in a certain spirit, above all a spirit of reverence, trust, and hope: a trust and hope that are not entirely dependent on earthly evidence, and can even persevere in its absence, or in the face of evidence to the contrary. Karl Rahner (1904–1984), a modern German theologian, calls this kind of hope and trust "primal," "total," or "absolute": "unbounded and unconditional hope which becomes a basic acceptance in trust of existence."[33]

In modern culture, when we use the noun, "religion," it turns these *acts* into a *thing* – and, moreover, a thing viewed from the *outside*. In doing so, it usually emphasizes some secondary intellectual content like "beliefs," dogma, or theology. That's one of the reasons, as you may already have noticed, I rarely use the noun "religion" in this book but prefer instead to use the adjective "religious," as in the expressions "religious practice" or "religious life," for example. Using the adjective instead of the noun helps remind us that "religious" is a quality we can see in certain kinds of actions or creative activities, actions carried out in the spirit of reverence, and constituting for the practitioner a genuine experience of spirituality, an authentic religious *life*. For that reason, from here on I will often use the word "religion" in quotation marks, to make clear when I do so that I'm deliberately using the word in the misleading way most modern people do.

For people in the West, especially those raised outside a religious tradition, or whose religious tradition is only skin-deep, this may come as a surprise, even a shock. It may even seem preposterous or a sneaky way to elude the key question, because they have grown up in a culture that thinks of "religion" in the very way I am rejecting. But if we look at other traditions, and recall the brief survey in the previous chapter, the point becomes almost self-evident. The Christian and Western emphasis on religious "beliefs" (especially since 1400) turns out to be the exception, not the rule. It's only Christian (or post-Christian, or anti-Christian) blinkers that blind us to the obvious.

In Judaism, for example, the ideas of God, Torah, the people of Israel, and the Holy Land "do not represent a catechism or a theology, for there is none such in Judaism." Jewish faith is something you *do*. Its focus is "neither on metaphysical speculation nor on dogma but on human action."[34] The Talmud (the oral law that accompanies the written

law of the Torah) avoids abstract language entirely.[35] Jews are defined
not by a canon of prescribed "beliefs" but by their actions, especially
their observance of the Mosaic law, the Torah (including dietary and
ceremonial laws), and of key rituals, including daily prayers, the
Sabbath, circumcision, annual festivals such as Rosh Hashanah, Yom
Kippur, Sukkot, Hanukkah, Purim, Passover, Shavuot, and once-a-lifetime rituals, such as the bar mitzvah. Similarly, in the case of Islam, as
we saw, its boundaries are defined by "Five Pillars," only one of which
– the *shahadah* – has any minimal belief content. The other four are
ritual activities of daily prayer, alms-giving, fasting (during the holy sea-
son of Ramadan), and a once-a-lifetime pilgrimage to Mecca.

If you recall our overview of the Eastern traditions, the point becomes
even clearer. They do not lack intellectual and metaphysical speculation:
the debates between Buddhist schools were at least as arcane as those
between medieval Christian theologians. But their final emphasis is not
upon belief systems, or on *defining* Nirvana, for example, but rather
"on *realizing* it within themselves."[36] Some of them, like Zen Buddhism,
do not have any of the things we in the West would expect to find in a
"religion." Much of Eastern spirituality consists of a variety of physical
and mental disciplines, practices, and rituals for exploring the spiritual
and psychic dimensions, and linking them, through meditation, both to
body and mind, in a spirit of unity and harmony.

Joseph Campbell tells an amusing story that illustrates the difference
not just between East and West, but also between someone who ap-
proaches religious practice from the inside and someone who does so
from the outside. A leading American academic at an international con-
gress on the history of religions approached a Shinto priest, at a garden
party in Japan:

> "You know," he said, "I've been now to a good many ceremonies and
> have seen quite a number of shrines, but I don't get the ideology; I
> don't get your theology." The Japanese (you may know) do not like to
> disappoint visitors, and this gentleman, polite, apparently respecting
> the foreign scholar's profound question, paused as though deep in
> thought, and then, biting his lips, slowly shook his head. "I think we
> don't have ideology," he said. "We don't have theology. We dance."[37]

The Shinto priest's response perfectly captures the heart of all religious practice, for those who know it, and live it, from the inside. True

religious life does not consist, primarily, in agreeing with or holding some set of intellectual concepts or ideas. It consists, instead, in reverent actions, which, in the case of the Japanese priest, were the stately, musical rituals of his tradition, which could not be reduced to words any more than one can express the "meaning" of a painting or a concerto.

If the concept of "belief" has any place close to the heart of faith, it too needs to become an action, or a verb rather than a noun. And, interestingly, it's in this form that it appears, almost exclusively, in the Christian scriptures. As a noun it seems to occur only once. As a verb, an *action* word, it occurs many times, and, even more interesting, it often appears as an *in*transitive rather than a transitive verb, that is to say, it is an action by itself, without a specific object. For example, immediately after Jesus tells the woman suffering from menstrual haemorrhages that her faith has made her well – in fact, while he is *still* speaking – a message is brought to another person in the crowd, named Jairus, that his daughter has died. As soon as he hears this, Jesus says to him, "Be not afraid, *only believe.*"[38] Obviously Jesus (or the writer of the Gospel) didn't mean that the man should recite a creed or accept some doctrine or dogma. The verb has no object. Jesus is telling the man to *do* something, just as the woman had done a moment before, to be inwardly transformed by doing something, not just with his mind but with his heart and his will also, and to do it with the same openness, the same spirit of trust. To be more accurate, Jesus is telling him to *continue* doing something, because Jairus had already come to him, seeking help, just as the women and Bartemaeus had done. However, the challenge for Jairus to continue acting with trust is even greater now, because any rational person would say that the chances of his hopes being answered have just been utterly destroyed.

If faith is a form of action or activity, or life – if it is something you *do* before it can become something you have, or hold, or mentally agree to – what is it that religious people do? This is a very large question. In a sense, the rest of this book is a partial answer to it. But I can perhaps suggest here, briefly, some of the types of action that faith might involve, that give shape to a life of religious practice.

As we have already noticed, the first type of action seems to be some kind of decision, an act of will.[39] The decision may be more or less explicit, depending on the context. In a homogeneous and deeply religious culture, it may not even appear on the surface, as a choice. It is a choice made largely by the culture itself. In a secular or mixed culture, the decision is much more explicit. In a predominantly secular culture like our own, where all the pressure is in another direction, it must be made or not made, consciously, by each individual.[40]

The decision is not made on the basis of knowledge or certainty, but rather on the basis of real, urgent human need, or some kind of encounter or experience in life. These may be the same thing, because the need often leads to the encounter. That the decision proceeds from the urgency of real experience doesn't make it an arbitrary one, however. On the contrary: that's what makes it *real*. As we discovered in chapters 2 and 3, this kind of decision is rooted in the natural human virtues of reverence, and in the way they inevitably point, or push, or pull human beings toward the discovery of the spiritual dimension that underlies everyday life. It's "the reverent attitude of mind," as Augustine said, "which leads them to choose God for their support."[41] We are led to God by reverence, not the reverse. We don't become reverent because we "know" God. It's in the practice of reverence itself that we encounter whatever it is that we call God, or that points to Him.

The decision is to *do* something, not to think something. The thinking is not unimportant, but it's "secondary." [42] It's a reflection *on* – or *of* – the action, not the action itself. Theology stands in relation to religious life as a music critic stands to music.[43] Which is to say, in a different space altogether, "external" to the "real basic phenomenon of spirituality."[44] The action that follows from the decision may take the form of a physical action, as in the case of the two women or Bartimaeus, or simply a mental action, like Jairus, after his daughter has died.

The external actions of a religious person might be conceived as a series of concentric circles, beginning, in the centre, with the spiritual practices of the tradition, including meditation, prayer, and worship, practices that are the natural human way to develop and exercise the virtues of reverence. "Religion has two kinds of acts," said Thomas Aquinas. The first are the actions of this inner circle, the specific exercises of reverence. And the second are the "other virtues" of "reverence" that flow from the first, virtues such as charity, mercy, and self-control.[45] So the outer circles of action will be the behaviours the person exhibits, as a result of the inner core in his or her personal life (diet, dress), in family life (respect for spouse and parents, the loving nurture of children), in his or her community (honesty, charity, and care for those in need, for example), in society as a whole (the pursuit of social justice), and even toward the whole natural world and universe.

The internal or mental actions are chiefly prayer and meditation – which are two sides of the same coin – and any other technique or exercise for exploring the depths of the spirit and connecting it to both body and mind, as well as to whatever the person may conceive as ultimate reality or the ground of all being.

But there is yet another kind or level of inner action that can be said to be the result of these external and internal activities. If I may use a physical image, we might call this a gradual *turning* or reorientation of the heart. The turning of the heart is a gradual reorientation toward the source of the spirit, toward the otherness of the spirit, and a reaching out to embrace it.[46] This third kind of action is essential, because it is the point of the other two, which are only means to this end.[47] A Jewish rabbinical teaching says that what really matters in a life is whether a person "directs his heart toward heaven."[48] As the great Jewish philosopher Maimonides (Moses ben Maimon) (1138–1204) said, "the Lord desires the heart, and ... the intention of the heart is the measure of all things."[49] Thomas Aquinas seems to have wanted to reserve the word "faith" specifically for this inner transformation, a reorientation of the will that not only "enlightens" the mind but "also warms the affections."[50] All of the religious traditions warn that, without this inner transformation, outward religious activity is merely a dry and meaningless husk.

Faith then is something that you do, internally and externally. But the way you do it is also important. Whatever is done to explore and express the spirit, in faith, is done in harmony with the virtues from which it springs, that is to say, reverently: "in reverence, awe and submission," in the words of the *Shulkhan Arukh*, a legal code authoritative for Orthodox Jews.[51] And, as the stories and excerpts we have just looked at show, it is also done in a spirit of trust and of hope.

Faith turns out, in the end, to be a decision to adopt certain virtues, to "put on" certain habits, habits both of feeling and behaviour.[52] You could almost say that the life of faith *is* the spirit of reverence, trust and hope in action.[53]

✳

But if faith is something you *do*, in a spirit of reverence, trust and hope, why do people do it? We already have part of the answer, in the first chapters of this book. But we will explore this question and its answer more fully in the next chapter.

# 6

# Encountering the Spirit

People normally initiate a life of religious practice because of some kind of experience or experiences.

I'm going to call this kind of experience an "encounter." That's what I think it normally feels like, or the shape it takes. As Martin Jay (b. 1944), an American historian of ideas, has said, what we call experience – any kind of significant experience – "is inevitably acquired through an encounter with otherness, whether human or not."[1] In the kind of experience that initiates a life of religious practice, people encounter someone or something – they come up against someone or something, or into their presence – and this encounter shapes their life, and the way they want to lead it.[2] They come into a kind of "presence," and they want to *continue* coming into that same presence.[3]

It's very important to emphasize right away that the kind of encounters I'm talking about don't have to be dramatic events. Life-shaking encounters and mystical experiences do occur, of course, and we will look at some of them in this chapter. But these are relatively rare, especially in our Western traditions. The vast majority of the encounters I'm talking about are much less dramatic, everyday events.

For example, most of us learned our basic habits of reverence by *encountering* them in the family. We became reverent beings by learning the habits and virtues of everyday reverence – manners, courtesy, respect, and so on – in our families, and we didn't even know it! We still don't. But we go on practising them, nonetheless. In the same quiet way, many people learn the more formal practices of reverence associated with religious life, because their families take them to church, synagogue, mosque, or temple, and perhaps also instruct the children in the religious rituals of the home. In this way some *encounter* the rituals and ceremonies that give formal shape to reverence and to spiritual life: they come to know these actions from the inside; they become familiar with the states of mind and feeling that accompany them. They may sense that these practices bring them into some kind of presence, and they may want to continue coming into it.

I will come back to these rituals and ceremonies, because they are a common and important kind of spiritual encounter. But first let's look at some others.

✳

One important kind of encounter is with a person.

This kind of encounter is not only very important, it's also very common. For example, the encounters we just talked about normally involve our parents and other family members. Research on child development has consistently shown that the relationship with parents – the love parents show their children and the example they give them – is by far the most important influence on the development of the personality. So the shaping encounter with influential people starts in the home, before we are even aware of it. It continues in our relationships with our friends – especially in a peer-oriented society like the one emerging at the beginning of the twenty-first-century – with other people around us, like school, college, and university teachers, and eventually with role-models in our workplaces and communities.[4]

From time to time, we meet figures who become especially important or influential for us. They seem to represent some kind of ideal. We are deeply impressed or moved by them – we feel the kind of *awe* in their presence I talked about in chapter 2 – and we want to become like them. They take the place in our lives that our parents originally occupied, as role models we can't help imitating. (In fact, the Talmud says these kinds of teachers are more important than parents.[5]) It's very important for us to find such models, because they inspire us to choose a profession or a way of life, and they fire us with eagerness and energy to live it in a certain way.[6] As American political scientist Hugh Heclo (b. 1943) puts it: "Real change comes when one person encounters another person who seems to be living out the truth of the matter ... so that in encountering them one senses a foundation that is like hitting a rock."[7]

Any relationship of this kind, between a "master" and a "disciple" is already, in some sense, a spiritual one, but sometimes it has an explicitly spiritual or even religious influence. The *Upanishads* (among the most important texts of the Hindu tradition) describe a series of encounters between students and teachers, some of whom are parents ("Upanishad" means "to sit down near to"); and the teaching sessions they recount are aimed at achieving spiritual insight. The tradition of the Tao has much to say about the forceful impact of a spiritual sage on others, and how that inner power is achieved. The encounter with a holy or spiritually authoritative figure, whether in person or second hand – through writings or stories, for example – is one of the most common and important starting points for a religious life.

In fact many, if not most, religious traditions begin through the encounter with a towering spiritual figure – Confucius, Lao Tzu, Chuang Tzu, Siddhartha Gautama Shakyamuni, Muhammad, Jesus of Nazareth – who may be an actual historical figure, but is soon transformed into something much more, as Gautama Shakyamuni became the Buddha, or Jesus of Nazareth became the Second Person of the Trinity. Jesus' encounters with Bartimaeus, Jairus, and the two women changed their lives, or we presume they did. These encounters certainly changed the lives of many others, and continue to do so. William Temple (1881–1944), a Christian writer who also became Archbishop of Canterbury, argued that "Knowledge of God can be fully given to man *only* in a person, never in a doctrine."[8] In these kinds of encounters, "we find ourselves face-to-face with a synthesis between norms that are ever valid and their unique model." But in these special encounters, it is the person who seems to validate the norms rather than the reverse.[9] A life-changing encounter with a person imbued, in our eyes, with a special spiritual presence or power, is one of the most common forms in which a religious life begins, or changes course, through a conversion, for example.

✳

Even in a largely secular society, people have many other kinds of encounters that direct their attention to the spiritual dimension of life, and may awaken a spiritual awareness or hunger.[10]

I have already mentioned the experiences of nature and of art, both of which may nourish a spiritual dimension that finds few other outlets today, and can awaken a deeper need or awareness. Those who are really attentive to the process of artistic creation, or who live close to nature, very often become alert to the fundamental mystery of creation that underlies them both. Where do artistic ideas and impulses come from? In certain moments of artistic creation, as Canadian literary theorist Northrop Frye (1912–1991) observes, there may be "a feeling of actual communication with a personal but not subjective presence. A writer who has once had such feelings can hardly pretend to himself that he has not had them, whatever the clamouring of ideologies and doctrines around him may say."[11] In his novel, *Doctor Zhivago*, Russian poet Boris Pasternak (1890–1960) gives a vivid description of this kind of creative encounter: "[H]e experienced the approach of what is called inspiration. At such moments the correlation of the forces controlling the artist is, as it were, stood on its head ... At such moments Yury felt that the main part of his work was not being done by him but by something which was above him and controlling him ... he felt himself to be only the pretext and the pivot setting it in motion ...'Lord! Lord!' he whispered, 'and all this is for me? Why hast thou given me so much? Why hast Thou admitted me to Thy presence?'"[12]

A similar kind of encounter can occur when people discover that ideas like justice, truth, or love are things that that can't be seen, but seem to be real nevertheless. They seem to live "outside" ordinary, earthly time, waiting for us to make them a reality in our own lives. So where exactly do they live, until we do so? Hugh Hood has expressed the quandaries that can fill a mind that encounters the mystery of eternal ideas, and asks how they fit into reality:

Is there anything that does not exist? Can something be and not exist? The square root of minus two, the idea of justice – they don't exist. At least they can't be found anywhere. What is the difference between being, pure and simple, and being in existence, actually existing or being present at some point in space and time? Can something be and not exist?

How can a mathematical idea be in my head? What do I mean when I say that? Does the idea of justice exist? And if it doesn't, how can something which doesn't exist modify the actions of beings who do exist and can be seen to exist? Granted that nobody ever conforms to a pure, abstract notion of justice in his conduct, never-theless the idea operates in conduct, allowing us to approach it or depart from it.

Where are the moral ideas of love, justice, truthfulness? Where do they come from?[13]

Just as we encounter something important when we confront these eternal truths, we meet the same thing, in reverse, when we come face-to-face with evil. In fact, the encounter with evil is one of the most com-mon sources of religious experience. No spiritual or religious tradition promises to banish evil, or pain or despair from this world. Indeed it is precisely the *encounter* with them that seems often to create awareness of the *need* for a spiritual life, and opens the door to one. It was Gautama Shakyamuni's encounter with the evils of disease, suffering, and death that set him on the road to become the Buddha. It was the total destruc-tion of their country that set the prophets Jeremiah and Ezekiel, and the exiled Israelites, on a similar journey of discovery, to a new spirituality of suffering, empathy, hope, and love: a turning of the heart. The en-counter with suffering and evil – "the mystery and the naturalness – the natural mystery, the mysterious naturalness – of suffering"[14] – is such an important part of the motivation for a religious life that Christians have taken as their central spiritual symbol an image of the most grue-some suffering imaginable. As the American philosopher Susan Neiman (b. 1955) observes, "the problem of evil is not derived from religion, religion is one kind of attempt to solve the problem of evil."[15]

An opposite form of encounter with the spirit can occur when people seek to lead an ethical life. It's not just that we seek some source of au-thority for our actions, or that we spontaneously seek to be accountable for them to someone or something. It seems to be more than that. There's something about serving "the good" that can't help making us aware of the *spirit* of the good, the spirit that underlies it or inhabits it. The struggle to lead a good or moral life necessarily leads human be-ings, as British writer Iris Murdoch (1919–1999) notes, to "encounter with an (unassimilable) external other": with whatever it is that "like a light shines through all the virtues," as the Roman philosopher Plotinus (204/5–270 CE) put it.[16] In the Jewish tradition, for example, obedience to the law of the Torah is "the way of regular encounter with God."[17] Even the Roman Stoic, Seneca (c. 3–65 CE), while warning about the supposed futility of prayer (as he understood it), found it hard not to acknowledge that living an ethical life leads to an encounter with the otherness of the spirit: "The god is near you, with you, inside you," he wrote to his young protégé, Lucilius. "A holy spirit is seated within us, a watcher and guardian of our good and bad actions. As this spirit is treated by us, so it treats us."[18]

This spontaneous, almost irresistible encounter with the spirit often takes place at key turning points in our lives, especially those that bring us face to face with the mysteries of being, when the miracle that things exist, or the poignancy that their existence may be short or finite, breaks though our normal, everyday composure. The miracle of a new birth, and the beginning of a new life, for example. Or a marriage, the moment when two people wager their whole lives, the only ones they have, on the outcome. Why do people find that both of these experiences bring them back to a synagogue or temple or church, even if they haven't been there for years? It's not just that they're falling back into a traditional cultural groove, though that's obviously a big element, too. It's something more, something that helps to *explain* the groove in the first place: the sense that these kinds of events have an unusual depth. Philosophers call this an "existential" depth, because these events confront us with the impenetrable mystery of existence. Events like these are lived therefore on a different plane from the normal daily routine, and need all the resources of symbolism and ceremony to express their significance, their relationship to something deeper or higher than ordinary, daily life.

Of course, for people unable or unwilling to use such spiritual resources, these events may be poignant and significant in another sense. They may bring them face-to-face with something that isn't there, a vacuum, an absence.

This presents us with yet another paradox, the kind of paradox with which this book seems to be crammed. Because another common form of encounter with the spirit is with a kind of *absence*. The encounter with absence is inevitable in life, because we can only see the physical world. The whole background of being *within* which everything exists – and without which nothing *could* exist – is, and must be, entirely invisible to us. Present, but invisible.[19] So human life, whether religious or not, is necessarily filled with a kind of *presence of absence*. A life of faith is simply a life more conscious of this inescapable presence of absence, a life centred upon it, a life whose stance toward this absence is an attitude of reverence. The prophet Isaiah declared that the God of Israel was "a God who hides himself."[20] The *Wen-tzu*, a Taoist text, says that the One "seems to be absent, yet it is there."[21] Almost all religious rites, such as the Christian Eucharist, for example, are therefore a complex intermingling of symbols of presence and absence.

In a secular age, this presence of absence is felt even more vividly, and painfully. Without the practices and reflexes that allow them to acknowledge this background presence and to participate in its mysterious power, many people experience an emptiness at the heart of things: an emptiness that makes them long for something to fill the void, to make them whole again.[22] This spiritual hunger can be encountered almost like a presence of its own. The Canadian novelist, Jack Hodgins (b. 1938), has written hauntingly about this kind of absence that has a palpable presence in modern life. In his novel, *Broken Ground*, one of the characters muses: "I began to suspect that I had already lost something important that I didn't even know about, before I was born or soon afterwards. We all had. And gone on losing even more of it ever since, whatever it was. Behind the colourful parade of this century's gains and losses was a huge absence of something that was neither identified nor regained nor replaced."[23]

Frederick Buechner (b. 1926), an American writer, has also spoken eloquently about the pervading presence of absence in our time, and interprets it as one of the ways we actually encounter the spirit, in the modern, secular world, through its very silence:

Each of us ... carries around inside himself, I believe, a certain emptiness – a sense that something is missing, a restlessness, the deep feeling that somehow all is not right in his skin. Psychologists sometimes call it anxiety, theologians sometimes call it estrangement, but whatever you call it, I doubt that there are many who do not recognize the experience itself, especially no one of our age, which has been variously termed the age of anxiety, the lost generation, the beat generation, the lonely crowd. Part of the inner world of everyone is this sense of emptiness, unease, incompleteness, and I believe that this in itself is a word from God, that this is the sound God's voice makes in a world that has explained him away. In such a world, I suspect that maybe God speaks to us most clearly through his silence, his absence, so that we know him best through our missing him.[24]

✳

This kind of encounter with the presence of absence is closely connected to (perhaps even at the heart of) many of the special, heightened encounters I referred to at the beginning of the chapter, especially those sometimes called "mystical." These heightened encounters seem to occur at several levels. At a first level, they may involve visions, or states of rapture and transport. In some cultures such experiences are more common than in our own. North American aboriginal spirituality reserved an important role for spirit visions, and a young person could not come to adulthood before encountering one. In Eastern spiritual traditions, the techniques and practices for the inner journey are designed to make possible the encounter with the depths of the spirit through meditation, sometimes leading (especially in their "Tantric" forms) to visions or deep and dream-like trances.

These kinds of experiences are much rarer in Western culture, but very influential. In the Christian tradition, there is a long history of visionary encounters, beginning perhaps with Paul of Tarsus's (c. 5–67 CE) conversion experience on the road to Damascus, and other visions he related in his second letter to the Corinthians.[25]

Beyond these first visionary experiences are the ones properly called "mystical." The mystical experience is a heightened form of the common encounter with what I called a presence of absence. That's what makes it "mystical." As an encounter with something ultimately unknowable, it is largely inexpressible, or expressible only indirectly through images and symbols. The psychological experience itself can be described but what is encountered cannot. The mystical impulse (like Eastern spirituality) seems to involve a straining toward pure reverence without any remaining trace of self-assertion.

For this reason, mystical experience also seems to occur on more than one level. At a first level, it is still a genuine experience. In late medieval Catholicism, there was a tradition of meditative practices leading often to "mystical" states or experiences, of which Ignatius of Loyola's "Spiritual Exercises" are among the best known. Ignatius (1491–1556) was the founder of the Jesuit Order, and had many mystical experiences himself, as did others such as Hildegard of Bingen (1098–1179), Teresa of Avila (1515–1582), and Marie de l'Incarnation (1599–1672).

At a second level, however, the mystical encounter – that of the Spanish mystic John of the Cross (1542–1591), for example – can no longer be properly described as an "experience." Because the striving for pure reverence – and thus for the elimination of all self-assertion (a goal that can never be fully achieved because the striving itself remains a form of self-assertion) – progressively takes the seeker beyond language, beyond even the "self" that could have, and could report, such experiences. If the first kind of mystical encounter is an experience of absence, the second is more like – as British theologian Denys Turner (b. 1942) puts it – an "absence of experience." This second level of mystical encounter can even seem like a critique or repudiation of the first, a kind of "anti-mysticism," because, from this second perspective, the previous level remains too much a form of self-assertion.[26]

Because of the growing split between spirituality and "belief" from the end of the fourteenth century, and the resulting undervaluing of spiritual practice I described in the previous chapter, it isn't easy to give an account of Christian mystical encounters. There is a risk of reading Christianity backward, and interpreting earlier spirituality as a kind of specialized mystical experience which only became more common after this divide took hold.[27] But either before or after the fifteenth-century watershed, what we now call mystical experience seems to be a more heightened awareness of some kind of invisible, unknowable "presence," an awareness that's part of all religious practice, and perhaps of all reverence.[28] Blaise Pascal left detailed notes of a profound religious experience that occurred to him on the evening of 23 November, 1654. It lasted for two hours, from 10:30 p.m. to after midnight, and during that time he had a vision of fire, together with feelings of certainty, joy, and peace, a sense of the greatness of the human spirit, a closeness to the God of Abraham (not the rational god of the philosophers), together with anxiety about losing or being separated from God, and guilt about his own unfaithfulness. His notes finish with expressions of total submission to God, and "eternal joyfulness for one day of life on this earth."[29]

At the end of the nineteenth century, as the reaction against the eighteenth-century equation of "religion" with theology was gaining ground, and there was a new interest in authentic religious life, William James (1842–1910), one of the founders of the American school of philosophical pragmatism, wrote a famous and surprisingly sympathetic survey of religious experience (and perhaps contributed inadvertently to creating the modern idea of a distinct religious "experience"). He noted that such encounters characteristically display that inner drive to unity and connectedness I identified as the animating spirit of the human instinct for reverence: "This overcoming of all the usual barriers between the individual and the Absolute is the great mystic achievement. In mystic states we both become one with the Absolute and we become aware of our oneness. This is the everlasting and triumphant mystical tradition, hardly altered by differences of clime or creed. In Hinduism, in Neoplatonism, in Sufism ... we find the same recurring note, so that there is about mystical utterances an eternal unanimity which ought to make a critic stop and think ... Perpetually telling of the unity of man with God, their speech antedates languages, and they do not grow old."[30]

As James observes, these mystical encounters don't tell us anything on their own. They can be expressions of mental disturbance as easily as anything else.[31] In fact, the visions of the mentally disturbed sometimes bear striking resemblance to mystical encounters, especially the first or visionary kind. "Mystical experiences are either very intensive cases of an experience of God which is basically open to all" says Karl Rahner; "or they arouse the suspicion that they are psychological phenomena which can be explained by particular psychical causes."[32] Visionary encounters can also be brought on by deliberate techniques of physical deprivation, as they often are in both aboriginal and Eastern spiritualities, as a way of gaining access to the deepest recesses of the psyche, or the spirit.

So mystical or deep spiritual encounters can't be evaluated by themselves. It is only by their fruits that we can really assess them, or by the stature of those who have them, and the meaning they attach to them. The way such encounters influence their whole lives, or how their whole lives and thought cast light on them.

In the case of Blaise Pascal, for example, we know that his was one of the most acute and discerning minds of Western culture, not only one of its mathematical pioneers, but also one of its greatest writers and observers of human nature. At thirty-four, he was at the height of his mathematical achievements, and his magnificent spiritual writings, the *Lettres provinciales* and the *Pensées*, were still ahead of him. So the significance of his experience may be estimated not only by the calibre of his mind but also by the momentous writings that followed.

In the case of Thomas Aquinas, it is rather the reverse. If we can evaluate Pascal's spiritual encounter in the light of what followed, we have to assess the significance of Aquinas's experience by what went before. In the early hours of 6 December, 1273, while it was still dark, he arose, as usual, to say mass before resuming work on his monumental *Summa Theologica*. But during the service, something happened to him. A vision, insight, or spiritual experience of some kind left him in a state of wonder. He did not return to his normal routine of dictation. When his secretary pressed him repeatedly for an explanation, Aquinas finally confessed: "I can't. Everything I've written seems no better than straw in comparison to what has now been revealed."[33] At the age of forty-nine, Aquinas had already written almost a hundred works, including the two great *Summa*, the *Summa Theologica*, and the *Summa Contra Gentiles*, each of which, in today's editions, amounts to over a thousand pages. Yet an encounter with something made him think that words were no longer adequate to express what he now knew. We can only guess the power of this revelation by the towering authority of what he now regarded as so much chaff.

The presence of absence experienced by all human beings may be especially poignant, painful, even insupportable, in the face of some kind of deep sorrow. In any moment of great pain, loss, or reversal of fortune, we encounter the need for something that speaks to the depth of our spirit in a way that ordinary thought and speech cannot. At these moments we encounter the reality that we are much more than our conscious minds or our restless, thrusting egos, that these can bring us no comfort in the face of something profound, especially something profoundly distressing. One of the reasons a person may encounter something beyond or inside himself, as Thomas Aquinas said, is "the deficiencies he feels in himself crying out for care and comfort."[34] Our "need to respond to a further reality than meets the eye and to grope [our] way towards it," Bernard Lonergan remarks, "tends to be shouldered out of the busy day, to make its force felt in the tranquillity of darkness, in the solitude of loneliness, in the shattering upheavals of personal or social disaster."[35] It is at moments like these, above all – the moments when we are weary and "heavy-laden"[36] – that we encounter the true depths of our humanity. "[T]he only time man pretends he does not need God," says Canadian novelist David Adams Richards (b. 1950), "is when he thinks or she thinks they are themselves God or are in a position of such comfort that God cannot trouble them or touch them. Once the man or woman finds himself or herself in deep trouble or despair, they search for what was always there."[37] At times like these, our urgent, unanswerable *need* forms a question for which we must have an answer. Not an answer for the mind, primarily. But an answer for the spirit, for our whole being. Something that answers our most authentic human need.

Need is not the whole story, however. Because with need comes opportunity, and discovery. In the moments when pride and self-sufficiency desert us, and we are defenceless, we can be thrown unexpectedly into a posture of humility, dependence, and reverence. And suddenly encounter both their comfort and their truth.[38]

Death is the greatest sorrow of all. Faced with the grief and anguish of losing someone they love, many people encounter again, or encounter for the first time, a side of themselves, and of the world, they had long neglected, or not given its proper due.

✳

Elaine Pagels (b. 1943) is a distinguished scholar of religion, the Harriet Speare Paine Professor of Religion at Princeton University. Since her first, best-selling book, *The Gnostic Gospels*, Pagels has written a series of very approachable books, popularizing advanced research on the first centuries of Christianity and on the formation of the Christian scriptures and dogma. In these books, the reader could sense Pagels' growing discomfort with beliefs formulated in the early creeds and doctrines, about such things as sexuality and the nature of evil, and a regret that the insights of the "Gnostic gospels," much closer in spirit to the "interiority" of Eastern religions, had not been more fully incorporated into "orthodox" Christianity.[39] The reader could not tell for sure, but sensed that this was leading to a growing alienation from the spiritual tradition of which she was a leading scholar.

But something happened. A death. The death of her son, her oldest child – the worst kind of sorrow any parent could imagine. As she absorbed the news of his fatal illness, and certain death, she rediscovered something. This rediscovery began, because two days after the first terrible news, she did something. As she recalls it:

On a bright Sunday morning in February, shivering in a T-shirt and running shorts, I stepped into the vaulted stone vestibule of the Church of the Heavenly Rest in New York to catch my breath and warm up. Since I had not been in church for a long time, I was startled by my response to the worship in progress – the soaring harmonies of the choir singing with the congregation; and the priest, a woman in bright gold and white vestments, proclaiming the prayers in a clear resonant voice. As I stood watching, a thought came to me: here is a family that knows how to face death ...

Standing in the back of that church, I recognized, uncomfortably, that I needed to be there. Here was a place to weep without imposing tears upon a child; and here was a heterogeneous community that had gathered to sing, to celebrate, to acknowledge common needs and to deal with what we cannot control or imagine. Yet the celebration spoke of hope; perhaps that is what made the presence of death bearable ...

I returned often to that church, not looking for faith but because in the presence of the worship and the people gathered there – and in a smaller group that met on weekdays in the church basement for mutual encouragement – my defenses fell away, exposing storms of grief and hope. In that church I gathered new energy to face whatever awaited us as constructively as possible.[40]

Elaine Pagels' rediscovery of the healing power of genuine human reverence was not immediate. For many years after the death of her son, she still found it difficult to participate in religious services. But by the time her second child, a daughter, had reached her sixteenth birthday, Pagels finally felt able to join wholeheartedly even in something as joyous as a Christmas service.

Attending to the sounds and the silence, the candlelight and the darkness, I felt the celebration take us in and break over us like the sea. When it receded, it left me no longer clinging to particular moments in the past but borne upon waves of gratitude that moved me toward Sarah, toward the whole community gathered there, at home, or everywhere, the dead and the living. For a moment I was shocked by the thought: We could have made this up out of what had happened in our lives; but, of course, we did not *have* to do that, for, as I realized at once, countless *other* people have already done that, and woven the stories of innumerable lives into the stories and the music, the meanings and visions of Jesus' birth. Thus such celebrations are borne along through all the generations that have shaped and reshaped them and those that continue to do so, just as encountering the tradition may shape and reshape us.[41]

What Elaine Pagels rediscovered, in the depth of the profoundest kind of grief any adult can feel, is something that will come as no surprise to the reader of this book. She rediscovered that, before it can become anything else, faith is something you *do*, not something you *have*. That a religion – because it is a deeper, richer form of spirituality – is not primarily about belief, at least not in the first instance, but rather about religious *practice*, and about leading a religious and spiritual *life*. She also rediscovered that the place where religious practice begins, and where a spiritual life is nourished, is by encountering something, by coming into its presence, often in reverent ritual and ceremony.

That brings us back to where this chapter began. I noted at the start that the place where many people encounter the spirit that draws them to, or holds them in, a religious life is in the practices of a religious tradition. The Jewish tradition, for example, recognizes some six hundred and thirteen ritual acts of obligation called *mitzvot* (or "commandments"). As we saw in the previous chapter, these actions more or less define what it means to be Jewish. In any religious tradition, that is to say, in any higher form of spirituality, such reverent practices always come – and should come – before dogma and doctrine.[42] In fact, as we saw, many religious or spiritual traditions seem to be able to get along without very much dogma or doctrine at all. And in others, like the Christian traditions, it's only within a prior life of reverence that dogma or doctrine can gain a hearing or acquire any deep meaning.

Religious practices such as ritual, ceremony, liturgy, sacraments, prayer, and meditation are at the heart of religious life, not at its periphery. Acts of reverence, as I noted in chapter 2, acknowledge superior worth. And that's both the meaning and function of "worship." Worship means "the assigning or acknowledging of worth."[43] If faith is something you *do* before it can become something you *have*, the rituals and practices of worship are often the primary things that you do. Or at least they are the starting point, the core to which all other activities (including theology) refer and to which they return. Ritual is the "scaffolding in which all religious thought has taken shape."[44] That's because ritual is at once the primary mode of expression for reverence, and a way to develop and explore it more deeply. Worship is "the summit of the heart habits we call virtue."[45] Places of worship and their symbols and ceremonies are designed to "create in the hearts of those who enter [them] certain feelings of awe and reverence," especially such virtues of reverence as "humility, mercy and soft-heartedness."[46] They allow us to express our deepest impulses of reverence by focusing and concentrating them, by giving them shape. They make reverent feelings and states of mind available to us, for deeper experience and reflection, empowering us for reverent and transforming action in the world and in ourselves.[47]

Religious rituals are the physical enactment of the myths that are the natural human way to interpret mystery. Those who participate in them are brought continually into an empowering presence: a presence embodied in their own reverence,[48] and in the patterns of symbols from which the rituals of their tradition are constructed. Such symbols serve not just "as verbal reports of historic events, either past or present or to be, but as revelations here and now, of what is always and forever."[49]

The symbols and symbolism of ritual express for us what rational concepts cannot. Its rhythms capture for us the deep rhythms we sense at the core of life but cannot reach in any other way. That is why, in many religious traditions, music and poetry play such important roles. By the way in which they engage our whole conscious and unconscious person, music, poetry, and other rhythmic forms come closest to reaching both the depths and the heights of our being: the deepest feelings and psychic forces, the highest yearnings and spiritual aspirations.[50] Music is, paradoxically, both "closest to us in its intense physicality and yet wholly open as to its significance." So it has a "natural capacity for the transcendent," which makes it the most natural form of spiritual expression.[51] Music, rather than conceptual speech, as William James noted, "is the element through which we are best spoken to by mystical truth. Many mystical scriptures are indeed little more than musical compositions ... Music gives us ontological messages which non-musical criticism is unable to contradict, though it may laugh at our foolishness in minding them. There is a verge of the mind which these things haunt; and whispers therefrom mingle with the operations of our understanding, even as the waters of the infinite ocean send their waves to break among the pebbles that lie upon our shores."[52]

For Confucius, music was an essential part of ritual, because it embodies the inner harmony at which his tradition of reverence aims. "[T]ake your stand on the rites," he said, "and be perfected by music."[53] Music and other forms of ritualized activity engage our whole person: the senses, the body, the feelings, and the mind. Their solemn, ordered patterns reflect the gravity at the heart of life, and simultaneously soothe and nourish us in doing so. They seem to capture both the sorrow and the joy deep down in life, the sorrow in the joy, the joy in the sorrow. At the heart of the solemn service for Rosh Hashanah, the Jewish New Year, for example, is the mysterious, primitive sound of the *shofar*, the ram's horn trumpet, "a sound that takes off where our words fail us."[54] Through participation in religious ritual and ceremony, especially music, we are able to come repeatedly into the presence of something religious people call the "sacred" or the "holy."

In 1917, fifteen years after William James published *The Varieties of Religious Experience*, a German scholar, Rudolf Otto (1869–1937), pursued the line of thinking about religious experience opened up by Schleiermacher and James. In *The Idea of the Holy*, Otto argued that (contrary to the rationalist view of religion as merely a set of doctrines, dogmas, or ideas) the essence or goal of religious life is to experience "the holy," or "the sacred." The holy or the sacred are what reverence, in its deepest spiritual form, seeks to encounter. They are the names we give to what we most want to be reverent about.[55] They *are* reverence in its deepest form of expression. They are therefore recognizable by states of feeling with the overtones of awe, fear, mystery, joy and power I already noted in our initial exploration of reverence in chapter 2. To designate the combination of feelings aroused by the encounter with the holy or the sacred, Otto invented the word "numinous," from the Latin word *numen* (meaning divine will, might, or majesty). The quality of experience this new word was intended to convey includes a sense of absolute dependence on something we did not create and do not control, something daunting but also fascinating, something fearsome but lovely, something (in Otto's words) that is "wholly other": the same thing to be found, he argued, behind all the experiences of both Eastern and Western mystics. Without this experience of the sacred, he concluded, human beings "can find no satisfaction in the mere allaying of the needs of our sensuous, psychical or intellectual impulses and cravings."[56] By experiencing awe in the presence of the sacred, human beings can draw upon its mysterious power to find the meaning and energy they need both to sustain their own lives and to make a difference in the world – to make even a different world.

Some spiritual traditions assume the inner action is the really important thing, and that the outer ones, the religious practice, are secondary, perhaps even a distraction or obstacle. Elaine Pagels admits her own

Protestant Christian upbringing had led her to think of ritual as just "empty form."[57] In this, her Protestant milieu was faithfully reflecting the impact of the two Reformations I noted in chapter 5. In such a view, ritual and practice are just outward and visible signs of an inward and spiritual grace. It's the inner state that counts.

This view isn't wrong, of course. In the end, it *is* the spirit that counts, as we saw at the end of the last chapter. That's the whole point of the life of the spirit, or spirituality. And it's why sincerity is so important in religious life, as I will consider again in the next chapter. Without sincerity, without a genuine hunger for insight or comfort or nourishment, without a sincere effort to turn your heart, religious practice *is* empty.

But thinking about ritual as merely "empty form" hides a key issue. What's the best way to reach your deepest inner spirit? Directly? Or indirectly? What's the relationship between inner states and outer actions? Do the former shape the latter? Or do actions also shape the inner person? These are critical questions not only for religious life but for our lives in general, and need to be thought about very carefully.

It would be a mistake to minimize the importance of outward actions, even for our inner or mental states. As I already noted, Confucius, Aristotle, and many thinkers since their times have emphasized that human beings are shaped much more by *habits* than by ideas. Or, rather, our ideas are often merely a reflection of our habits. Our mental attitudes, our stance toward the world, the overall cast of our temperament, character, and outlook are shaped not just by what we think but equally – or even more – by what we do. "Our deeds determine us as much as we determine our deeds," as the English novelist George Eliot (1809–1880) put it – a theme I shall have occasion to come back to in later chapters of this book.[58]

From this point of view, actions are not secondary. They are the place to start. Habits of reverent action are the best way to begin nourishing true inner spirituality. That's why religious practice, including ritual, comes before religious dogma or rational thought.[59] Because that's where we are most likely to encounter what we are really searching for, not just in a religious life, but in life itself.

# The Way: Life as Pilgrimage

The best way to think of a life of religious practice is as a journey. A journey in search of something – something that is never completely found. But the search for it can give direction and shape to a life. In religious language, this kind of journey is often called a pilgrimage or a quest.

✳

In the Christian *Gospel According to St John*, the most symbolic and least historical of the four accounts of Jesus' life, the author attributes to him the famous words: "I am the way, the truth and the life."[1] "The way," "the truth," and "the life" are terms found in many other spiritual traditions also; and they capture some of the key features of any religious life. So I'm going to use them as the framework for the next three chapters, starting with "the way": the journey that gives a characteristic shape to any life of religious practice.

The idea of "the way" seems to be almost inevitable in any spiritual tradition. The teaching of the Buddha, for example is also called "the way," because he believed the actual goal of the spiritual journey – what the Buddhists call the state of "enlightenment" – can never be taught but must be discovered by each individual person. What *can* be taught are the practices and disciplines that will help the seeker to move forward in his or her journey *toward* enlightenment. What *can* be taught is "the way": both the methods for getting there, and the road to travel.

The meaning of the Chinese "Tao" is also "the Way." It is a way of approaching and revering truth, but truth is a force, a living reality, that cannot be caught in words, much less in a system or concept. To approach it is an art, not a science. This art has something to do with learning to perceive, to cherish, and to *live* the human paradox discussed in chapter 1, the inseparable contradictions expressed so vividly by the *yin yang* symbol: fire and water, hot and cold, wet and dry, man and woman, permanence and change, heaven and earth, union and non-union, and so on. To learn the *way* of living all these endless dualities in a wholeness, a totality of flowing motion, is to find the way to the truth of life.

In the *Quran*, the spiritual life is referred to as the "straight path" or the "right path."[2] In Islam's mystical tradition, Sufism, life is conceived as a journey of spiritual exploration called the *tariqah*, "the way." This journey is a long and difficult one, leading to the moment of enlightenment, which brings about the extinction of the individual personality in its union with the divine reality.

The Hindu *Bhagavad Gita* also calls the spiritual journey "the way" – the Way of Love – and its chapters describe the various means through which human beings can search for or strive toward the ultimate reality, the "good of all beings" that lies behind the screen of the senses and "beyond the reach of thought and feeling": selfless service, wisdom in action, discipline and renunciation, and meditation.[3] Clearly the concept of "the way" is essential to most spiritual traditions. For a religious mind, life *is* this kind of journey: a journey of discovery, of exploration, of learning, always conscious of the objective, always looking toward it, or for it.

In the *Bhagavad Gita*, the Lord Krishna uses the image of climbing a mountain to describe the journey toward spiritual awareness.[4] The same image is used to describe the Sufi journey by Reza Aslan (b. 1972), an Iranian/American writer, and might well serve as a description of any life of genuine spiritual or religious practice:

As with all journeys, the Way has an end, though it should not be imagined as a straight road leading to a fixed destination but rather as a majestic mountain whose peak conceals the presence of God. There are, of course, many paths to the summit – some better than others. But because every path eventually leads to the same destination, which path one takes is irrelevant. All that matters is to be on the path, to be constantly moving toward the top – one measured, controlled and strictly supervised step at a time – passing diligently through specific "abodes and stations" along the Way, each of which is marked by an ineffable experience of spiritual evolution, until one finally reaches the end of the journey.[5]

✳

As you already saw in chapter 3, a spiritual "journey" can be thought of as having both internal and external forms. The inward spiritual journey often appears to have different stages, or levels, the same levels glimpsed in mystical encounters. Sometimes these levels are formally laid out, especially in Eastern spirituality. In the Jain tradition, for example, "the way" begins with twelve vows, and proceeds through eleven orders of virtue. In chapter 4, I already noted the various levels through which the discipline of yoga, employed in both the Hindu and Buddhist traditions, seeks to lead the spiritual traveller from lower to higher forms of spiritual life. The fourth of the Buddhist tradition's four holy truths is the "eightfold Path" along which the spiritual traveller proceeds, through the three stages of morality, meditation, and wisdom, a path that is "holy, incorruptible and straight," and leads to Nirvana.[6] The Hinayana Buddhist tradition identifies ten stages of insight through which the yoga practitioner must pass to achieve Nirvana. The Mahayana Buddhist *Guide Book to Meditation on Amida* describes in detail the step-by-step "way" to the saving vision of the Buddha, starting with ten "negative precepts" (bearing some resemblance to the biblical Ten Commandments), and proceeding through seven meditations, to set the stage for the visionary coming of the Buddha into the mind of the seeker.[7]

Christian thinkers (such as the anonymous fifth-century writer known as "Pseudo-Dionysius," the thirteenth-century theologian, Bonaventure [1221–1274], or John of the Cross) often referred to a "three-fold way" – purification, illumination, perfection/union – similar to the Buddhist three-stage progress to Nirvana. Bonaventure also doubled the steps in each of these stages, and added a final unknowable one, to identify (like Teresa of Avila) seven steps in the ascent to God.[8]

"The Way" as set out in the Sufi epic, *The Conference of the Birds*, describes a journey similar to those of Bonaventure and Teresa through seven treacherous valleys, beginning with the Valley of the Quest, followed by the Valleys of Love, Mystery, Detachment, Unity, Bewilderment, leading finally to the Valley of Nothingness. Each stage in the spiritual journey must be accomplished in sequence until the traveller achieves an ecstatic self-annihilation, drowning in God, and in the love of God.[9]

The concept of spiritual journey is fundamental to the Jewish scriptures. Their narrative shape is that of a mutual quest: the quest of God for his wayward people, and the quest of the people of Israel for their

God. Within this overall narrative can be found a number of other allegorical quests, especially the apparently foolish journey of the already aged Abraham to find the promised land. Another archetypal journey in the Jewish tradition is the Exodus, the Israelites' forty-year wandering through the wilderness searching, again, for the promised land.

There are at least four Christian versions of this same archetypal quest narrative. The first are the accounts of his own spiritual journey and of the collective "pilgrimage" of all Christians as set out in Augustine of Hippo's two masterpieces, the *Confessions* and *The City of God*. The second are the medieval cycles of romance which "all exhibit in one degree or another the pervading idea of quest,"[10] especially the stories of the quest for the Holy Grail, whether those involving Parsifal, or the many versions of the legends of King Arthur and the Knights of the Round Table. A third quest narrative is the journey through hell and purgatory to heaven, as told in *The Divine Comedy*, by the Italian poet, Dante (c. 1265–1321). A fourth, that has had a profound influence on the English language and imagination, is *The Pilgrim's Progress* by John Bunyan (1628–1688). Perhaps the first English novel, *The Pilgrim's Progress* relates the arduous journey of a man named "Christian" from the city of "Destruction" to the "Mount Zion," the "Celestial City." His journey is full of perils, temptations, and difficulties, including the "Slow of Dispond" and the "Hill called Difficulty," but Christian gradually overcomes them all to achieve his goal, though he must leave this life to do so.

While Bunyan's work is an allegory of the *inward* journey that gives shape to any religious life, it was based on a long tradition of *external* or physical "pilgrimage" that is also an important part of many religious traditions. As I noted, one of the "Five Pillars" of Islam is the pilgrimage to Mecca that must be made by every faithful Muslim at least once in a lifetime. Especially in the first five hundred years of the Buddhist tradition, large numbers of monks and laymen made regular pilgrimages to the holy sites of Magadha, in north-east India, where the Buddha was said to have lived and where his relics were claimed to have been found. In the Christian tradition, pilgrimages to Jerusalem or to other holy sites were an important feature of Christian spirituality for many centuries, especially during the Middle Ages. Throughout western Europe, pilgrimage routes led to major holy shrines, such as Santiago de

Compostella in north-west Spain, with many sites, such as Chartres, France, along the way.

Until its destruction by the Romans in 70 CE, the great Temple in Jerusalem was the focal point of worship for the people of Israel. Sukkot, Passover, and Shavuot were originally three annual pilgrim festivals when all adult males were required to journey to the Temple. A visit to the Temple was also required at certain stages in life. After the destruction of the Temple, pilgrimages also took place to local sites like the Synagogue of Moses at Dammuh, near Cairo in Egypt, as a substitute for pilgrimage to Jerusalem.[11] But the place of the Temple was also taken, more generally, by all the local synagogues that gave rise to Judaism as we know it today.[12]

As the increasingly important role of synagogues suggests, a physical or "external" pilgrimage can be thought of in many ways, and does not have to be a momentous journey to a distant place. A weekly or daily visit to a synagogue, or temple, or church is also a kind of pilgrimage, a visit to a holy place, to heighten the sense of the sacred by coming physically into its presence. In fact, this kind of routine doesn't even have to involve a change of place at all. For example, one of the other Five Pillars of Islam is the duty of daily ritual prayer, or *salat*, performed five times a day: at sunrise, noon, afternoon, sunset, and evening. Only the noon prayer on Friday is supposed to be performed in a mosque; the others can be carried out wherever the faithful are to be found, though it is preferable for them to be performed in groups, reflecting the principle of unity or connectedness at the heart of reverence.

So "external" pilgrimage doesn't have to involve a change of place, even if it is a physical or bodily act. It can take place anywhere, without any change of location. Saying a prayer is also a form of pilgrimage: a mental journey. Prayer to God, as Thomas Aquinas says, "brings us into his presence."[13]

As the Five Pillars of Islam help to remind us, a religious life is best thought of as a life of religious *habits*. It is the habits – *not* beliefs – that make it a religious life, or a life of religious practice. And the habits, taken as a whole, constitute the journey – at least the "external" journey – that is the characteristic shape of a religious life. A religious life is given its shape and rhythm by the way religious habits cluster into natural cycles: daily, weekly, monthly, and so on. The five daily prayers of the Muslim *salat*, like the *tefilot*, the morning, afternoon, and evening prayers of the Jewish tradition, or like the eight traditional "hours" or "offices" of the Christian day – matins, lauds, prime, terse, sext, nones, vespers, compline – give a shape to the daily cycle of life: the faithful journey through each day, in a regular cycle of religious activity or "actions." In many religious traditions, the weekly cycle is punctuated by at least one, if not more, visits to a holy shrine: mosque, temple, synagogue, or church. The monthly cycle may reflect one or more religious "seasons" or solemn festivals or fasts, such as Ramadan, or Yom Kippur, or Passover, and by special days or "feasts," such as the celebration of a "saint" or a "high" holy day. And taken all together, these various seasons and feasts make up an annual cycle, so that the faithful live their religious life by "journeying" through the familiar, cyclical, seasons of the religious year. A Christian, for example, lives not just through the workaday cycle of the calendar year, from January to December, in unvarying routine, but journeys instead (or rather in parallel), like a pilgrim, through the great cycle of religious seasons, each with its own decorations, colours, rituals, prayers, symbols and events that recall for him or her the drama and the purpose of their faith: Advent, Christmas, Epiphany, Lent, Holy Week, Easter, Ascension, Pentecost, Trinity.

The external spiritual journey or "pilgrimage" embodied in religious habits is both the expression of and the occasion for an inward journey, just as the outward physical exercises and controlled breathing of yoga are the supports for an inner transformation. External religious habits are the outward and visible signs of something inward and spiritual.

It would be wrong and misleading, however, to say that they are *only* outward and visible signs. This would imply that they are secondary and dispensable, that you can have a spiritual life without spiritual habits. This is one of the great errors of our time. If either were more important it would probably be the habits, because they are the condition for the other, inward journey. But the truth is that they are inseparable. A spiritual life without spiritual habits would be a shallow thing, unlikely to sustain, or to persist. A seed thrown upon dry ground.

But religious habits without a genuine inward and spiritual journey would be, as I said at the end of the last chapter, an empty shell, the form without the substance. That's why inward sincerity is so important in religious life. All of the world's great spiritual traditions talk about the emptiness and falsehood of a religious life that is nothing but outward form without the inner spirit. In fact most of them warn against the dangers of this kind of false "religion." In the Christian scriptures, for example, external religiosity without inner sincerity is often associated, unfairly, with the "Pharisees," a word that became a synonym, in the Christian tradition, for hypocrite (although the Pharisees were actually one of the most spiritually advanced groups of their time). The *Quran* also warns about hypocrites who "pray for the sake of ostentation and remember God but little."[14]

Hypocrisy is a big issue for many young people today. That's largely because, as Lionel Trilling noted, "sincerity and authenticity" are two of the central but ambiguous demands of modern culture, beginning in the seventeenth century.[15] Their growing importance for us parallels the rise of the virtues of self-assertion. We now live in what has been called a "culture of authenticity," reflecting the "expressive individualism" I noted in chapter 1, one of the most common forms the virtues of self-assertion take today.[16] This demand for authenticity is often a reason or excuse for the young to turn away from their own spiritual traditions, because they think they see people observing outward forms without any apparent impact on their real lives. If that's where you're coming from, you're right to be concerned about genuine hypocrisy.

But you need to be discerning and charitable, too. We can never know the struggles that go on in someone else's heart, or what they've had to overcome, even to be as they are. In the Christian scriptures, there's a famous story about a disreputable low-life and a very devout, rather stuck-up person, who both happen to make their pilgrimage to the great Temple of Jerusalem at the same time. As they stand in prayer, the devout one prides himself on his religious life and thinks to himself, "Thank God, I'm not like this other guy, and immoral people like him," while the low-life can only hang his head in shame and ask mute forgiveness for being what he is. Jesus (to whom the writer of the gospel attributes this story) makes it very clear that it's the low-life character not the devout man who understands the real meaning of religious life. The respectable guy only apes the outward forms while betraying their inner spirit. But the low-life makes a genuine pilgrimage, sincerely seeking for the help and forgiveness he so desperately needs.[17]

David Adams Richards reminds us that self-righteousness is "much graver an error than hypocrisy." The feeling of superiority many people have about hypocrisy in others is often an even worse form of the very sanctimony they think they're opposing. Richards says he had to over-come this kind of hidden smugness in himself.

> It was only later I began to see that I was blaming people for being people, and transferring that blame to the very hope for transcen-dence that these people had in their hearts. I was looking at people and blaming them for their hope and their prayers even if they could not manage to live up to them ... [I]f people fail at this transcen-dence, should they or others not seek to try? In fact, the very fact others still seek to try, and that some succeed, shows not only the necessity of continuing to try, but the truth of the ultimate quest.[18]

People can and do try to become better than they are through some-thing we might call "creative hypocrisy." By assuming or "putting on" virtues that aren't natural or authentic, at least not at first, people can become what they aspire to be.[19] In fact, that may be the only way to do it. "Fake it 'til you make it" is a contemporary expression with great moral truth and power. If someone acts "as if" they were kind, or pa-tient, or generous, or brave, and does so consistently and for a long time, they end by becoming kind, or patient, or generous, or brave, be-cause these virtues can't be disentangled from the actions or habits through which they're expressed.

If they are to mean anything at all, the outward religious habits must be the means and occasions for the inward journey; the means through which we constantly explore and experience our faith, hoping, waiting and preparing to rise to some new level of spiritual insight or awareness or behaviour, as the Sufi or the Buddhist aims to rise through the different levels of consciousness toward the spiritual goal of enlightenment. The sincere spiritual traveller is always preparing for spiritual progress: "day by day a sense of spiritual advance."[20] He or she hopes that, through regular practice, and through regular reflection on the practice, they may be able to say, I realize that I see things differently now than I did a year ago, or that I am a "different" person. Or some reading, event or experi-ence has just raised my understanding to a new level of insight. That's one of the reasons for the repetitiveness of religious ritual. The "words and motions" of religious ritual, as the American economic historian Deirdre McCloskey (b. 1942) remarks, "give the faithful repeated chances to get it right ... for the first time grasp, really grasp the meaning."[21]

One day, for example, Martin Luther (1483–1546), the initiator of the Protestant Reformation, was listening to another monk recite the portion of the Christian creed about the "forgiveness of sins," when suddenly he saw the Scripture in an entirely new light: "and straightway I felt as if I were born anew. It was as if I had found the door of paradise thrown wide open."[22] Similarly, at the age of seventeen, Jonathan Edwards (1703–1758), the great American theologian, was reading a passage from Paul's first letter to Timothy when "there came into my soul, and it was, as it were, diffused through it, a sense of the glory of the divine Being; a new sense quite different from anything I ever experienced before."[23] In the Christian tradition, these moments of insight, moments of spiritual growth that take one to an entirely new level of understanding, are sometimes called revelations or "epiphanies" (as when Jesus was revealed to the Three Kings, in the original Epiphany). In the Buddhist tradition (especially in its Mahayana version), these are the moments of "sudden" enlightenment, when "meditation becomes ripe. Abbot Rei-Un, seeing the peach flowers became enlightened, and Zen Master Kyo-Gen at hearing the crack of a bamboo ... Heaven and earth are split apart in an instant; as if a sluice had been opened, suddenly we attain bliss and life infinite."[24]

One way to think about the spiritual journey is to think of it as a constant process of readying yourself (through worship, reading, reflection, meditation, prayer, or something else) for an epiphany; for the moment of insight, when you will "see" things in a new light. One of the most important forms of preparation is the formulation of the right questions. For without questions, there can be no moments of answer.[25]

Equally, the spiritual journey may be thought of as readying yourself for the many periods, whether short or long, when the answers don't come, when everything seems dark and confusing, when evil rather than goodness seems to be rewarded, when you feel like an outcast, when you are tempted to despair. Such times are part of the journey. They are foreseen in all spiritual traditions, and are integral to them, whether described as the "Valley of Bewilderment," or the "Slow of Dispond," or what John of the Cross called "the Dark Night of the Soul."[26] That they are an essential part of any authentic spiritual life – not its opposite or negation – can be clearly seen in the great treasury of spiritual poetry shared by both the Jewish and Christian traditions, the Psalms of David. The Psalms illustrate that one of the fundamental rhythms of religious life (perhaps especially in the Western traditions) is a regular oscillation between doubt and despair on the one hand, and ecstatic conviction and praise on the other, with little, if any, middle ground in between. At their depths, even doubt and despair are open to doubt. As the Sufi master-piece, *The Conference of the Birds*, puts it: in the Valley of Bewilderment, "I doubt my doubt, even doubt is unsure."[27]

The lesson of all pilgrimage narratives is that true spiritual life lies in pushing through these dark moments to the farther shore. The value of a spiritual life lies precisely in the resources it gives to do this. A life lived in a spirit of reverence, trust, and hope, as a journey of faith – that is to say, as a journey of religious practice and exploration – provides the spiritual resources to cross over these valleys of sorrow and loss, of doubt and despair, to the other side. As I noted in chapter 4, the Sanskrit words *Hinayana* and *Mahayana*, the names for the two main traditions of Buddhism, are different sizes of "vehicles" or "ferry boats," to carry the traveller to the other side of the river of life.

From a spiritual perspective, these moments of darkness can also be viewed as times of testing in which new depths of awareness or experi-ence are achieved, new realities encountered, new meaning revealed. With need comes opportunity and discovery, as we saw in the last chap-ter. In *The Pilgrim's Progress*, when Christian plunges into the final river of his journey, he is tempted to despair, and indeed does so. But he learns that the waters become deep or shallow depending on his own attitude to them, his own degree of trust and hope, his own faith.

In the Eastern traditions, as you have seen, the "way" leads normally to some degree of extinction of the individual in an *identity* with being whereas the Western journey leads normally to some kind of loving *re-lationship*. But for the purposes of this chapter, the differences are less important than the similarities. Almost all of the world's great spiritual traditions conceive of a life of religious practice as a journey in search of something. And almost all of them assume that, except perhaps for a handful of exceptional individuals such as the Buddhas, the journey is one whose object can never be fully achieved. For this reason, the jour-ney *itself* becomes the point. The journey is, in a sense, its own arrival. As the Sufi poet Jelaluddin Rumi (1207–1273) expressed it, "when you look for God, God is in the look of your eyes, in the thought of looking, nearer to you than yourself."[28] One of the key sayings of the Soto Zen tradition of Buddhism is that "the practice *is* enlightenment."[29] Being, or truth, or eternal life, or ultimate reality, or *nirvana,* or whatever is the object of the quest, are not to be found only at the *end* of the journey, but *in* and *through* the journey itself.[30]

If faith is something you do, this "doing" takes the form, primarily, of a journey or a pilgrimage; a spiritual quest which not only spawns the religious "habits" that give shape to a religious life, but is also the purpose of such a life. It *is* the life. "[T]he good life for man," as the British/American philosopher Alasdair MacIntyre (b. 1929) observes, paraphrasing Aristotle, "is the life spent in seeking for the good life for man."[31]

But if the religious life is a search for something, it would be a contradiction to think that the thing sought must first be found for such a life to begin. This is where so many conventional ideas about "religion" prove to be utterly mistaken. They assume that to lead a religious life, a life of religious practice, one must first have found something called "faith." But this is backward. As Wilfred Cantwell Smith remarks, "it is seriously misleading to suppose that the way to get religious faith is to find out what it is and then go in pursuit of it. Rather, *faith is the name we give to the fact that one is in pursuit of something (or Someone) else.*"[32]

One thing such a life is in search of is the truth. We will consider how that search differs from other ways of seeking truth, and how it relates to them, in the next chapter.

# 8

# The Truth: Reason and Revelation

A religious life is a search. A search for, among other things, truth.

This may surprise you. Since the eighteenth century, it has become commonplace to assert or assume that religion is a set of comforting fairy tales fit only for the credulous whose only continuing purposes are to keep the lower classes in their place (as both the French *philosophe* Voltaire [1694–1778] and Karl Marx [1818–1883], the German founder of communism, suggested, from very different perspectives), or to provide an emotional crutch for those too weak to lead their lives in the cold light of truth.[1] German philosopher Ludwig Feuerbach (1804–1872), for example, who played a key role in inventing the modern Western concept of "religion," also dismissed it as nothing more than "the projected personality of man"; a cultural relic from pre-history, one that should be superseded by the new human sciences. "That which to a later age or a cultured people is given by nature or reason," he argued, "is to an earlier age, or to a yet uncultured people, given by God ... Only when we abandon a philosophy of religion, or a theology, which is distinct from psychology and anthropology, and recognise anthropology as itself theology, do we attain to a true, self-satisfying identity of the divine and the human being, the identity of the human being with itself."[2] Similarly, Sigmund Freud (1856–1939), the father of modern psychoanalysis, dismissed religious teaching as "fairy tales" held over from an earlier, more primitive age, whose origin lay in the initial twin needs of "defending oneself against the crushingly superior force of nature" and "rectify[ing] the shortcomings of civilization."[3]

But those who dismiss religion as "untrue" still have to answer the perennial question attributed in the Christian Bible to Pontius Pilate:

what is truth? And a second, equally important question: how does one get hold of it, or know it to be true? British philosopher John Stuart Mill (1806–1873) noted that there are two questions you can ask about anything. One question is "Is it true?" The other is "What does it mean?"[4] The problem with so many modern examinations of "religion" is that the first question is normally asked before the second. Yet the second, as Mill conceded, is logically prior to the first. You can't decide the truth of something until you have enquired deeply into its meaning. A refutation of something understood only superficially, or from the outside, or from your own perspective alone, is no refutation at all.

There is no clearer demonstration of this than Sigmund Freud himself. Freud based his criticism of "religion" on the assumption that "the only religion which ought to bear that name" was the anthropomorphic* religion held by the "common man," in which "an enormously exalted father" looks after the needs of his "children," but must be "softened by their prayers and placated by the signs of their remorse." "The whole thing is so infantile, so foreign to reality," Freud commented, "that to anyone with a friendly attitude to humanity it is painful to think that the great majority of mortals will never be able to rise above this view of life."[5]

The problem with this kind of criticism is that it attacks something few serious religious thinkers have ever maintained. Fifteen hundred years earlier, Augustine had already explained that "it is man not God, who is benefited" by exercises of "reverence," such as prayer and worship.[6] Aquinas agreed.[7] And he didn't need Freud to tell him that the highest stage of spiritual development is reached when the mind perceives divine truths (as Aquinas himself said) "without anthropomorphism."[8] Similarly Maimonides (a near-contemporary of Aquinas) wrote his celebrated *Guide for the Perplexed* precisely to show that the language of the scriptures should be interpreted "in a figurative sense," not literally, and that therefore reason and revelation are *not* in conflict.[9]

Even Augustine (who sometimes interpreted biblical language in a remarkably literal way, to modern ears) also observed that much of religious language needs to be interpreted "in a metaphorical sense, not literally."[10] Long before Freud, Augustine had already asserted that to think of God as "a kind of man or as a vast bodily substance endowed

---

\* In this context, "anthropomorphic" means thinking of God as if God has human attributes or characteristics.

with power," or to interpret the Creation story of Genesis literally, as something that happened in "time," is to act "like children." And he warned against those who "in the stupidity of pride" despise religious language "as language fit for simpletons." To Augustine, the "simplicity of language" of religious texts makes them meaningful and sustaining to those who cannot approach them in any other way, including children. And, for others, more discerning, "the words of Scripture are no longer a nest but a leafy orchard, where they see the hidden fruit," the spiritual meaning.[11] Perhaps the definitive rebuke to critics like Freud was provided, almost a hundred years before he wrote, by Samuel Taylor Coleridge (1772–1834): "Whatever must be misrepresented in order to be ridiculed is in fact not ridiculed; but the thing substituted for it."[12]

So we still need to sort out what kind of "truth" is conveyed by different human ways of knowing and experiencing the world, such as reason, or science, or "religion." And how do these different ways of knowing and expressing truth relate to each other?

❊

As I already suggested in the Introduction, reason and religious insight don't inhabit the same space. That doesn't necessarily make religious practice *ir*rational – though it *can* be irrational, just like any other human activity, including reason itself: an "excessive investment in reason" turns it not into reasonableness but into "rationalism," "the old enemy of reasonableness."[13] But the important point is that reason and "religion" don't cover exactly the same territory. A traditional way to put the relationship between reason and religious insight is to say that one begins where the other leaves off. A better way to put it, as I suggested in the Introduction, might be to say that religious insight *includes* reason but also goes beyond it. Your view of the relationship between reason and revelation ultimately depends on whether your idea of reason is broad enough.

Our modern idea of reason, which dates back to the seventeenth century, has gradually become very narrow. When we think of reason today we think of the discursive, calculating, everyday kind of reason. The models for this are mathematics and empirical argument: the kinds of thinking that seek to know and control the physical world.[14] But throughout history, thinkers have usually recognized that this is only one form of reason, and not the deepest. They have identified another form, a reason that recognizes its own limits, and then seeks to go beyond them by means other than itself. Aristotle called it "contemplation."[15] Thomas Aquinas and other medieval philosophers called it "intellect."[16] Blaise Pascal called it the "heart" or the spirit of "finesse" in contrast to the "geometric spirit" of discursive, calculating reason.[17] Many thinkers of the Enlightenment and its Romantic aftermath called it "Reason," in contrast to "Understanding" (which is what they called discursive reasoning, reversing common-sense usage).[18]

This distinction between two different types of reason is largely alien to our modern minds. We don't often acknowledge that there is another kind of thinking that goes right up to the limits of our ordinary, everyday reason – the limits imposed by the virtues of self-assertion that underpin it – and then seeks to go beyond those limits by transcending or subverting itself, pointing beyond the limits of the knowable world, "gesturing toward what it cannot know."[19] In order to understand where instrumental reason's exclusive writ runs out and additional spiritual insight becomes necessary, we need to recognize that both science and ordinary rational thought have limits. There are boundaries beyond which they cannot go to explain reality, even the physical reality, of the universe. As far as science is concerned, the British physicist, Stephen Hawking (b. 1942), has described its limits in this way: "Even if there is only one possible unified theory, it is just a set of rules and equations. What is it that breathes fire into the equations and makes a universe for them to describe? The usual approach of science of constructing a mathematical model cannot answer the questions of why there should be a universe for the model to describe. Why does the universe go to all the bother of existing? Is the unified field theory so compelling that it brings about its own existence? Or does it need a creator, and if so, does he have any other effect on the universe? And who created him?"[20]

Since the seventeenth century, science, by definition, can only answer "what" questions (*what* happened?); it does not and cannot answer "why" questions (for what *purpose* or *end* did it happen?). The decision to eliminate "why" questions from science (questions about the "final" causes identified by Aristotle, discussed in chapter 3) was part of the scientific revolution that created our modern world. So the only way science can deal with "why" questions is to convert them into "what" questions. In doing this, it has often made important contributions to our understanding of the world, because many "what" questions had previously been framed wrongly as "why" questions. Still, there remains a whole category of questions about which science can offer no help. "To account for one happening by appealing to another is to change the topic without meeting the issue," as Bernard Lonergan points out.[21] So the suggestion that science can or could replace "religion" is simply what is called a "category mistake": a case of mistaken identity.

Similar limits apply to other forms of rational human thought better equipped to address "why" questions, such as philosophy. There is only so far they can go, before the track begins to disappear. "The beginning," as Iris Murdoch says, "is hard to find."[22] Part of this difficulty has to do with the nature of language itself, because to explain something rationally you need words, and you need to use them in a rational way. But eventually the words run out, or start to run in circles. To explain the meaning of some words, you need other words, which need to be explained in turn, and so on, *ad infinitum*.[23] Another part of the problem is that, as we began to see in chapter 3, ultimate truth involves the totality of what is. And no particular thing can explain the totality: it would always be "influenced and threatened" by other things which aren't included. You can't get "outside" the totality to explain it.[24]

So any process of thought needs to start from some assumptions: assumptions that are normally invisible to the thinker, and almost impossible to excavate, or bring into the light of day. They are simply given, or taken for granted. And what is taken for granted is the hardest thing of all to see. In the Hindu tradition, these kinds of hidden assumptions are called *shraddha*. British philosopher R.G. Collingwood (1889–1943) called them "absolute presuppositions": "absolute" because you can't normally get behind them, or can only do so with great difficulty. They are the starting point for the whole life of the mind, the basic building blocks, the raw material of thought.[25]

Where does this raw material come from?

One good answer might be that it comes from the ongoing human conversation itself, the one we joined at birth.[26] But that answer only brings us back to the same point, by a long, though illuminating, detour. To understand what the assumptions of the ongoing conversation are, let alone where they came from, we would have to trace the conversation back over an enormous span of time. Unfortunately, "[w]e can never stand near the beginning," as Karl Jaspers said.[27] And even if we could, we would still want to ask where or how to ground our assumptions about ultimate truth.[28]

So to begin to answer this question, I will use three different images.

For the first one, let's go back to the image of the mountain climber in search of ultimate reality, in the last chapter. If truth is the peak of the mountain, the climber finds that, as he or she climbs higher toward the summit, the track of clear, rational thought begins to run out. The "highest peaks," as Thomas Aquinas said in his inaugural lecture at the University of Paris, "are beyond all human reasoning."[29] In fact, the climber finds they are enveloped in deeper and deeper obscurity, an impenetrable fog or cloud – which is exactly the image Aquinas and many other Christian thinkers used to describe the experience of approaching absolute truth.[30] The summit of human thought turns out to be "a kind of non-knowledge," or *un*knowing.[31]

Human life is surrounded on all sides by deep and impenetrable mystery. Buried in this mystery are both the beginning and the end, the origins of life and its purpose or meaning, the origins of thought itself. So we peer obscurely into it, and try to make out what we can. "We are like those," said Maimonides, "who though beholding flashes of lightning, still find themselves in the thickest darkness of the night."[32] We send scouting parties up the mountain into the enveloping cloud, and we get back their garbled, partial, and often baffling reports through the fog. Their messages are like sudden lightning flashes, as Maimonides said, or like brief, static-filled radio messages that we try to piece together, to make sense of them. Because they come from beyond the rational, in the cloud of mystery, they take a different, non-linear form.

The language of religious practice almost never takes the form of rational, discursive prose. Instead it takes the forms of myth, symbol, story-telling, poetry, music, and art. And also the language of paradox: "True sayings seem paradoxical," says the *Tao Te Ching*.[33] Or the language of declaratory, prophetic aphorisms, statements, and commands, such as that a man must lose his life to save it," or "Honour thy father and thy mother," or "Let there be light."[34] In the Islamic tradition, these kinds of prophetic utterances are called *hadīth*. "An utterance of this sort is one charged with such intensity, urgency or authority," Northrop Frye explains, "that it penetrates the defenses of the human receiving apparatus and creates a new channel of response."[35]

Because they come not from our everyday, wide-awake perceptions but rather from pre-rational encounters in the cloud of mystery, let's call these dreamlike and poetic messages "revelations." In the Hindu tradition, they are called *shruti* which means, literally, that they are *heard*, rather than learned. They simply come to us, often unbidden. They simply *are*. But they are not unreal. In fact, they are every bit as real as anything in our waking world. As Maimonides said, they "teach things beyond the reach" of the rational mind.[36] Revelations are another form of the "encounters" I discussed in chapter 6. They are just as much the product of human experience as anything to be found in a laboratory. They are the data of our spiritual experiments, the raw material for human thought.

But like any data, they need to be interpreted with care, and in a way that takes account of the kind of data they are. Because the language from our scouting parties into the cloud of mystery consists of myth, symbol, and metaphor, it needs to be interpreted "figuratively," as Maimonides and Augustine said, or "spiritually," as Paul said.[37] People like Freud who insist on interpreting literally what is not literal are simply missing the point.

✳

So far I have been using the image of a mountain, because we often associate a spiritual quest with a climb. But a second metaphor that may be helpful is the image of a plunge into the ocean, because the mystery that surrounds us is both above and below: it is the mystery of origins as well as the mystery of destination; the mystery of the feelings as much as the mystery of the mind. The deep ocean of feeling on which float our conscious minds is as much a mystery to us as the highest purposes of life. So our scouting parties can be imagined as deep-sea dives quite as much as alpine expeditions.

This mysterious ocean of feeling on which sail the frail barks of our "selves" is the domain explored by psychology and psychoanalysis, but also by myth, art, music, poetry, metaphor, and story. These symbolic modes of expression are our most reliable informants about our deepest feelings and our deepest intuitions. Many writers have tried to explain the difference between rational and religious life by contrasting "thought" and "emotion." Margaret Donaldson, for example, describes the difference between the "intellectual" mode (that gives rise to rational thought and science), and the "value-sensing" mode (from which we get art, music, and religious experience) by saying that, in the first, thought is dominant, with emotion a secondary component. In the other, emotion is dominant, with thought as a secondary component.[38]

There is obviously some truth in this. Like poetry, music, and art, religious life seems both to give and require more direct access to some feelings than can be obtained in other ways. As Charles Taylor reminds us, religious impulses like the Christian virtue of charity don't seem to proceed from the mind or the brain but "from the guts; the New Testament word for 'taking pity'... places the response in the bowels."[39]

But on the other hand, religious life can be highly intellectual: not everyone who embraces religious life does so in the grip of strong emotion. Thomas Aquinas said that religious virtue is *not* tested by "emotion" but rather by the "*actions* we offer to God."[40] Moreover, the use of nouns like "thought" and "emotion" makes them sound like "things"; things that you "have." But thinking and feeling are things that you *do;* they are forms of action. "Thought" is what's left over when an *activity* of thinking has already occurred. Thought may be logical, but logic is *not* a way of thinking.[41] It's merely a standard you apply when the thinking has taken place.

And what if these two forms of human *action* – thinking and emotion – were not as different as we often assume? What if, as Susanne Langer suggests, they're actually both higher forms of one common type of activity: the activity of feeling?[42] What if our supposedly rational thinking processes "are continually moving in relation to more affective or instinctive levels of thought and feeling," as Iris Murdoch puts it?[43] The life of reason, said Lionel Trilling, "begins in the emotions." What we call an idea comes into being, he suggested, "when two contradictory emotions are made to confront each other and are required to have a relationship with each other."[44]

So-called rational and even scientific thought seem to be almost as much activities of feeling as emotion itself. As N.T. Wright (b. 1948), a British theologian remarks, "something like [love] is already at work when the scientist devotes himself or herself to the subject matter so completely that the birth of a new hypothesis comes about not so much through an abstract brain (a computer made of meat?) crunching data but through a soft and mysterious symbiosis of knower and known, of lover and beloved."[45]

Consider for a moment what really happens in your own mind when you try to think rationally about something, especially something difficult or obscure. First of all, you have to be motivated to think about it. Reason "does not come with its own motivation," Deirdre McCloskey observes, "thinking requires emotion."[46] So there has to be some strong feeling that starts the process, and keeps it going. The thinking itself usually begins in hunches and intuition – that is, with certain feelings.[47] It then proceeds in a shifting whirl of ambiguous words and images, with many levels and rich overtones.[48] The depth of your thinking will depend on how carefully you can listen to each of these confusing and often contradictory promptings. It often succeeds through unexpected leaps of imagination or flashes of insight, when bits and pieces of your thinking suddenly connect or snap into place, sometimes when you're not consciously thinking about the problem at all, or are only half-awake. And it ends in judgements of truth. But what is truth? It's a "metaphysical" not a logical concept. That is to say, truth isn't simply delivered by the structure of thought in a straightforward way: instead, your unexpected encounter with it, and your decisions about it, determine that very structure.[49]

And, in the end, how do you know something is true? Because you are convinced. That is to say: you have a *feeling* of conviction.[50] In the "rational" mode, your conclusion should be related to some kind of "evidence," but it's still an act – almost an aesthetic act – of *feeling*.[51] Afterward you can – and must – go back and arrange your thoughts or arguments in a "logical" manner, to support your conclusion. But that's not how you got there in the first place.

The same point can be made in reverse. How do you know something *isn't* true, no matter how impressive the supposedly "rational" arguments that can marshalled in its defense? Because something in your gut tells you it can't be true. As William James pointed out, the place that "rationalism" occupies in our whole mental life is "relatively superficial."

> It is the part that has the *prestige* undoubtedly, for it has the loquacity, it can challenge you for proofs, and chop logic, and put you down with words. But it will fail to convince or convert you all the same, if your dumb intuitions are opposed to its conclusions. If you have intuitions at all, they come from a deeper level of your nature than the loquacious level which rationalism inhabits ... [S]omething in you absolutely *knows* that that result must be truer than any logic-chopping rationalistic talk, however clever, that may contradict it.[52]

So instead of contrasting thought and emotion, it may be better to say there are two higher activities of human *feeling*: the "intellectual" or rational activity of feeling, and the "value-sensing" activity of feeling. In each of these, some feelings are suppressed and others are enhanced. In the first, the feelings that are encouraged are those that allow this external world to be properly observed, recorded, and controlled – or at least those that don't get in the way of that purpose. Feeling itself becomes objectified. It builds up "a whole objective world of perceptible things and verifiable facts."[53] This is the beginning of rational consciousness.

In the second case, different feelings are enhanced, especially feelings of belonging and relationship *to the whole*. Focussing on the mystery and meaning of *being* – rather than on the *thing* that exists – fosters the impulse to identity and participation rather than the impulse to analysis and control. The focus is no longer on things and their impersonal impact on each other, but rather on their significance or importance, their relationship to each other and to the whole. Artistic understanding, for example, "is not a question of fact," as Lionel Trilling said, "but of value."[54] The basis of both art and religious spirituality is "the joy of revelation, the vision of a world wholly *significant*."[55]

✳

So the images of both mountain and ocean can help us to think about the challenge of approaching ultimate truth. But we could also employ a third image, an image from outside our earth altogether. In modern astronomy, a "black hole" is an imploded star whose mass is so great that it sucks everything nearby into its centre, including light waves. Because no light is emitted from this kind of star, it can't be detected by conventional astronomy except by its effects on the things around it that we *can* observe. Light waves, for example, passing not so close as to be sucked into the imploded star, may still be bent from their course by the gravitational pull of a black hole. The effect on what we *can* see gives us clues to the presence and nature of what we *cannot*.

We could use this celestial example as an image for the mystery that surrounds and underlies our lives, the mystery neither our science nor our rational intellects can penetrate. In fact, this thoroughly modern image has religious antecedents: in many spiritual traditions, divine reality is described as a light so powerful and blinding that it appears to human sight as an impenetrable darkness: a "black light," as some Sufi writers put it.[56] Christian mystics also used the image of darkness to convey the idea of a light too bright to see.[57] For example, the anonymous fifth-century writer known as "Pseudo-Dionysius" described the "dazzling obscurity" of the "divine darkness." Nicholas Cusanus (1401–1464), a remarkable thinker who was also a cardinal of the Catholic Church, spoke of "a light that is dark."[58] And English poet Henry Vaughan (1622–1695) said that there is in God a "deep, but dazzling darkness."[59] The tradition of the Tao uses the same imagery. "The Way of illumination seems dark," says the *Tao Te Ching*.[60] "Look at dark empty space," says the *Book of Chuang Tzu*. "It's in this emptiness that light is born."[61]

We cannot look directly into this mystery. But, like a "black hole," we can learn something about it from observing its effects, especially its effects in human lives, one of the most common sources of religious insight. Thomas Aquinas, for example, argued that the existence of God, even though it's not self-evident to us, can be discerned "from those of his effects which are known to us."[62] We might then think of spiritual practices and experiences as "experiments," or perhaps "space probes," designed to inform us better about the nature of this mystery at the heart of things.

Here, however, the analogy would start to run out of gas, because the data gathered by our "probes" informs us of two important facts. The first is that, because this mystery has an impact on human lives, a key issue turns out to be the attitude that we adopt toward it, specifically, whether our attitude to the mystery is reverent or not. And the second fact is that this attitude, and the behaviour that flows from it, actually determine how much we can learn about the mystery of this particular "black hole."

The relationship between reason and revelation has often been presented as a quarrel between "science" and "religion." But there can *be* no genuine quarrel between science and religion, because they each deal best with different aspects of human life. The investigation of the material world, said Thomas Aquinas, "is the physicist's job. The philosopher should accept his findings."[63] Science is also essential to religious insight because it has to complete its work in order to show the limits of its own kind of knowledge, the point where a certain kind of rational knowing fails and non-knowledge or unknowing begins. Science is "the only way to genuine non-knowledge."[64] But, for that very reason, science needs the help of something else to explore what lies beyond its own realm.

Science and religious insight reflect two equally advanced ways in which human beings engage with the world. A fully developed person or culture needs both, and they suffer when one is missing, or not adequately developed.[65] The faith that goes beyond reason doesn't abandon or exclude reason. It embraces and includes it. And takes it, in all of its manifestations – history, philosophy, science, social science – beyond where they can go alone.[66]

So science and religion cannot "quarrel" but should instead assist and support each other, which includes challenging each other when need be. But this kind of necessary challenge isn't a quarrel: it's a partnership. We might even call it an "educational contract," a relationship in which the partners are bound together by a mutual obligation to help each other acquire a richer understanding of reality than they can achieve alone.

The quarrel, if there is one today, is between twenty-first century science and the science of 300 BCE, or whenever religious scriptures were written. Writers employ the scientific assumptions and images of their day, as I have been doing in my use of the black hole as metaphor, and these assumptions grow outmoded, as scientific understanding advances. Contrary to popular assumptions, it's scientific knowledge, not religious knowledge, that becomes rapidly outdated, and unreliable. The authentic spiritual insights of 300 BCE are still valid today, while a scientist who obtained her PhD in the 1960s has probably seen many if not most of the theories she was taught in graduate school already overturned.

However, the ways of knowing in science and religion differ. Scientific rationality is not the only or even the best tool for exploring the kind of truth that lies in the background of our rational knowledge, beyond all sight. "Those who seek it by reason," says the Taoist *Book of Chuang Tzu,* "use reason where reason has no place."[67] In matters of the spirit, the scientific model of the neutral or "disengaged" observer doesn't work very well, because the attitude of the observer seems to make a difference. Plato and Aristotle both agreed that true philosophical enquiry begins from, and must be rooted in, a spirit of awe and wonder.[68] In matters of the spirit, the observer is also the observed, and therefore can't, by definition, be "disengaged." The observer is concerned about, and concerned in, what he or she observes. It's a mistake to think that spiritual or religious knowledge is any less empirical or "fact-based" than so-called scientific or rational knowledge.[69] But the site of the observatory or laboratory is different: it's located in the individual human heart. What goes on there, and the attitude we take to it, are critical to the outcome. In order to *see* certain things, we have to *be* certain things.

✳

There appear to be at least four conditions for approaching and obtaining spiritual knowledge and truth. The first has to do with the kind of people we are, and the intentions we have. That is to say, there are moral conditions to the knowledge of ultimate truth. We can illustrate this by a simple example. If you want to lead a life devoted to sexual pleasure (as the modern culture of self-assertion encourages you to do), you are unlikely to be open to the spiritual insights, to be found in virtually all the world's great spiritual traditions, about the necessity of some sexual restraint for the good condition of the human spirit.[70] These are truths you will be almost certain to avoid encountering, or acknowledging. To put it crudely, if you want to go to a club or pick-up bar to find someone, anyone, to have sex with tonight, you are unlikely to go to church tomorrow morning to be told that your wishes were contrary to any kind of truly good life.

In the Western spiritual tradition, the classic case illustrating this particular example is that of Augustine of Hippo. He became convinced that it was the power of his sexual and other appetites that had prevented him for so long from seeing truth. Classical Greek philosophy, especially that of Plato, had often taken for granted that human beings can't help loving what is good and what is true. But Augustine's personal struggles taught him that the impulse to self-assertion can make us unable – unable because unwilling – to see the truth, or to act on it. That, in fact, the pleasure of self-assertion can make us resist truth just for the pleasure of resisting. In other words, human beings will resist truth, or do evil, just for the pleasure of exercising their own wills. They will do evil, literally, just for the hell of it.[71] Augustine's insight, as Charles Taylor puts it, was that "the will is as much the independent variable, determining what we can know, as it is the dependent one, shaped by what we see. The causality is circular, and not linear."[72]

The world is not just given to us, and registered by us, in some neutral, objective process. There is a direct connection between our actions and what it is possible for us to know. Thus, it is a truism in all the world's spiritual traditions that only "those who *do* what is true, come to the light."[73] In the Buddhist tradition, for example, "morality" is the

first of the three divisions in the eightfold path to enlightenment, because it alone can clear the mind of all the "defilements" that "attack"
the mind, and prevent it from advancing on the path to enlightenment.[74]
Similarly, Maimonides warned that the seeker after ultimate truth must
first "most thoroughly refine his moral character and subdue his passions and desires."[75] There's an intimate "internal relationship between
truth and goodness and knowledge," says Iris Murdoch. "[W]e establish
truth and reality by an insight which is an exercise of virtue."[76] In other
words, if you *act* in certain ways, there are some things you will never
know, or can never *see*.[77] Even Aristotle agreed that the "eye of the
soul" can't function in the absence of virtue, because "what is best ... is
not evident except to the good man; for wickedness perverts us and
causes us to be deceived." Therefore it's impossible to be wise "without
being good."[78]

A second condition for approaching spiritual truth seems to be the
need or urgency of doing so. This requirement is rooted in both (what I
might call) visual and psychological conditions. By "visual" conditions,
I mean the conditions for "seeing" or perceiving things.[79] By psychological conditions, I mean the urgency of resolving some real and pressing issue in your own life, your real life.

As far as "visual" conditions are concerned, I already noted that we
live in a world constituted by questions and answers. We are not neutral
pieces of blotting paper, objectively registering an endless amount of
data from our senses, as some modern philosophers have suggested. If
we were, we would go mad, from data overload. Instead, we live in a
world already constituted for us by the conversation of our family and
our culture. The conversation has already selected for us the meaningful
things in our environment we need to pay attention to, and why. As we
learn to formulate our own questions, we begin to notice other features
of the environment that have significance for us. But, unless something
hits us, literally, on the head, we only see things – *really* see them, in a
meaningful way – in response to questions we have already formulated,
or our "intentions" in the world. And even if something does hit us on
the head, forcing us to pay attention, we will only be able to attach
meaning to it within the web of our already formulated questions and
intentions. Remember the apple that fell on Isaac Newton's head. It
wasn't the apple that delivered the theory of gravity. It was Newton's
own pre-existing mental conversation, into which the apple fell. If the
conversation of your culture or your family has eliminated all reference

to the spiritual dimension of life, it may be very difficult for you even to name, much less to explain, the strange hunger and thirst you feel, the underlying disquiet or dissatisfaction with a life lived only in the everyday, and in the prison of the modern self.

As for what I called the psychological conditions for approaching truth, certain kinds of truth appear only to be available to us when there is an urgent and pressing need for them in our lives. In chapter 6, I included the arrival or appearance of such a need in a human life among the "encounters" that initiate or fuel a life of religious practice. These encounters may be something deeply sorrowful and troubling, like a death, or some other kind of profound, perhaps inconsolable loss, or a shattering setback or disappointment or betrayal, a personal failure or breakdown, or any other kind of grievous suffering. Or they may be the opposite: some kind of deeply joyous, hopeful, or meaningful encounter like a marriage or a birth. Friedrich Schleiermacher called these kinds of encounters "openings into the Infinite." Confronted with events like birth and death, he observed, it almost seems "impossible to forget that our own self is completely surrounded by the Infinite ... they always stir a quiet longing and a holy reverence."[80]

These encounters are every bit as real, as "empirical," as anything a scientist deals with. But they are also very personal, and therefore not easily transferable. What one person can learn or know from them may not be available to someone else who has not encountered the same need, and therefore has not had the same experience – especially if the surrounding cultural conversation provides no language for expressing the content of these encounters. At such moments we are like mountain scouts ascending through the cloud that obscures the peak, shouting to each other through the fog, "Do you see what I see?" And all you can do is look, and see. Or not see. In your own part of the fog. And nothing is easier to deny than what is only self-evident.[81]

A third condition for approaching or acquiring truth seems to be the attitude or posture that we bring to the search. We can put this in a very straightforward way: to see the truths revealed by the virtues of reverence, you have to approach them reverently. The virtues of self-assertion, by definition, *assert* themselves *against* reverence. That is what they are supposed to do, what they *have* to do. But the corollary is that if you approach truth with the aggressive, demanding, necessarily sceptical posture of modern science and philosophy, if you put truth on the rack (to paraphrase Francis Bacon), then you are most unlikely, by definition, to be able to encounter or to see a certain portion of truth, perhaps the largest or most important part of it. To see this part of the truth, you need to approach it from a posture of reverence. "If there's no true centre [to welcome it]," said the Taoist sage Lao Tzu, "Tao will not stay."[82] When Canadian communications theorist Marshall McLuhan (1911–1980) was asked why he was a practising Catholic, he replied: "I sought for truth, and the only way to truth is on your knees."[83]

A final condition for approaching truth is the kind of activity through which you seek it. One of the most important is what, in many spiritual traditions, is called meditation or contemplation. In medieval Christian thought, contemplation is the highest form of thinking, above both intellect and what we now call "reason," in its modern sense.[84] On the Buddhist "eightfold path" meditation is the next of the three stages, after morality, and includes both "right mindfulness" and "right concentration." Contemplation and meditation are reverent forms of thinking. The difference between these forms of thinking and the more assertive thinking characteristic of our rational minds is the spirit of openness, receptiveness, respectfulness, commitment, engagement – in short, reverence – that the thinker brings to the exercise. He must not "direct his thoughts or *force* them to obtain knowledge of the Creator," Maimonides said, "but he must *wait* modestly and patiently, and advance step by step."[85] The thinker does not force the pace, or put truth on the rack, as if it owed something to him or to her, but rather *listens* with an eager heart, as if he or she owed something *to it.*[86]

John of the Cross distinguished between meditation and contemplation.[87] For him, meditation is the first stage, for beginners, and involves conscious focus on specific "forms, figures and images." Those who become proficient in meditation can then move to the higher level of contemplation, in which the mind becomes less active and cultivates instead a passive emptiness, "refraining from the desire to see or feel anything," and waiting for the mind to be filled with the divine.[88] The similarity between the description of contemplation in the Christian spiritual tradition – with its emphasis on "emptiness" – and the language of the Eastern meditative traditions is very striking.[89]

In these kinds of thinking, the thinker is not a disengaged, neutral observer. On the contrary, you must be *fully* engaged, as if not just the outcome but the thinking itself, and the manner of its doing, mattered deeply in your own life. As if your whole life depended on it. As if it *were* your life. "The thing to be kept in mind in meditation," says a Zen

Buddhist text, "is to have the great conviction that this is the path that can save me, and it is only this path that can save me."[90] In this kind of thinking, the searcher after ultimate truth is not aiming to deduce or analyze or catalogue or classify, but rather to *live in* the truth, gradually learning to experience its riches.[91] Analysis and logical deduction are necessary, but they're secondary. They come later. They can only work, or work best, when they support and follow that meditation on the core mysteries of life from which they derive all their substance, and what I have called their raw material.

Another word for this kind of meditation and contemplation, in many spiritual traditions, is prayer. Prayer is not primarily a way of asking for something. That's only the beginning. We start to pray in this way, because it's something we can't help doing. In need, we can't avoid spontaneously reaching out for help. This kind of prayer may be an implicit affirmation of God's goodness, but it only makes spiritual sense when it's also an act of "absolute surrender," giving ourselves "unconditionally" to God, just as we are, with all the pressures, needs, and anxieties of everyday life.[92] It's also the part of prayer we need to get over as quickly as possible, so we can get on to the more serious parts, which include preparing our wills to answer our own prayers, as Thomas Aquinas noted, but also, and even more important, *listening* to the messages that come to us from the cloud of mystery.[93] The serious part of prayer, as W.H. Auden remarked, "begins when we get our begging over with and listen for the Voice of what I would call the Holy Spirit, though if others prefer to say the Voice of Oz or the Dreamer or Conscience, I shan't quarrel, so long as they don't call it the voice of the Super-Ego, for that 'entity' can only tell us what we know already, whereas the Voice I am talking about always says something new and unpredictable – an unexpected demand, obedience to which involves a change of self, however painful."[94]

Meditation, contemplation, prayer, and other spiritual disciplines provide the raw material for reason to work on. These activities are the first step in reason's reflection on the even rawer material of dream, poetry, symbol, and myth. In the search for truth, reason's job is to take our intuitions about the nature and purpose of life and put them into some kind of coherent, logical form, subjecting them to critical and logical analysis, and transmuting them into theology, philosophy, ethics, and other forms of rational thought. Our spiritual intuitions – the "revelations" of spiritual encounters and experience – must meet reason's reasonable tests. Faith must be reasonable as well as holy.

But this is a two-way street. If the spirit must meet reason's needs, so must rational thought meet spiritual standards. Spiritual insight provides the raw material, the content for thought, but it also *grounds* reason, giving it a foundation in authentic human experience[95] Reason's conclusions must be consistent with deepest prophetic insight. Where they are not, there are "reasonable" grounds to suspect that they are not true.[96]

\*

The role of reason in subjecting spiritual insights to logical analysis, or arranging them into coherent, rational patterns, helps to explain the essential role of doubt in a life of faith. Many people assume that doubt is the opposite of faith. In reality, doubt is not alien to faith but integral to it: an essential component of religious life, one of its most regular and characteristic moments.[97]

In the last chapter, I noted that the Psalms of David alternate regularly and abruptly between despair and doubt, on the one hand, and ecstatic praise and affirmation, on the other. Psalm 42, for example, the beautiful psalm which begins "Like as the hart desireth the waterbrooks, so panteth my soul after thee, O God," shifts abruptly in its very last verse from expressions of doubt and disquiet to expressions of trust and thanks. Similarly, the familiar twenty-third psalm, a surpassingly lovely pastoral evocation of loving-kindness and trust ("The Lord is my Shepherd") comes immediately after the equally moving cry of despair, "My God, My God why hast thou forsaken me?" in the twenty-second psalm, a cry of such agonizing desolation that Jesus himself is said (by the Gospel writers) to have remembered it (but perhaps also what follows it, as we may be tempted to forget) on the Cross.

These abrupt mood shifts can be found throughout and within each of the Psalms, because they reflect one of the fundamental rhythms of religious experience, especially in its Western version.[98] They show that doubt is not alien to religious practice but rather, one of its most intimate components, "a condition of all spiritual life."[99] What John of the Cross called the "dark night of the soul" or what the Sufis call the Valley of Bewilderment – the moment when meaning cannot be found, when you feel lost and abandoned, when you doubt even your doubt – is a familiar, recurring and essential part of the spiritual journey.

In this, as in other ways, the truth of religious experience expresses both psychological truth and the truth of the intellect. Psychologically, it reflects the real experience of anxiety at the core of our lives that all our busyness and insatiable appetite for things are designed to keep at bay, the deep loneliness our restless sexual energy tries to cure but only feeds. Intellectually, the role of doubt in religious life reflects reason's assertive demand for an explanation or argument that will satisfy the rational mind. Rational consciousness is, in Bernard Lonergan's words, a "self-assertive spontaneity"; that is to say, it "demands" explanations for everything "but offers no justification for its own demanding."[100] This is actually one of the real *virtues* of self-assertion, one of its essential contributions to life in general and to spiritual life, in particular. Doubt is one of the ways the virtues of self-assertion express themselves in spiritual form. Doubt is the element that enables us, and forces us, to check, clarify, deepen and, if necessary, revise the understandings we derive from our raw spiritual experience and material. Every authentic religious life is a mixture of true faith and false belief: a mixture of true reverence and false ideas about what that reverence reveals or means. While the decision, commitment or "act" of faith holds us constant, doubt helps us to sift the false belief from the true.[101]

In the Talmud, voicing doubt is one of the essential conditions for learning.[102] As a result of confronting doubt, spiritual matters are (as Augustine said) "more carefully examined [and] more clearly understood."[103] It's doubt that helps us, for example, to separate reverence from superstition, its opposite and counterfeit, which is, in Thomas Aquinas' words, "worship offered to the wrong objects or at the wrong time or in the wrong manner."[104] Without the creative force of doubt, there would be no serious intellectual content to religious life at all, only thanks and praise. And by appealing to standards like truth or justice, the exercise of doubt may actually serve, paradoxically, to confirm the very realities it purports to deny. As French philosopher L.-B. Geiger notes: "[P]eople sometimes believe they hate God ... when they really only hate and persecute a certain false idea of him they have created in their own minds. Those who attack God in the name of truth or justice are only attacking the idea of an unjust God, or the enemy of truth, while they are really serving the true God – who is nothing more than Justice and Truth themselves – by their very devotion, even if misplaced, to truth and to justice."[105]

The famous lines from Tennyson's *In Memoriam* -"there lives more faith in honest doubt, believe me, than in half the creeds" – can be read from this point of view as well.[106] Not only are creeds less central and doubt more central to faith than is commonly supposed, but doubt is actually prior to the creeds. It is what causes them to be created. It is what pushes some of those who lead lives of faith to give that faith an articulate, rational (and therefore contestable) form. That's why the famous prayer, "Lord, I believe; help Thou mine unbelief," can and should be prayed in two ways – *for* unbelief as well as against it![107]

※

Recognizing the essential role of doubt in spiritual life brings us face-to-face with yet another paradox. It should by now be apparent that reverence is capable of recognizing the essential role of doubt: in fact, properly conceived, reverence must reach out and embrace reason and doubt, as essential parts of itself.

But the relationship is not mutual. Doubt, by itself, naturally resists reverence. That is, after all, its role in the scheme of things: to *assert* itself, to challenge, to resist. Reverence reaches out, doubt retreats. Reverence embraces, doubt resists. Reverence longs to link, to engage, to unify. In fact, reverence is little more than the spirit of union itself. Doubt pushes back. And, in fact, it expresses little more than the spirit of "pushing back" itself![108]

So our exploration of reason and revelation, of doubt and faith, of reverence and self-assertion should have begun to give you greater insight into at least part of what Hegel may have meant by the puzzlingly abstract aphorism I quoted in chapter 1: "Life is the union of union and non-union." Human life, like the universe itself, is made up of two parts: the reality of unity, of wholeness – the fact that every individual thing is a part of a larger whole – which, in human terms, expresses itself in the spirit of reverence; and the reality of division – that every thing is the individual thing that it is, distinct from the whole – which, in human life, expresses itself as the spirit of self-assertion.[109]

These two go together, as we saw in chapter 1. But Hegel's starkly abstract way of putting it helps to show how this relationship is structured, and what our discussion of doubt has also just demonstrated: that one of these two has, and must have, priority, because it is the very ground of the relationship. It's not simply the fact that without the whole, there can be no part, although that is certainly true. It's more than that. It is that union itself furnishes the principle – the dynamic – that binds union and non-union together.[110] Or, to put this in human terms once again, that the virtues of reverence are prior to, and provide the ground for the virtues of self-assertion to operate. Without the spirit of reverence, the virtues of self-assertion would be virtues no longer. They would be like a monster eating its own tail, eventually eating itself up.

The image is a Hindu one. But the insight is also a main argument of one of Hegel's best-known books. For him the French Revolution, and especially the self-destructive slaughter of the Terror, illustrated what happens when the spirit of self-assertion frees itself entirely from the virtues of reverence.[111]

This is an insight of the greatest importance not only for our own, human lives but also for the physical universe in which we live, as we will see in chapter 12.

✳

If human reason is a "self-assertive spontaneity" – if the virtue of self-assertion we know as reason is a spontaneous, unquenchable demand to explain everything – its own demand will push it to go beyond itself. The characteristic mood of reason is one of "perpetual dissatisfaction."[112] So it can't be satisfied with its own limits. Its own demands will require it to subvert or transcend itself in order to go further. Its own demands will oblige it to adopt or embrace another kind of thinking based on another kind of virtue: the virtue of reverence that is the human response to the *un*knowable world of being within which everything we *can* know exists.[113]

"Rational" thinking that insists on clarity, and wants to extract conclusions in a straightforward way from demonstrated "facts" and well-defined principles, soon loses touch with deep feelings of value and significance. It leads to a limited, reductionist kind of thinking in which the deepest promptings of the human spirit are ignored. It needs to ally itself with a more sensitive kind of thinking that remains open to all the mysterious, contradictory promptings of what Pascal called the "heart." This kind of thinking relies on feeling and judgement more than brilliance or cleverness. It feels intuitively – often at a glance, with sudden insight or revelation – the subtleties and complexities of the human world to which the "geometric" spirit, with its literal, linear, utilitarian mindset, is often blind. Blind even to the very feelings that drive it, and play a role in shaping its supposedly rational conclusions.

As Pascal argued, the human world needs both kinds of thinking, and should yoke them together. Complete success in the modern, utilitarian form of reason that Pascal called the "geometric" spirit will depend on not losing touch with its counterpart, the one he referred to as the spirit of "finesse." Without the spirit of "finesse," thinking leads to false conclusions, ignoring the deepest promptings of the heart. Without the "geometric" spirit, it may lack rigour and depth, and can lose its way in the speculative imagination. A kind of human wisdom that links both the rational and value-sensing modes – the geometric spirit and the spirit of "finesse" – doesn't make a sharp distinction between subject and object, between you and your surrounding world, but sees them instead as parts of a meaningful whole in which they both *participate*.[114]

✳

The narrower form of reason – rational thought that doesn't point beyond itself to revelation – is not sufficient for a good life, either of individuals or of communities, for at least three reasons.

First, the limited form to which human reason has been reduced in the modern world may not be able to provide all the things the Enlightenment sometimes thought it could.[115] Herbert Simon (1916–2001), a Nobel Prize-winning social scientist, points out that what we now think of as reason depends on premises (or what I called presuppositions), on so-called "facts" (that are themselves the products of hidden premises and values), and on rules of inference, none of which reason itself can supply. As a result, this kind of reason can be helpful in deciding on means to achieve certain ends, but "it has little to say about the ends themselves." All reason (in this sense) can do, Simon says, "is help us reach agreed-on goals more efficiently."[116] The goals themselves have to come from somewhere else.[117]

Second, rational thought, in its narrower form, goes neither deep enough nor high enough. This kind of reason speaks adequately neither to the depths of the psyche, the deep ocean of feeling within us, nor to our highest spiritual aspirations for fullness. Reason, by itself, can teach only Confucius' and Aristotle's "golden mean," not prophetic, counter-intuitive revelations (from the cloud of mystery), such as measureless, self-sacrificing love.[118] In its narrower forms, reason doesn't fully engage the imagination and the aesthetic faculties. It does not – perhaps cannot – normally engage all the senses, the whole physical, embodied person. It doesn't go all the way down. As a result, reason, by itself, will always be a weak reed for achieving a true change of heart, a transformation of the will. That's what's wrong with the modern reliance on pure "reasoning" alone, says Deirdre McCloskey. "It is *reasoning*. Not a cause for action."[119] Paul of Tarsus expressed this failure of reason succinctly in his single, agonizing cry: "I do not understand my own actions. For I do not do what I want, but I do the very thing I hate ... wretched man that I am! Who will deliver me from this body of death?"[120]

A third reason rational thought won't lead our modern world to the good life we seek is that rational thought, by itself, can be as corrosive as it is nourishing. It's not just that reason isn't enough. It seems to be much more than that. For reason divorced from reverence can turn into its very opposite. American Shakespeare scholar Harold Goddard (1878–1950) noted that the character of Iago in *Othello* "is perhaps the most terrific indictment of pure intellect in the history of the world 'pure intellect,' which as [American philosopher Ralph Waldo] Emerson said, 'is the pure devil.' 'Think and die,' as Enobarbus [in Shakespeare's *Antony and Cleopatra*] puts it, though he may not have realized all he was packing into three words. The intellect, as all the prophets have divined, should be the servant of the soul. Performing that function it is indispensable. There can scarcely be too much of it. Indeed, the primacy in the world of art of men like Beethoven, Michelangelo, and Shakespeare himself is that their imaginations are held in check by their critical power. But the moment the intellect sets up a sovereignty for itself, it is the slave in revolt, the torchbearer turned incendiary, Lucifer fallen."[121]

Reason that cannot bend to worship the Good may well be condemned – or even drawn, irresistibly – to worship the reverse. "Primitivism," Terry Eagleton remarks, "is the flip side of rationalism."[122] Death, violence, and other forms of degradation may be where we end up when the ineradicable human impulse to reverence is "stifled."[123] The great German novelist Thomas Mann (1875–1955), described this process forcefully: "The intellect longs for the delights of the non-intellect, that which is alive and beautiful *dans sa stupidité*, in love with it, oh, in love with it to the point of idiocy, to the ultimate self-betrayal and self-denial, in love with the beautiful and divinely stupid, it kneels before, it prays to it in a ecstasy of self-abnegation, self-degradation, and finds it intoxicating to be degraded by it."[124]

The experience of modern culture since the mid-nineteenth century seems to confirm Mann's instinct. Reason may be the first victim of a world in which it rules alone. If reason is one of the virtues of self-assertion – if it is a "self-assertive spontaneity" – its power to control the very spirit of self-assertion from which it flows, of which it partakes, is likely to be very low. A world in which *nothing* is sacred is likely to be a very irrational world. In a world devoid of reverence, reason becomes a self-devouring monster.[125] There are many reasons for this, but one of them is that human beings are quickly bored by the known. "When someone knows the causes of things, then he at once tires of them," the great Dominican preacher, Meister Eckhart (c. 1260–c. 1327) observed.[126] And boredom is one of the things that lead most directly to corruption, and to lack of concern.

As we saw in chapters 2 and 3, reverence is the posture we adopt when we become conscious of our place in a larger order we did not create and do not control, about which we have little, if any free choice. You can't feel reverence for what you yourself create, control, and understand. From this point of view, the mystery that surrounds and penetrates human life turns out to be not just the source of human reverence but one of the conditions of human goodness. We humans *need* that mystery to counteract our temptation to arrogance and to what the Greeks called *hubris*, the overweening confidence in our own powers that leads to so much evil in the world. It is actually a kind of "not-knowing," as Eckhart said, that "keeps the soul constant and yet spurs her on to pursuit."[127] The dangerous temptations of self-assertion are kept in check, and transformed instead into the highest human virtues, by mystery, awe, and reverence. Paradoxically, as we have seen, we become most human when we are able, with dignity and conviction, to acknowledge our submission to something beyond ourselves.

For this reason, Ernest Becker (1924–1974), a Pulitzer Prize-winning psychologist, argued that a religious life "solves the problem of human dignity at the highest level." First of all, the two basic "motives of the human condition" – the ones that, in this book, I have called reverence and self-assertion – "are both met: the need to surrender oneself in full to the rest of nature, to become a part of it by laying down one's whole existence to some higher meaning; and the need to expand oneself as an individual heroic personality." But, equally important, a life based on religious practice embraces and gives meaning to the mystery that is both ineradicable from this world but also indispensable to any kind of good human life we can conceive: "[R]eligion alone gives hope, because it holds open the dimension of the unknown and the unknowable, the fantastic mystery of creation that the human mind cannot even begin to approach."[128]

✳

In the next chapter we will explore this, the greatest mystery of all.

# 9

# The Life: The Mystery of Being

The greatest mystery is that there is anything at all, rather than nothing.[1]

"Fact explains nothing," says the American novelist, Marilynne Robinson (b. 1943). "On the contrary, it is fact that requires explanation."[2] The prior and fundamental question is: why are there any facts to explain? Why does the universe go to all the bother of existing, as Stephen Hawking asked?

This is the greatest mystery. But it is also the most important fact about the world, and, at the same time, the one that is hardest to grasp or articulate. The reality of our existence, of our *being*, is so close to us, so immediate a truth that it's almost too close to see. When we find that life is surrounded by an impenetrable cloud of mystery, it's not just because things are very far away from us or very complex, though some truth may be like that. It's also that things are too simple and too close for us to grasp. My being is so close to me – closer than my skin, or my thoughts, closer (as the *Quran* says) than my "jugular vein,"[3] more intimate to me than I am to myself[4] – that it's normally invisible to me. And if I do become aware of the simple but absolutely fundamental fact that "I am," I can't give that fact any content. It's too transparent. In fact, it doesn't seem to be a thing at all.

However, one place where you may come face-to-face with your being is in your life, and in the choices you must make about it.

✳

The fundamental question for all of us is: how am I to live?[5] What am I to do? But this is closely connected to another difficult question: who am I? Which also implies: who do I *want* to be?

Each of us is confronted by the puzzle of our own individual selves. We assume there is or must be an "I," but we can't locate it very easily, especially when we are young, when we are starting out in our lives. There seem to be so many "me's." There's the me that loves a party, but there's also the me that wants to be alone. There's the me that wants to be a great success in life, and make lots of money, but there's also the me that wants to sleep in until noon. There's the me that loves having friends, but there's also the me that's careless and lazy about them, sometimes mean or even cruel. There's the me that's loud and boisterous with some people, and quiet and serious with others. Sometimes there are so many "me's," it seems like there isn't any "I" at all. There's no actual centre, just a lot of random behaviours and impulses. This can be a source of great anxiety, even frightening, at any age, not just when you are young. Maybe there's actually no real me at all. And, even worse, maybe other people will find out!

How can we explain this strange jumble of potential persons and personalities that make up the self? And how can we do something about it? How can we unify them into something more like an authentic, consistent self?

Modern science is a help here, because it has required us to relearn that there are no "things" in the universe, only events and acts. In the world described by relativity theory and by quantum physics, the things that we see are merely the outward manifestation of events and acts in a field or flow of energy. Biological life emerges out of this totality of activity as a special field of rhythmic events. In these special rhythmic events that herald the emergence of biological life, a choice appears: for the first time, there is an option. The appearance and resolution of such options is both the sign and the reality of transition to biological, animate life, the transition from inanimate matter to organism. The resolution of these options in specific choices is what gives biological organisms their distinctive direction, vitality, or what we call "life."

From the most primitive form in which it appears, life is made up of these acts of choice, which also exhibit an ability to connect themselves into larger and larger clusters, in which a lead act, if you like, "pulls" others along with it, or into its orbit. Larger acts are composed of smaller ones. Primitive organisms, like cells, combine into more complex organisms. Susanne Langer has called this process "entrainment" (from the French verb "entraîner"), and the image of a train can perhaps help us imagine how it works.[6] If you think of the locomotive as the lead "act," the other railway carriages are the other subsidiary acts it pulls along behind it, or that make up the over-all organism. But this image will only take us so far, because you have to imagine that each one of the boxcars could be yet another train, and each one of its carriages could contain still more trains. Maybe the image of a Russian doll, or of a giant magnet pulling long chains of magnetized iron filings, could help to expand our mental images of the characteristic structure of animate life.

A large organism like a dog is a complex hierarchy of such clusters of biological acts. Most of them occur below the level of feeling – digestion, breathing, blood circulation, for example – and are resolved automatically or reflexively by the organism. But as they rise into higher and more complex clusters, such biological acts begin to make themselves felt – they cross the threshold of feeling – and issue in the level of acts we call behaviour. Augustine suggested, with great insight, that these first acts of self-assertion are what give rise to feeling: that it is in the encounter with various objects that are "pursued or shunned" that self-assertion "changes and turns into feelings of various kinds."[7] But feelings themselves are still acts, acts of self-assertion. To feel, as Susanne Langer said, is to *do* something, not to have something.[8] And feelings themselves eventually cross other thresholds, introducing yet other levels of acts, including the very high forms of feeling we know as rational mental acts, or thoughts.

This brief sketch of the continuum of acts, from the first biological process to the highest mental acts, should help to shed light on both the dilemmas facing any person and the common framework underlying all of them.

First of all, the fact there's no automatic "I," but rather a wide range of potential and actual "me's" – which is so disturbing when we first notice it – reflects nothing more than the biological reality that we are (from a purely biological perspective) merely a "cluster of clusters," of physical, psychical, and mental acts.[9] This huge cluster that we are has no necessary or automatic unity, especially at the higher levels of feeling and thinking, except for one absolutely crucial fact – or rather, "act" – which, like most of them, is entirely invisible to us. This vast and complex train is given its initial, primitive unity and direction by the locomotive that pulls it, by the lead act that pulls all the other act clusters along with it. This is the fundamental act of our being, the fact that "I *am*."

So we shouldn't be surprised to discover that the unity of our identities is not a given; that we are, each of us, dozens if not hundreds of

potential personalities walking around together in the same being. In
this area, modern psychology has got things backward. The unified,
single personality is not "normal" and the multiple personality "abnor-
mal." It's the other way around. The integrated personality is a high
moral achievement, a struggle, "a climb from the many to the One."[10]
When we say that a person has "integrity," that's what we mean. The
English word "integrity" has its root in the Latin word "integer," meaning "whole." When we say someone has integrity, we mean that their
being is consistent and unvaried; that what you see is what you get; that
we can count on them to act in a certain way.

But this is one of the highest human virtues. It's not where we start.
We start in the messiness of the multiple act clusters that constitute our
being, which may or may not have any unity or consistency at all. We
can't really understand the function of religious life until we fully recognize what Iris Murdoch called "the illusory whole of the unified self."[11]

Of course, most of us are lucky. We have the good fortune to start life
in families or communities that help us, initially, to establish some basic
act clusters, the large, repetitive patterns of acts we call "habits." These
basic patterns are the essential building blocks of our lives. They are
what make life possible. Without them, we would swim in a buzzing
anarchy of options, and would go mad.

The initial collection of habits we acquire from our families gives us
the early impression that we are an integrated personality, that we have
an identity. We think we *are* our habits. That each of us is an "I," not
just a collection of "me's" – although we may already have some misgiv-
ings about why some of our habits seem at odds with others. For example, you may want to think of yourself as a "nice" person, but you
know very well, in your heart, that you are consistently mean to Terry
down the street, or to your brother.

As soon as you move beyond the orbit of your family, these misgiv-
ings increase. If you are at all sensitive or self-aware, you begin to notice
that some of the habits you acquired in your family (habits of thought
about other people, for example) are not ones you want to maintain.
They aren't "you," and they aren't good. Some other habits you may
*want* to maintain, but find it very hard to do so. These habits (getting
out of bed in the morning, and working or studying hard, for example)
were given to you by others. They came too easily, and are not necessarily "you." They have to be re-appropriated, or re-earned, if that's really
the person you're going to be. There may also be new habits you want

to acquire, habits your family didn't give you, that express the person you now want to be, but that aren't easily compatible with the habits you've acquired so far. Maintaining, discarding, and acquiring the habits that will define your life may be a real struggle, and this struggle may bring you face-to-face with the fact that you aren't really who you thought you were. There may not even be a "you" at all. Just a jumble of contradictory desires and actions.

This moment of confronting, for the first time, the abyss of existence, the real struggle involved in becoming a unified, effective human being, can be very traumatic. Some people don't survive it. But, fortunately, most of us have been sufficiently equipped by our families: the habits we learned – especially the underlying habits of feeling – sustain us, and we are able to make this difficult passage to adulthood. But the process of doing so may also bring you face-to-face with the contradictions between your various selves, and the difficulties of choice and of will. At the highest moral peaks of our lives we come back to where biological life on earth started, in the resolution of options.

✳

If you're lucky, this encounter may also bring you face-to-face with something else.

In the encounter with choice, we encounter something we don't find in thought. In thinking, we can maintain any number of possibilities and contradictions. We can even make them a virtue, as Hegel did. But in real life we can't always do so; we have to make choices, whether we like it or not. And even whether we *do* make a choice or not: because *not* making a choice is also a choice. "Sooner or later," as C.G. Jung said, "the decision is simply there. Practical life cannot be suspended in an everlasting contradiction."[12]

The central role of choice in life was much emphasized by Aristotle and the ancient Stoic thinkers. "Consider who you are," said the Stoic philosopher Epictetus (55–135 CE). "First of all, you are a human being, that is, one who has nothing more ruling than choice, and all else subordinate to that."[13] But in discovering the centrality of choice in human life, you may also discover the *reason* why choices are so crucial in your life, in contrast to your thought. The reason is that you are a finite being, with only one life to live. When you make a choice, you make it for life, because you can't live the moment over again. "[T]here is not the smallest

point of time," said Samuel Johnson, "but may extend its consequences
either to our hurt or our advantage, through all eternity, and give us reason to remember it forever, with anguish or exultation."[14]

This was the objection Danish philosopher Søren Kierkegaard (1813–
1855) brought against thinkers like Hegel who, in his view, confused the
realms of life and thought. In thought, you may be able to hold two
contradictory truths in your mind at the same time, but in real life you
can't do two contradictory things at the same time. You have to choose.
So the truth about lived existence, can only be found in "the reality of
the act of choice," an "absolute either/or" with which "philosophy has
nothing to do."[15] And in this "act of choice" (which, as we have seen, is
also the defining character of all biological life), you may also – if you
are alert – come face-to-face with the deeper reality that forces such a
choice upon you, the fundamental reality that otherwise might remain
invisible to you, that can't be turned into a concept: the reality of your
existence, the fact that you *are*.[16]

Another way in which we can and do encounter the reality and mystery of being – of *our* being – is in the mystery of non-being, the mystery
of death. The loss of someone we love is the hardest thing we have to
bear in life, that a beloved person, so much a part of our life, no longer
*is*. With particularly vivid, lively people, their death not only brings us
grief but plunges us into a state of wonder and perplexity. How could
someone in whom there was so much life no longer be alive? It seems an
impenetrable contradiction. The loss of others naturally leads us to
think also about our own death, something that is both difficult and
painful to do. It's almost impossible for us actually to imagine our *not-
being*. If and when we try to do so, we often experience a kind of deep
anxiety, a dread in the face of this future state of non-being.

When we face death, or in the inevitable choices we are forced to make
about our lives, we encounter the mysterious fact of our actual existence
and, by extension, the existence of the world around us. "Man alone of
all beings," wrote German philosopher Martin Heidegger (1889–1976),
"experiences the marvel that what-is *is*." He called this experience being
"addressed by the voice of Being."[17] When we are "addressed" in this
way what we discover is that things *are*, that the world really *exists*, and
that this is the most important fact about it, and about us, even though
there is almost nothing we can say, or even think, about it. Without our
existence, thinking would not even be an option. But it is still the greatest
mystery of all, even though everything else depends on it or flows from it.

It's only one step further to consider the nature of being itself. Is being simply a characteristic of things or does it have a reality of its own? Sometimes, we may have the feeling, or perception, or "experience of Being," in Heidegger's words, "as sometimes 'other' than everything that 'is'."[18] Many thinkers, from Plato and Aristotle through Augustine and Thomas Aquinas to Heidegger himself, have in fact concluded that whatever lies at the heart of the cloud of mystery, behind the reality we know and in which we live, one of its characteristics is, and must be, *being*. One of the essential characteristics of everything that is is that it *is*.

This recognition may seem like progress, but it immediately raises other questions, including the obvious one: what is being? It's important to ask this question, because we use the word "being" in several different ways, for instance as a noun (human *beings*) and as a verb (to *be*, the act of being). So is the reality underlying things *a* being – or is it an *act* of being?

Aristotle seems to have straddled these two usages. For him, the *cause* of being was its "form," specifically a particular form combined with particular matter. But existence itself was also a kind of action. And the *notion* of being was a concept based on an *act* of understanding: the highest form of reality, "on which depend the heavens and the world of nature," was a divine "*act* of contemplation" or thought.[19] Thomas Aquinas agreed with Aristotle and went one step further. For him, "being" itself was an act: the *act* of being. As he put it, "to be" is the *act* by which something is the thing that it is.[20]

Aquinas' formula seems to come closest to the personal experience we already explored. But this insight makes being hard to think or to talk about, because the Western cultural tradition makes it much easier for us to talk about concepts than about something that seems to be nothing more than a verb. The supreme Act of existing that holds reality in being must therefore remain in the cloud of mystery, to be approached only by our scouting parties, not by our conceptual reason. Heidegger himself said that the closest you can get to this kind of mysterious truth is a kind of "reserving proximity," meaning that "something is near and yet remains at a distance," ultimately unknowable – a kind of "black hole," as I suggested earlier. But as we draw nearer to it, even though its mystery is preserved, we find ourselves, in Heidegger's words, "at home."[21] As the gentle Brahman Uddālaka Aruni explains to his son in the Hindu holy book, the *Chandogya Upanishad*, "all creatures have being as their root, being as their home, being as their base."[22] This is where rational thought has to point beyond itself, and religious life takes over.

But rational thought has not yet said its last word. Because if the ultimate reality underlying the universe and ourselves has something to
do with a supreme Act of existing, other things follow, two of which we
can mention now, leaving the rest until chapter 11. If ultimate reality
has the nature of Being, then it must also be *one*, as Plato suggested, and
it must also be *true*, as Aristotle emphasized. Whatever *is* is part of the
totality of being itself, and whatever really *is* is true, because it *is*.[23] So
ultimate reality must have at least these characteristics (though, as we
shall see, it may have more): being, unity, and truth.

About these three characteristics, the Eastern and the Western spiritual
traditions are in agreement. In fact all this seems much more self-evident
to the East than it does to the West. The *Upanishads*, for example, central
texts of the Hindu tradition, might almost be described as a series of
meditations on the nature of being. But because of the process of "mythic
dissociation" discussed in chapter 4, our separation of subject and object
and our heavy investment in the power of rational thought, the rediscovery of being seems to be very disorienting for the modern Western mind,
and requires enormous mental effort.

That's why the mystery of being is often expressed in the Western
spiritual traditions in a disguised form such as the creation story in
Genesis, the first book of the Jewish and Christian Bibles. Serious thinkers in both the Jewish and Christian traditions recognize that such stories need not be interpreted as depicting something occurring only or
necessarily "first in terms of time," however.[24] That is, creation narratives are a figurative way of expressing the insight that a mysterious
power holds things in existence, "not only when things first begin to be,
but so long as they continue to be."[25]

The mystery of being is equally central to Islam. In fact, the very first
words dictated to Muhammad by a mysterious presence – the first
words of what was to become the *Quran* – were: "Recite in the name of
your Lord *who created*."[26] Not surprisingly, then, being is one of the
dominant themes of the *Quran*. On page after page, the repeated response to the rhetorical question to unbelievers – "How can you deny
God?" – is a recitation of the mysterious reality of being: "Did he not
give you life when you were dead ... he created for you all that the earth
contains."[27] A phrase repeated almost like a mantra throughout the
*Quran* is: "If He decrees a thing, He need only say: '*Be*,' and it *is*."[28]

Both the reality and mystery of being explain the absolutely central
position occupied, in the three great Western spiritual traditions, by the

story of the encounter between Moses and God on Mount Sinai, when God, speaking out of the midst of a burning bush, reveals his name: "I AM THAT I AM," and instructs Moses to tell the Israelites, "I AM hath sent me to you."[29] In this, one of its most defining mythical moments, Western spirituality declares that, whatever else it may entail, "God" is a name it gives to the mystery of Being, and not a name for a thing but rather a name for an act or an action, for a verb not a noun, for the mystery that things *are*, that we *are*, that "I AM."

As a result, any atheist, or, for that matter, any believer, who turns God into a thing is barking up the wrong tree. God does not and cannot "exist," in the sense in which the modern world poses the question of his existence. Because to "exist" He would have to be a thing. But no existing thing, says Iris Murdoch, "could be what we have meant by God."[30] God is "not a particular entity like Australia or a blackbird," explains Karl Rahner (echoing Aquinas and Pseudo-Dionysius), "but supports everything, is the origin of everything, permeates everything."[31] God does not exist, because whatever we mean by that name is something more like existence itself, or even the possibility of existence. As the French philosopher Étienne Gilson (1884–1978) remarked, "any religious God whose true name is not 'He who is' is nothing but a myth."[32]

✳

Awareness of the mystery of existence, the mystery of being, emerges, then, from humankind's deepest experience of life itself, and of its opposite, death. The great spiritual traditions are rooted in our encounter with both these challenging realities, and so both have a spiritual as well as a literal meaning, especially in the Western traditions.

Psalm 19 declares that "The words of the Lord are spirit and life," and language like this can be found throughout the Jewish and Christian scriptures. In Deuteronomy, for example, "life" is contrasted with its opposite: "See, I have set before you this day life and good, death and evil. If you obey the commandments of the Lord your God which I command you this day, by loving the Lord your God, by walking in his ways, and by keeping his commandments ... then you shall live ... But if your heart turns away, and you will not hear ... I declare to you this day that you shall perish ... I have set before you life and death, blessing and curse; therefore *choose life*."[33]

Clearly here the injunction to "choose life" has a spiritual meaning as much or more than a literal one.[34] What the scriptures seem to be describing are two kinds of options for life itself, one option that leads to a real and true kind of living – "the life that is really life"[35] – and another which leads to a kind of living death.

This symbolic or metaphorical meaning of life and death is carried forward into the Christian scriptures. In his letter to the Romans, for example, Paul explains that "if you live according to the flesh you will die; but if by the Spirit you put to death the deeds of the body, you will live."[36] Obviously Paul is talking here about a kind of "life" and "death" that take place within life itself – a life and death that are "here and now."[37] This is one of the reasons the Crucifixion is such an important symbol for Christians: because it symbolizes not just something that *has* taken place but also something that *continues* to take place, metaphorically, in the lives of all genuine seekers after truth. Christians, as Paul explained in his second letter to the Corinthians, are "always being given up to *death* for Jesus' sake, so that the *life* of Jesus may be manifested in our mortal flesh."[38]

As Northrop Frye has suggested, Christian teaching seems to be trying to express that "human life ... is a confused and inseparable mixture of joy and suffering, good and evil, life and death, and that the eternal realities of this life are two poles, worlds of life and death which are outside time. The Bible ... is traditionally called a revelation, and the 'spiritual' kingdom of God of Jesus' teaching is primarily, from the Christian point of view, what it has to reveal ... the apocalyptic world, the ideal world ... which human energy tries to bring into being ... the vision, the model, the blueprint that gives direction and purpose to man's energies."[39]

This ideal world of the "kingdom of God" is found in the Jewish and Christian scriptures in many metaphorical forms, as Frye points out, including the Garden of Eden, the Promised Land, the New Jerusalem, and even "eternal life" itself.

✳

There are at least two ways to think about the possible meanings of "eternal life." One is the spiritual meaning we already glimpsed in Deuteronomy and other Jewish and Christian texts. And the other meaning is literal.

In the literal version, "eternal life" occurs if not within time, at least after time, or after our time, after our physical and literal death. There are some good reasons why we often wish to think of "eternal" life in this literal way. One is the sheer difficulty, for living beings, of doing otherwise: our "natural revulsion from annihilation," as Augustine put it.[40] Because of the way the "feeling of Life," like all human feelings, has a tendency to make us think it "lasting and for ever," as Samuel Taylor Coleridge noted – and because of the difficulty for humans to imagine how their very "Being," the basis of "all our Thoughts, Feelings, Acts and Experiences," could pass "from Something to Nothing." The natural human instinct to look for a life that is not ended by death "is therefore no arbitrary fancy conjured up by our desires – but a necessity inwoven in our Being."[41]

Another good reason for human beings to entertain the hope of an eternal life that continues after this one is the role of hope in mortal life itself. As we have already seen, hope is such a necessary ingredient of a good human life that "faith" may be just another word for it, a way of describing a life lived in, and filled with, hope and trust. A life lived without hope is already a hell, a living hell.[42] This is true throughout our lives. But nowhere must it be truer than at the end. To live the last years of life in dignity and joy seems far more likely when they are illuminated by a reasonable and spiritual hope in a life that is not ended by death. "When the fire of our own lives grows cold," says Kathryn Tanner, a contemporary American theologian, "we come to burn with God's own flame."[43] Samuel Johnson may have exaggerated the alternative scenario, but he was driving at something important when he observed: "Piety is the only proper and adequate relief of decaying man. He that grows old without religious hopes, as he declines into imbecility, and feels pains and sorrows crowding upon him, falls into a gulph [sic] of bottomless misery, in which every reflection must plunge him deeper, and where he finds only new gradations of anguish, and precipices of horror."[44]

For modern ears that find Johnson's description of an old age lived without religious hopes exaggerated,[45] we can turn the same insight around, and put it positively. The tradition of the Tao describes the great advantage of a life and old age based on a "supreme reality ... ever-constant and enduring":

My life is spent working on it.
My old age seeks ease in it.

At death I find rest in it.
That which makes my life good also makes my death good.[46]

The Jewish rabbinical sages said that this kind of death is "nothing but a kiss."[47]

A third reason for human beings to conceive an eternal life not ended by mortal life is the instinctive human demand for accountability and justice: for others, of course, but also for ourselves. Our minds revolt at the possibility that the intrinsic quality of our actions and those of others, regardless of outcome, may not matter, in the sum of things. We spontaneously resist the possibility that the only thing that matters is whether someone else finds out about our deeds, that, if no one else knows, or no one else is harmed (as one modern test, derived from John Stuart Mill, puts it[48]), then it doesn't matter what we do. We want to believe that someone *always* knows. That we are acting "under the Eye of Omnipresence."[49] That "*somewhere* it must be justly recorded."[50] And that therefore we are under an obligation to act morally, even in the most private and even secret parts of our lives.[51] This human impulse seems to be most powerfully expressed in the Islamic tradition. If one of the strongest recurring themes in the *Quran* is the mystery of being, a second theme is that "God is watching all your actions" and that "God will call you to account for them."[52]

The Islamic tradition expresses in perhaps its starkest form a universal human demand for justice. The idea of a "last judgment" expresses a deep human longing that, despite so much evidence to the contrary, "what is hidden is just."[53] We want to see justice in the universe. Or rather, our insistence on seeing justice in the universe is the expression of our belief in Justice itself.[54] Which is why the religious mind spontaneously concurs with Paul's assertion that "each of us will be accountable to God."[55]

All three of these are good and sound reasons for humankind to embrace what the Anglican Book of Common Prayer calls a "reasonable, religious and holy hope" for a life that isn't ended by death.[56] A life lived in the light of such a hope is a life transformed.[57] This kind of life is what, in chapter 5, I called faith. And the transformation is more than enough to justify the hope. As Paul said, "we are saved by hope."[58] If we are indeed heirs of an everlasting kingdom, as the scriptures proclaim, we can only be "heirs through hope."[59] Because, as the first letter of

John, in the Christian Bible, puts it, "we are God's children *now*; what we *will* be has not been revealed."[60] In other words, we don't and can't "know" what awaits us after death.[61] But what can be asserted from a spiritual point of view is that "we are God's children *now*." And, in this light, "eternal life" takes on a new and important spiritual meaning, a meaning not dependent on the future, but one that is truly eternal; that is to say, *outside* of time altogether, but therefore also *inside* every moment of present time.

This way of thinking about "eternal life" is a very old one. Augustine said that "eternity is not in the past or in the future," but in another realm altogether, "outside time."[62] And therefore also inside time, "existing in every new moment."[63] As the *Quran* says, "*This* is the Day of Resurrection: yet you did not know it."[64] To live in or for "eternal" life is to live every moment as if it were a door to eternity, as if eternity were already in the very heart of it, as if it *were* eternity itself.[65]

One way to do this, as you saw in chapter 2, is in the way you view time. If you see the present moment as simply a point in time, without any strong connection either to the past or the future, then you aren't living in "eternal" life. But if you see the present moment as including, in a profound way, all past time, and all future time, "that whole amplitude of time, which is eternity" (as Whitehead put it), then you can be said to be already living in "eternal life."[66] And to live this way has consequences. Living *this* way is living spiritually, because the moment must be lived respectfully, reverently – not for itself alone, but for its meaning, its significance, in the light of all that has come before, and all that will follow, to the end of time, and beyond.

Another way to live in "eternal life" now – today – is to live in the light of what Plato called "ideas," or Aristotle "final causes." Truth, goodness, beauty, justice, mercy, and so on, are "eternal" ideas. They live outside of time, waiting for us to make them our own, to make them real. To live a life in their light, to genuinely love them, and to strive to make them real and alive in this world is *already* to live in eternal life.[67] This is what the Bible (as Frye noted) calls the "kingdom of God," the vision, the model, that gives, or can give, direction to our lives.

Living this way has consequences too, including for our idea of ourselves, or of the "self," as we shall explore in the next chapter.

✳

Our exploration of "life" and of "being," in this chapter, has begun to bring us full circle. And also to the end of a road. For if, as we saw, life begins in the rhythms that give rise, first, to biological life, then to feeling, and finally to the high form of feeling we call mind, intellect, or thought, this is not a one-way street. The ultimate encounter with the mystery of being, and with "eternal life," radiates back down the causal chain, trans- · forming what is below – just as the body and psyche support, nourish, and provide the raw material for what is found above, even the images, dreams and symbols to express it. That's why Aristotle called the ideas associated with eternal life "causes": to suggest that they have as much influence on what happens in the world as those material or "efficient" causes that can be studied by science. The ideas, values, and aspirations that *pull* us forward into the future are just as important as the other causes that *push* us, from behind. Perhaps more important.[68]

Of course, words like "forward," "behind," "above," "below," are merely spatial metaphors, images human beings can't seem to avoid using to express these kinds of truths.[69] We seem spontaneously to think in terms of a spatial "hierarchy," where "higher" is fuller or richer or better than "lower." But, behind and through these images, human beings struggle to express the idea that our lives can be transformed, and made more "true," by living in a way that unites our "highest" aspirations and dreams with the realities of body and psyche from which they grow: by living spiritually, by living *in* the spirit.

The writer of the Christian Gospel of John attributes to Jesus the saying that "no one can see the kingdom of God without being born *from above*."[70] In the light of the discussion in this chapter, this spiritual insight becomes almost self-explanatory. No one can see – let alone enter into, or live in – the metaphorical "kingdom of God" who has not passed the phase of living only in the physical world, the world of material and efficient causes, who has not been renewed, or "reborn," through some kind of vision or pursuit of a greater or "higher" reality.[71]

For many people, however, as we shall see in the next chapter, the starting point may well be the absence of any such thing.

# 10

# An Adult Faith

In the Introduction, I compared the difficult transition from childhood to adult faith to a journey over a treacherous mountain pass, in which the traveller (like a knight on a medieval quest) must meet and undergo trials along the way, especially the trials of reason. In our modern culture, as I remarked, most don't make it to the other side of the mountain.

※

In the modern world, almost every young person does – and probably must – live through a period of life when they reject the religious tradition, if any, of their family or their culture. Wilfred Cantwell Smith has explored this almost inevitable dynamic of modern life through a meditation on the Islamic *shahadah*, the simple declaration – "There is no god but God" – which, as we saw in chapter 4, is one of the Five Pillars of Islam. True religious life, he observes, is "a process, a movement in faith." From this perspective, the declaration needs to be "taken in stages."

No man, this reading suggests, can legitimately and truly say "God" who has not previously said, and meant, "no god." To arrive at true faith one must first pass through a stage of unbelief. "There is no God": this comes first, and must be lived through in all sincerity, and all terror. A person brought up in a religious tradition must have seen through that tradition, its forms and fancies, its shams and shibboleths; he must have learned the bleakness of atheism, and experienced its meaninglessness and eventually its dread. Only such

a person is able to go on, perhaps only years later, to a faith that is
without superficiality and without merely cheap and secondhand
glibness.[1]

The period of life in which a young person rejects religious practice
and religious truth is made almost inevitable by the assumptions and
prejudices of modern culture, especially its bias in favour of "scientific"
forms of reasoning and evidence and also the widely-held assumption
that there is something naive about religious practice. But, as I also suggested in chapter 8, doubt is also an essential feature of the rhythm of
religious life itself. It is a reflection of the genuine virtues of self-assertion,
the rational mind's demand for a clear and convincing account of things.
Without this kind of demand, there would be no continuing effort to sift
truth from error or illusion, or to deepen and clarify understanding.
There would be no possibility of an adult faith.

Such a period or movement of rejection also corresponds (at least
distantly, or in anticipation) to what in religious language is called the
"dark night of the soul," or the "valley of bewilderment," the inevitable
and recurring moment – in a religious (and perhaps in any kind of) life
– when we feel abandoned, and alone in the universe. So the falling
away from religious practice that most young people experience today
may not be a bad thing, in itself. It may even be a good thing. Without
it, you may never reach a fully adult faith. You may remain in a kind of
suspended childhood, in what Smith refers to as "superficiality" or
"cheap and second-hand glibness," the kind you see all the time on religious TV shows. Since doubt is a necessary and essential part of a true
religious life, adolescence and early adulthood are the time to explore
doubt to the full, to the very depths. Without it, you may never achieve
a true and adult faith. You may never see things as they really are.[2]

Of course, this stage may not feel at first like being abandoned. On
the contrary, it may feel like a brave adventure, a courageous looking
at life and truth in the face. And also a liberation, a new freedom to do
and think what you like (including, of course, the delicious pleasure of
sleeping in on Saturday or Sunday morning). This is all the more likely
as modern tradition encourages us to see the rejection of religious practice in exactly these ways. But doubt, lived to the full, also points the
way back. That is, if it is genuinely "lived through in all sincerity, and
all terror." Because an alert mind will probably begin to notice things
that make this kind of adventure rather less appealing and self-evident

than it first appears, and more costly in human happiness and fulfil-ment, and perhaps in truth itself. The first is the prospect of living in a meaningless universe.

A truly secular world is one in which everything happens by accident, necessity, or fate, as the ancients believed, or that is "absurd," as many modern writers have put it. This is a world in which there is no meaning written into the universe, but also no genuine freedom either, only the illusion of freedom. Doubt, by itself, doesn't lead anywhere, except to a wasteland, a meaningless universe.[3] And if you are honest about your doubt – if you don't try to eat your cake and have it too, as so many people do – this is where you will end up. That's what Smith means, I think, by "the bleakness of atheism ... its meaninglessness and eventu-ally its dread." A truly meaningless world is a, literally, terrifying place to be The natural reaction to this kind of world is fear or terror, as Smith said, or "nausea," as so many twentieth-century writers, like the French writer Jean-Paul Sartre (1905–1980) put it.[4] So living in it re-quires a strong dose of courage, or a strong sedative, or simply an ability to be distracted from the truth – by pleasure, or conspicuous consump-tion, or busyness, or alternative sources of meaning, such as art or na-ture, or by something else.

Or else it requires bad faith. This is very common. Many people at-tempt to hang onto the values and visions of a meaningful world, while pretending not to do so.

But someone who honestly confronts this kind of world may shrink from the abyss, and may start to consider the alternatives. As Susan Neiman remarks, "the search for reason in the world is not derived from religious notions of Providence. Rather, the invention of Providence arises from the search for reason in the world."[5]

For all of these reasons, someone entering adulthood (or already well into it), who is honestly trying to lead a purely secular life, may experi-ence a growing restlessness, a feeling of not being fully satisfied by the normal pleasures of everyday life.[6] They may feel that something is missing, may feel in fact an unnameable hunger for something that ad-dresses the challenge of life in a deeper, more nourishing way, something that speaks as much to the spirit as to the body or the mind. Ordinary human "flourishing," as Charles Taylor puts it, may not bring a feeling of human "fullness," or fulfilment.[7] The constant, inevitable "swinging of the *I* in its lonely truth" – back and forth between the two poles of reverence and self-assertion – is "the place where the desire is formed"

for something fuller, richer, more genuinely fulfilling.[8] Augustine thought
that this state of restlessness and unslakable thirst was one of the most
evident signs of God's "grace," his merciful kindness in ensuring that
human beings would miss him, and search for him, until they found
their heart's desire: "By the misery and restlessness which they then suffer you make clear to us how noble a being is your rational creation, for
nothing less than yourself suffices to give it rest and happiness."[9]

A religious life (like everything else, for that matter) is an answer to a
question. You have to ask the question before the answer can become
relevant, or meaningful. This kind of persistent hunger for something
more fulfilling than ordinary human satisfactions may begin to form
such questions for you. Another kind of experience that can do so is the
experience of reaching the bottom, or hitting some kind of wall in your
life. "In the experience of failure," Leszek Kolakowski observes, "in seeing Being defeated by nothing, the knowledge of being and of good
emerges ... the Sacred is revealed to us in the experience of our failure.
Religion is indeed the awareness of human insufficiency, it is lived in the
admission of weakness ... Thereby it *is* a cry for help."[10]

For some people, of course, this only shows that (what they call) religion is false; that it's just a "crutch" for those not strong enough to live
life without it. But people who think in this way are not consistent. They
appeal to the facts of the "real world," but they choose to overlook or
dismiss the most important of those facts. What you can't help needing,
what you can't do without, is *real*, just as real as anything else, certainly
just as real as the supposed facts of a material world; maybe more so.
Moreover, as we saw in chapter 6, it's not just a question of need alone.
Because with need comes opportunity, and discovery. Our moments of
greatest need can also throw us into new encounters, encounters that
suddenly reveal new truth.

When hunger, or thirst, or doubt, or despair, or failure, or loneliness,
or anxiety, or evil, or joy – or whatever it may be in your life – has finally broken through your self-defences, or your self-sufficiency, your
initial assumption that you were cast in the leading role in the movie of
Life, when experience has finally formed the question in your mind, you
may be ready for the answer or, rather, for seeking it.[11] You may be
ready to set aside the biases of the modern world, and pay closer attention to the real facts, of the real human world.

In this state, you may be prepared for the kind of encounters I described in chapter 6, including the encounters with "being" in the

mysteries of birth, marriage, and death. And you may be ready to see the deeper spiritual meaning or potential in each of these encounters, to see the eternal lurking in the folds of the present moment.[12] Having rejected a religious view of the world as fairy tales fit only for children but not for the adult you have become, yet discovering the unsatisfying, unfulfilling, painful, or even terrifying character of a truly secular world, you may be ready to rethink, ready to reconsider the claims of the spirit; to explore the eternal, not just the particular self.

If you have reached this point, you stand on the threshold of the potential second stage of Wilfred Cantwell Smith's progressive interpretation of the Islamic *shahadah*. As you will recall, Smith suggests there are several distinct stages or processes that must normally be gone through, in our modern world, on the way to a truly adult faith. One is gaining an adult understanding of religious language.

The problem of religious language is one of the main reasons modern people usually don't survive the dangerous mountain journey to adult faith. As I remarked in chapter 4, the great religious forms of spirituality have the weaknesses of their strengths, and the strengths of their weaknesses. One strength is that religious truth is not expressed in conceptual language but rather (as I discussed in chapter 8) in myths, stories, symbols, images, and so on.[13] Religious expression takes this form for many reasons, including (as we saw) the difficulty of penetrating mystery in any other way, but also because of its origins deep in the psychic constitution and experience of humankind, and because of its purpose: to support and nourish all sorts of people, and all parts of them, at all stages of their lives, from birth to death.

This is a great strength. It means, among other things, that religious language and practice engage not just (or even primarily) the conscious, rational mind but also the imagination, feelings, intuition, the subconscious, and the body itself: movement, gesture, smell, sight, hearing, taste, voice, and so on. Like art and literature, to which it is so closely connected, religious practice "moves us more because it moves more of us."[14] As a result, religious life is open to everyone, not just to the learned or the intellectual, or to those who love abstractions. To the simplest as to the most sophisticated.[15] That makes it as accessible to children as to adults. Any child can absorb the stories, myths, and symbols of religious practice, and can draw something from them. And as the child grows up, "these books grow with him," as Augustine said.[16]

But these strengths have their corresponding weaknesses, especially in the modern, rationalist world. One of them is that people often think that they can and should outgrow this kind of language and practice, that religious texts are merely "fairy tales," as Freud said, designed only for the credulous or the weak.[17] The result is that many young people, even if they have had a religious upbringing (which is less and less frequently the case) fall away, sometimes wistfully, from religious practice as they grow up, because they can't see how it fits with the rationalist assumptions and language of the modern world. Since the words don't mean what you thought they meant, maybe they don't mean anything at all.

So gaining a truly adult understanding of religion means going beyond a childish understanding of those sacred stories and symbols which were no doubt entirely literal for you when you first heard them, if you ever heard them at all. In childhood, their simplicity and directness served an important purpose. It made their meaning directly accessible; the "numinous," resonant, mysterious, powerful quality they may once have had for you is exactly the point. You want to hang onto that, or recover it, or discover it for the first time. But now you need to understand the words differently. You need to learn to understand them "figuratively," as Augustine and Maimonides said.[18]

Some well-meaning adults insist on interpreting scriptural narratives of events like the Creation as factual accounts, though the greatest religious thinkers made it clear that such stories "cannot be taken literally," as Maimonides said, but can and should be interpreted spiritually.[19] "In the Beginning," in religious language, means something deeper and richer, and possibly quite other, than simply "in the first place."[20] As we saw in chapter 9, even "life" and "death" may not have a literal meaning in a religious text, and often don't. "One should therefore not rely on mere words," as the Buddha explained, "but everywhere search for the intention behind them."[21] In Augustine's view, scriptural texts were meant to be mined for "every truth that we can deduce from them and ... others besides that we cannot, or cannot yet, find in them but are nevertheless there to be found."[22]

This doesn't mean religious texts stand in need of "demythologizing," as some modern theologians and writers have put it.[23] Using mythological language in spiritual and religious life seems to be almost as unavoidable, Maimonides said, as following "the laws of nature in relation to the body." Because if we were to approach them "without the use of parables and figures, we should be compelled to resort to expressions both profound and transcendental, and by no means more intelligible than metaphors and similes." In fact, without the knowledge imparted by "tradition" and by symbolic images, he observed wryly, "most people would die" before ever attaining the insight – into ultimate things – on which to base their lives![24]

To think that religious language must be demythologized is to fall into the trap of thinking that rational, linear speech is the only true kind of speech, and that everything else needs to be somehow translated into it in order to be "true." We have already seen how little this way of thinking does justice even to secular modes of expression such as poetry, art, or music, the kinds of expression with which religious language has most in common, and whose form it often takes. For religious language, this kind of assumption is even less appropriate. "Something about prose is inadequate, even blasphemous," says Susan Neiman, "because it is insufficiently awed by the task."[25]

In chapter 8, I suggested the feeling that emerges from our physical bodies builds up two inseparable and interpenetrating worlds of fact and value. So we could perhaps think of language as a continuum between these two worlds.[26] At one end of the spectrum, "scientific" language tries (sometimes in vain) to make a sharp distinction between understanding and valuing. But even in everyday speech this distinction doesn't hold true, because, in normal speech, "facts" and "values" are not sharply separated. When we see acts of bravery or cowardice, we call them acts of bravery and cowardice: the seeing and the evaluation are not separate, and language would not allow us to separate the two easily, even if we wanted to.[27] "Almost any description involves an evaluation," as Iris Murdoch remarks. "Perception itself *is* a mode of evaluation."[28] In the language of poetry, the distinction between perception and value has begun to disappear altogether. A poetic symbol, as Coleridge famously observed, "always partakes of the reality that it renders intelligible."[29] Religious language takes this tendency even further.

In religious language – at the other end of the spectrum from "scientific" language – you can no longer distinguish the symbol from the thing symbolized at all. On the contrary, as Leszek Kolakowski says, in religious language "signs *are* – instead of simply representing – what they signify."[30] This is because religious language is primarily the language of religious *actions*, acts of worship, ritual, prayer, meditation and so on. In this context, religious words are not so much signifiers as *transmitters* – transmitters of the realities and the power toward which religious reverence is addressed. They are the means for religious people to *participate* in something. In religious language "the understanding of words and the feeling of participation in the reality they refer to merge into one."[31]

In other words, religious language may be "figurative," as Augustine and Maimonides said, but it is not really allegorical, or even strictly metaphorical. Religious symbols are "consubstantial* with the truths, of which they are the *conductors*."[32] Religious language cannot be demythologized without being destroyed, because myth is the language of mystery. But even though religious language can't be demythologized, neither is it literal. And developing an adult faith is partly a matter of learning to listen to religious language, texts, poetry and stories in a new and more perceptive way, hearing them as full of multi-layered symbolism, and seeking to find in them, in Augustine's words, "every truth that we can deduce from them." As Wilfred Cantwell Smith said, "people take their religious symbols from their fathers, but ... every man must find out for himself what those symbols mean."[33]

In the modern world, you are unlikely to do this until some things have happened to you. The first is what Smith calls "seeing through." That means not only seeing all of the weaknesses, failures, and shortcomings of your own religious tradition (there are bound to be lots of them) but also seeing that your initial understanding was mistaken, or insufficient. Doubt, lived honestly, and to its bleakest depths, can make you reconsider things. It can push you to go further, to listen again to the words and symbols of genuine religious practice, and hear them anew, or for the first time, in their true light, to discover the truly adult meaningfulness of religious language. I am not just talking here about "intellectual" or abstract meaning. That's important, but only in a secondary way. I'm talking about the meaning necessary for living. "The only serious enterprise," says English philosopher Bernard Williams (1929–2003), "is living."[34] As we saw in chapter 9, religious practice is about life, it *is* a way of life, a way of living. And it grows out of the needs of real people, in their real, adult lives. The meaning and truth of

---

* "Consubstantial" means being of the same substance as something else, or being the same thing.

religious language are rooted in these practical needs. If you don't feel the need, chances are you won't see the meaning or the truth, either.

✳

Another process you normally have to go through on the way to a truly adult faith is the search for, or encounter with, your own elusive "self." "To thine own self be true, thou canst not then be false to any man," says Polonius to his son, Laertes, in Shakespeare's *Hamlet*. And although they are put into the mouth of someone perhaps incapable or unworthy of understanding their full meaning, as happens so often in Shakespeare (Portia in *The Merchant of Venice* is another good example), most readers spontaneously recognize the deep truth of these words, and their importance for a young person, like Laertes, setting out on life's journey. But what, or where, or who is the "self" to whom you should be true?

As we saw at the beginning of the last chapter, the self is not the "given" that we thought it was when we were children. There's no necessary unity or consistency to the personality: there's no natural "I," just a lot of random "me's." A famous American jazz musician once said: "When I play, I'm trying to play the truth of who I am. The problem is that I'm changing all the time."[35]

Constructing an authentic and consistent "I" is not something that comes easily or naturally. It's a high moral challenge, perhaps the highest there is; a challenge many people may not feel up to. For example, in attempting to cobble together a genuine self, you may find yourself up against the problem of the will, or rather of the weakness or absence of will that has puzzled philosophers since ancient times.[36] Not only may you be unable to do what you want to or should do but, even worse, you may find (like Augustine) that the will can be perverse: it delights in doing the opposite just to relish its freedom, its own self-assertion.

Many young people discover this, with a shock, once they are no longer sheltered by the habits of their home. It can be a scary experience. They may find themselves repeating Paul's heart-rending cry: "I do not understand my own actions. For I do not do what I want, but I do the very thing I hate ... wretched man that I am! Who will deliver me from this body of death?"[37] There seem to be so many potential selves, and finding or constructing a consistent one seems to be hard enough, let alone being true to it.

Although the discovery that you don't seem to have a genuine self is scary, it also helps to know that it's not a new one: people have been encountering this same personal void for thousands of years. The Buddha called it *anatta* ("no self"), and he thought its discovery was an essential step on the road to enlightenment.[38] As you struggle with this same problem, it may occur to you that there's more than one way to think about the self, and that the way we normally think about it may be misleading or, at the very least, incomplete.

A distinction between two different ideas of the self can be found in all the great religious traditions of humankind, especially the Eastern traditions. The Buddhist *Tibetan Book of the Dead*, for example, distinguishes between "your illusory ego" (which is a "separate self") and "your own true self," through which shines "the boundless light" of "true reality."[39] This distinction between the two selves is also one of the main themes of the Hindu *Bhagavad Gita*. In that great dialogue, the Lord Krishna repeatedly instructs the young warrior prince Arjuna in the vital difference between the particular, changing self identified with the body and the senses – with pleasure and power, and the "fever of the ego" – and another, quite different self, the eternal self, the "Self of all beings, living within the body," that is "everlasting, infinite, standing on the motionless foundations of eternity."[40] As we saw in chapter 3, this other self, beyond the ego, is the one the Hindu tradition calls *Atman*, and the Tao calls the inner, real, or true self. The real person, says the *Book of Chuang Tzu*, is "pure spirit."[41]

These two different ideas of the self can help us to distinguish the modern from the pre-modern mind. It has been remarked that one could draw a line through the eighteenth century, a line between Samuel Johnson and his biographer, and much younger contemporary, James Boswell (1740–1795), whose great *Life of Johnson* created the model for all modern biographies.[42] This line would divide the emergence of the modern idea of the self from the pre-modern idea. On this, the modern side of the line – Boswell's side – the "self" is conceived as everything particular, individual and unique about the person. On the other, the pre-modern side of the line – Johnson's side – the self is conceived, instead, as everything that is universal and eternal in the person.[43] Being true to this second kind of "self" is obviously very different than being true to the first or modern "self." The eternal or universal self is as unchanging as the specific or unique self is unstable, divided, and variable. Finding and being true to eternal values is not exactly an easy task. But it is conceivable. And in the pursuit of these eternal values, in the quest for the eternal "self," the problem of the particular or unique self may simply be dissolved, as all the potentialities of the individual are pulled along (or "entrained") – and thus *pulled together* – in this pursuit. When we are pulled together in this way, by our "'deepest' or most serious" self, we no longer feel we're merely "a collection of heterogeneous impulses."[44]

Discovering this other, eternal self also helps solve the challenges of sincerity and authenticity I discussed in chapter 7. As Lionel Trilling suggested, the modern pursuit of sincerity is often self-defeating, because self-assertion, by itself, simply dissolves the self into conflicting acts of self-assertion.[45] Absolute freedom can only lead to what Hegel called the "disintegrated" self, which can't really be sincere or authentic, because there's no longer any self to be true to, there's no "there" there.[46] In pure self-assertion, paradoxically, "selfhood is lost, and all that remains is different roles played in different situations."[47] So the endless pursuit of sincerity and authenticity in modern culture is a symptom of a deep problem, not simply the means of its solution. Genuine sincerity and authenticity require a self that only the virtues of reverence can construct.[48]

✳

The eternal self may furnish the key that allows you to escape from the dead end of the particular or modern self.

But to do this may require a third process, another one that must normally be gone through on the way to a truly adult faith. As you begin to pay closer attention to the facts of the real human world, you are likely to encounter the "hierarchy of goods" I already pointed out in chapter 3. What this means is that things are not all worth the same. They have different values. Some good things are *more good* than other good things. The things you once thought were really important – like cars, or being popular, or getting drunk, or wearing the right clothes, or having lots of money – these things may be good in their own way, but they're not as good as other things. They don't have any staying power. They can't sustain you, or satisfy you, over the long haul. They eventually leave you feeling empty, or unsatisfied. In fact, in comparison to some other things, they don't turn out to have nearly as much "good" in them as you once thought. They don't have any real "depth" of good in them at all.

This discovery is painful enough, on its own. But discovering the hierarchy of goods also compounds the problem of the will with the related problem of guilt. This second problem is built right into the structure of the world, and of actions themselves.

From its first and simplest forms, as we saw in chapter 9, life is defined by the arising and resolution of options, most of which occur below the threshold of feeling, but many of which arouse our strongest and most painful feelings. The problem is that every choice necessarily excludes another option, or options. Even if our own choice was a good one, in the hierarchy of goods the other options, the ones we excluded, were, in their own way, or from another perspective, *good ones too*. But these options don't just disappear. They remain like shadows on the chosen path; shadows of all the good things we chose not to do. Even when we chose for the best, we had to exclude many good possibilities along the way. "[W]hatever I do," as Alasdair MacIntyre observes, "I shall have left undone what I ought to have done."[49] And this "remaining presence of the negative in every choice"[50] means that even a "perfect" life, if there were such a thing, could not be lived without a growing burden of guilt, guilt for all the good things undone, the paths not taken, the rich possibilities excluded. The "force of the losing claim" creates what Martha Nussbaum (b. 1947), a contemporary American philosopher, has called an inescapable "demand of good character for remorse and acknowledgement."[51] This may be part of what Christians mean by "original sin": the structural impossibility of leading a blameless life. Dealing with the inevitable problem of guilt in a creative way is one of the functions of the major religious traditions, and someone who has become aware of this fundamental human predicament may begin to consider these spiritual resources with a more open mind.

If awareness of the hierarchy of goods deepens the problem of guilt, it also offers a way to solve it, and the related problem of the will, so agonizingly described by Paul. The distinction between the particular and the eternal selves begins to resolve the problems of identity and will, and another step forward is the identification of the "eternal" values that constitute the true self. A third is the means for making them real in our lives.

A basic human problem is how to turn "potentiality" – the things you could or should do, or wish you could do, or dream of doing – into "act." Part of the solution to this central human problem, as discovered by all the religious traditions, is the awe-inspiring and therefore empowering encounter with the sacred. As a result of coming into the presence of the sacred, human beings find the strength to turn what is only a possibility into an act, or a lifelong series of actions. A Buddhist text explains this by saying that faith "*leaps forward*." Inspired by some example or vision, the seeker "leaps forward, by way of aspiration, to the various Fruits of the holy life, and he makes efforts to attain the unattained, to find the yet unfound, to realize the yet unrealized."[52]

Among the "fruits of a holy life" are religious practices such as prayer and meditation that help to unlock the problem of the will (as so many recovering alcoholics and drug addicts have discovered). Bonaventure said that prayer is the "source of all lifting up."[53] Prayer and meditation fix our minds and hearts on whatever is to be found at the top of the hierarchy of goods – on what is most worthy of our love.[54] They bring us into its empowering presence.[55] In doing so, they become, as Coleridge explained, "the medium between mere conviction and resolve, and suitable *action*."[56]

Whatever creates the empowering experience of awe in your life is what may be called sacred or holy for you. It is the source from which you can draw the inspiration, motivation, and energy to act. An inevitable question for you, then, is whether the source of your own empowering awe is truly worthy or not: whether it is at the top of the hierarchy of goods and is therefore really worthy of your reverence, or whether it is only an "idol": that is to say an imitation or substitute.

In an adult journey of faith, we gradually learn the true value of things. Even – or perhaps especially – in the pettiest wrongs we commit, we explore the gradations of the good and discover that, as Leibniz said, "a lesser evil is a kind of good, just as a lesser good can be a kind of evil, if it becomes an obstacle to a greater good."[57] Once you have noticed this, you are ready to follow your thinking to its logical conclusion, and to ask yourself: so, what things really do have genuine value? Seeking an adult answer to that question begins a lifelong quest for the answer.

If you seek it with any sincerity at all, your experience will begin to show you that what (in chapter 1) I called the "virtues of self-assertion" express real goods, but they aren't enough. They aren't the whole story, in the "hierarchy of goods." To lead a genuinely adult life, even a secular life, you also need to learn and practice the virtues that express other goods, those that (in chapter 2) I called the virtues of reverence. You need to practice them in your family, in your work, in your profession, with your friends, in your community, and even (as we will see in chapter 12) in relation to the natural world. This is very likely something you have already learned, implicitly, from the modern "expressivist" culture in which you grew up, with its strong, underground spiritual yearnings – but without recognizing these virtues for what they are.

As you proceed on your adult journey, you may now be open to discover you can't practice these necessary virtues, or do it well, or sustain it, without help. Because reverence, like other goods, has a hierarchy too. Some things are *more* worthy of reverence than others. To be any good at the virtues of reverence, we need the help that comes from practising them in a regular, structured, habitual way, and doing so for the things that are *most* worthy of our reverence, for whatever lies at the top of the hierarchy of goods, and which we therefore call sacred or holy.[58]

That's where a life of religious practice comes in. The highest good, the realm of the sacred, must always remain a mystery to us. But the attitude we take to it, the posture we adopt toward it, the things we say about it, and the search we undertake for it, affect everything else in our adult lives. An adult faith is a search for that truth. A search conducted with hope and with trust, in a spirit of reverence for the truth that is sought.[59]

The kind of help religious practice offers is not just on the big stuff – like the meaning of the universe or the meaning of life – though there's always a necessary connection with these things. But, perhaps because big questions can't be answered any other way, religious practice also offers help, more immediately, on the little stuff: the challenges of our everyday failures, and of everyday living, in an adult world. Like the problems of identity, will, and guilt discussed in this chapter.

The problem of the will begins to be dissolved by encountering the hierarchy of goods, the eternal self, and the true meaning of things like prayer. And the problem of guilt begins to find a solution (as we will see again in the next chapter) in the discovery of forgiveness and how essential it is for us – in a world where the hierarchy of goods excludes the possibility of a blameless life. Essential, of course, to receive, but far more (as we also discover) to give. This further discovery reveals yet another paradox – that you must lose your life to save it – a paradox that reason alone could never have discovered for us, nor ever endorse, on reasonable grounds alone. It is in "dying" to our particular or modern selves that we are born to what is called "eternal" life.

Thomas Aquinas said that the Christian Lord's Prayer is a "perfect" prayer. Maybe so. But a close contender would have to be the prayer known as Francis of Assisi's Prayer, which comes about as close as you can come to a successful formula for everyday living, based on this profound, spiritual paradox.

> Lord, make me an instrument of Thy peace.
> Where there is hatred, let me sow love,
> Where there is injury, pardon,
> Where there is doubt, faith,
> Where there is despair, hope,
> Where there is darkness, light,
> Where there is sadness, joy.
> O Divine Master, grant that I may seek
> Not so much to be consoled, as to console,
> To be understood, as to understand,
> To be loved, as to love.
> For it is in giving that we receive,
> It is in pardoning that we are pardoned,
> And it is in dying that we are born to eternal life.

There is not much theology here, or not at first. Only the deepest lessons of a truly adult life. And Francis' prayer makes crystal clear, again, that an adult religious faith must be something you do before it can become something you might be said to have or believe. It is not a set of propositions. It is something you *do*. Something you do in your relations with other people and with your community. Something you do in your relationship with the natural world. Something you do in sacred ritual, meditation, and prayer. Something you do in your own mind, and spirit. And because you do these things – and *in* doing them, and *through* doing them – you cannot help encountering the truth that lies behind the universe.[60]

# Learning from Each Other

I hold this truth to be self-evident, that all of the world's great religious traditions are created equal.

But it's important to say immediately what this statement means, and what it doesn't mean. It *doesn't* mean that truth is relative. The word "truth" loses all meaning as soon as you admit anything but one standard of truth that all must meet. How to do this is another and much more complex question. But a single standard of truth is an ideal that must be maintained if our human dialogue and our human community are to have any foundation at all. "That truth, even moral truth, exists I have no doubt, for I am no relativist," says Stephen Carter (b. 1954), an American novelist and legal scholar (and I agree with him); "but we weak, fallen humans will never perceive it except imperfectly, a faintly glowing presence toward which we creep through the mists of reason, tradition, and faith."[1]

What I *do* mean is that each of the world's great religious traditions is a valid path for a serious spiritual journey, a genuine revelation of a common truth about human life, and about reality, that all are seeking to reveal, and have revealed, in their own ways.[2] And if I am right, this is of the utmost importance for the future of our world.

✳

One of the greatest challenges of our modern world – a challenge splashed across the pages of our newspapers and websites every day in the first decades of the twenty-first century – is the existence, and necessary co-existence, of different traditions, including religious traditions.

For some people, the religious motivations that seem (at first) to be behind so many terrible conflicts in the world today serve only to show that "religion" is the root of all evil. If only we could get rid of "religion," they say, then we could get rid of all these conflicts too, and could get on with living reasonably with each other, and in peace.

For many of these same people, the importance of religious issues in the daily news also comes as a surprise, even a shock, a very disagreeable shock. Weren't all these religions supposed to die out? What are they still doing here, they ask, rather angrily? Often "with a contempt they would be ashamed to show toward other cultures."[3] In the last half of the twentieth century, even scholars (perhaps especially scholars) convinced themselves that the world was undergoing a process of "modernization," in which the forces of industrialization and urbanization were leading inevitably to secularization, with the resulting decline and disappearance of "religion" as a major force in the world.

Obviously it hasn't quite worked out that way, except in the West. And even here, the process has not gone as far or as fast as the prevailing biases of intellectual and media culture, the prevailing public discourse, would lead you to expect. Equally obviously, the assumptions that lie behind these reactions to the re-emergence of religious issues are deeply flawed. They are based on an unexamined and unjustified assumption that "religion" is self-evidently false, and therefore destined to evaporate with the spread of education and literacy. This is a partially self-fulfilling assumption, of course, once it takes hold. And people who hold it therefore also mistakenly presume that religious practices and experience are merely a passing phase in the history of humankind. Reality is quite otherwise. In chapter 4, I already recalled Mircea Eliade's observation that "the 'sacred' is an element in the *structure* of consciousness and not a stage in the *history* of consciousness."[4] "Religion," as William James said, is "an essential organ of our life, performing a function which no other portion of our nature can so successfully fulfill," and, for that reason, "must necessarily play an eternal part in human history."[5]

But precisely because religious practice and experience are, and are likely to remain, permanent and necessary features of the human community, the challenge of religious diversity is one of the most pressing issues in a globalized world. In a world where each culture stayed more or less within its own geographic sphere, the issue of religious plurality might have been less urgent. But even if the world had ever actually been such a place, it certainly is one no longer. The realities of population migration, economic globalization and global communications, including the Internet, mean that different religious traditions and practices – including non-religious and secular traditions – are now confronting each other, sometimes angrily, around the world and within the borders of many countries. This means that one of the most important tasks of religious persons today is to reflect on the conditions and priorities for understanding between different religious traditions.

Before exploring those conditions and priorities, however, let's pause to consider whether "religion" really does contribute to human conflicts and, if so, how, and why. This may help us to address them.

First of all, it's important to recognize that many of the conflicts raging in the world in the name of "religion" are actually conflicts arising from other sources, including colonialism and anti-colonialism, nationalism, ideology, cultural differences, ethnic, tribal, and class power struggles, greed, demography, poverty, unemployment, alienation, and so on: conflicts in which religious language and symbols are merely some of the weapons, and some of the excuses, not necessarily the "real" source of the conflict. That doesn't mean appeals to religious motivations can't be used to fuel a conflict. They certainly can. But that doesn't always make "religion" the root source of the conflict, either.[6]

Second, there is no reason whatever to believe that a world without "religion" would be a world without conflict. Quite the reverse. There is every reason to believe that religious experience is the soil in which the concepts of peace and love and brotherhood have entered the conversation of humankind, and that religious practice and religious taboos constitute one of the most potent constraints on violence in the world. A world totally bereft of religious practice and values – a world, therefore, in which nothing is taboo and nothing is "sacred," not even human life – far from being a garden of brotherly love, would more likely be a war of all against all.

Having said all this, however, is there some way in which "religion," by its very nature, contributes to human conflict? The answer, I think, would have to be contradictory, both yes *and* no. The reason for this self-contradiction is rooted in the "human paradox" itself, and the way humankind's conflicting impulses of self-assertion and reverence have played themselves out, since pre-historic times, in religious life as in all other dimensions of human culture. Early religions incorporated the practices of killing, sacrifice, and violence that were part of the cultures in which they grew, and from which they were inseparable. And though they also helped gradually to tame these instincts, later traditions never entirely lost the connection to the deep psychic forces from which they arose.[7]

So even though the mature religious traditions we have been considering in this book turned the earlier ones upside down, rejecting the idea of divine violence, they still exhibit the initial paradox in a specifically religious form, one that I will call the "religious paradox." (There's also a paradox of self-assertion, but I won't be able to explore it in this book.) The religious paradox arises partly from the fact that religious traditions are founded on revelation. It's important to recall here the argument of chapter 6, that religious practice and traditions grow not out of abstract reason, like philosophy for example, but rather from actual experiences, concrete *encounters* with the spirit and with the "sacred." This is one of their advantages, as a form of expression for authentic human experience. They are empirical, like science, rooted in specific events and circumstances, including specific cultural circumstances.

Revelation occurs in the particular, not in the general. That's one of its strengths. But it is also one of the ways in which it may contribute to conflict. *Because* a revelation is particular, many people who see or experience its truth assume that this particular revelation is the whole truth, or that other revelations cannot also be true.[8]

To be fair, this is not just a problem for religious truths alone. It is equally the case in other areas of human life, including philosophy. Philosophers are often just as guilty of being blinded by their own insights, and therefore unable to credit the truths seen by others. John Stuart Mill observed that, in philosophy, "the besetting danger is not so much of embracing falsehood for truth, as of mistaking part of the truth for the whole," because in all the major philosophical controversies the participants have been "right in what they affirmed, though wrong in what they denied."[9]

The problem of narrow-mindedness isn't limited to "religion." And neither is the violence that can flow from it. The twentieth-century has been called "a ravaged century," perhaps the most violent in history, the one that invented the word "genocide" to describe its own terrible crimes. Yet the slaughter of over twenty million people in Eastern Europe and another thirty million or more in China during the last century wasn't the result of religious ideas or conflict: it was a pure product of secularism and of secular ideologies, often invented or inspired by social scientists and philosophers, like Karl Marx or German philosopher Friedrich Nietzsche (1844–1900), who had nothing but contempt for religious traditions. It has been called "mindslaughter."[10]

So the secular thinkers who attribute violence to religion are simply blind to the beam in their own eye. The temptations of intolerance and violence are a problem shared equally by both secular and religious traditions. Both find it very seductive to enhance their own conviction of being in the right by demonizing and attacking their opponents.

Nevertheless it's entirely fair to recognize that because religious revelations are so strongly charged and energizing, they can be easily exploited to mobilize groups and communities, and to raise emotions, including violent emotions like righteous anger, to a fever pitch. That's one of the reasons the world has witnessed so many so-called "wars of religion" throughout history, wars that often had many other, nonreligious causes too, but where religious feelings certainly played their part. In fact, exhaustion with European "wars of religion" was one of the things that led many thinkers of the eighteenth-century Enlightenment to reject (what they took to be) "religion."

This side of the "religious paradox" is also reinforced by the close connection between religious traditions and culture. Because religious revelation is revelation in the particular, not in the general, it is embodied in practices and traditions reflecting that culture. This doesn't mean a religious tradition can't transcend cultural boundaries, or evolve from one culture to another, or absorb and respond to changing cultural circumstances or challenges. It certainly can, as the Buddhist, Christian, and Islamic traditions, among others, clearly show. But it remains the case that specific religious traditions are closely tied to specific cultures, mostly for better, as we shall see again, but also for worse.

The "worse" is that cultural difference reinforces difference between religious traditions. And, because human beings are always suspicious of the different and the strange, cultural conflict can heighten and inflame religious conflict. It's sometimes hard to distinguish the one from the other.

Both revelation and culture combine, therefore, to reinforce one side of the "religious paradox," the side that can contribute to conflict and violence, if it isn't counterbalanced by something else. But it *is* counterbalanced by something else. In fact, it's counterbalanced by the very

substance of the revelation itself. All of the world's great religious traditions (this is one of the things that qualifies them as "great") teach lessons
of peace, tolerance, and reconciliation between all living persons. "Be self-
controlled! Give! Be compassionate!" says the Hindu *Brhadaranyaka
Upanishad*.[11] One of the strongest themes of the *Bhagavad Gita* is the
teaching of "selfless service" to others.[12] The *Quran* teaches "charity,
kindness, and peace among men."[13] "Loving people and aiding things is
goodness," says the tradition of the Tao.[14] Even the Buddhist tradition,
which goes further than any other in advocating "detachment" from
this world, also bears a powerful message of compassion and pity for all
living beings. The two Buddhist teachings of *ahimsá* and *maitrí* are exactly the same as Augustine's two basic rules of "do no harm" and "help
others."[15] As the Buddha himself explained, "It is for the weal of the
world that a Buddha has won enlightenment, and the welfare of all that
lives has been his aim."[16]

British writer Karen Armstrong (b. 1944) reminds us that the world's
great religious traditions all "share an ideal of sympathy, respect and
universal concern."[17] In fact, it is from our religious traditions that these
ideas have entered the conversation of humankind, and it's far from
certain that they would long survive the demise of these traditions. So
when religious persons use the revelations of their particular religious
traditions as incitements, excuses, or weapons for conflict, let alone for
violence, they are betraying the very substance of the revelation they
claim to uphold.

This is one of the reasons that what I called the "religious paradox"
is indeed a paradox. Because the *substance* of true religious revelation is
in tension with the fact that it *is* a revelation. Understanding this paradox is an important step to solving the otherwise puzzling fact that
revelations of compassion and concern can be exploited to incite exactly the opposite. The problem for the world today is not "religion"
itself, much less an excess of it, but rather a *lack* of it, a failure to be true
to authentic religious revelation. As Friedrich Schleiermacher put it, the
"spirit of division ... is not brought about by religion but by the want
of religiousness."[18]

For another thing, understanding the religious paradox also reminds
us how much more the world's great religious traditions have in common than what divides them. In practice, as William James pointed out,
"the feelings on the one hand and the conduct on the other are almost

always the same, for Stoic, Christian, and Buddhist saints are practically indistinguishable in their lives."[19] Thus, the great revelations all point in the same direction, and are all particular revelations of one common truth.

❊

The fact that all religious revelations are "particular" points to something that should bind them together: the opportunity and the need to learn from each other. Since each of the revelations is particular, it can reveal only part of the whole truth.[20] Religious traditions therefore need each other. They need to learn from each other, so that each of their particular revelations can be completed and deepened by the others. In other words, the world's great religious traditions – like all human beings – should regard themselves as bound to each other by the same kind of "educational contract" I described in chapter 8. You will recall that this kind of contract is a relationship in which the partners are bound together by a mutual obligation to help each other acquire a deeper understanding of reality than each can achieve alone. The great religious traditions need to listen and learn. But they also have an obligation to share their own unique revelations, so that others may deepen theirs. They need to engage in the ongoing conversation that is the foundation of human life.

This kind of "educational contract" between religious traditions might be called a "new ecumenism." The word "ecumenism" comes from Greek words meaning the "inhabited world" or "house," and has been used, especially since the beginning of the twentieth century, to describe movements which strive for Christian unity. There are two sides to this movement. One works for the structural unification of Christianity, seeking to break down the walls between separate denominations, and to merge them into a "united" church, or churches. A second has more modest goals, and seeks only to achieve agreement among Christian denominations on matters of doctrine and practice, and mutual recognition of the validity of each other's sacraments.

In speaking of a "new ecumenism," I mean something that is both less and more than this "old ecumenism." Less, because the ideal of structural unity seems not only unattainable but possibly undesirable. More, because the old objective of agreement among Christians does not go far enough.

It's certainly desirable that different Christian traditions should strive, with all their heart, to overcome the differences between them. They should also develop and express mutual respect and fellowship; an open-hearted welcoming to each other's rites and sacraments. Anything less is a scandal. But in the kind of world reflected in today's headlines, understanding and respect between Christians may seem very small potatoes, given what is at stake. While this aspect of ecumenism is very worthy and should be sustained, it seems obvious that the world now needs a "new ecumenism" in which priority is given to the interfaith dialogue that has always been a strand in the traditional movement.

✳

In a secular world, people who live a life of religious practice share a common outlook and common challenges, including the challenge of living with, or in, secular cultures. The *fact* of living in or beside secular societies suddenly makes former mountains of difference seem like molehills. It highlights the remarkable similarities between different spiritual traditions, especially in comparison to modes of thought that make no explicit room for the life of the spirit, or for reverence.

This recognition is not as new as you might think. Over fifteen hundred years ago, Augustine observed that "although there are many great peoples throughout the world, living under different customs in religion and morality and distinguished by a complex variety of languages," those who "live by the standard of the spirit" form nevertheless one single community, especially in relation to those who live by another standard.[21] In other words, the world's religious traditions not only share common ways of relating to the world, they share a common challenge of dealing with those who don't – or think they don't.

That's part of the problem, of course. A secular frame of mind is itself a kind of faith, – simply a "different faith" – though those who view the world through secular glasses don't recognize the fact.[22] "The agnostic and especially the atheist, unaware of the god he believes," says Deirdre McCloskey, "is as uncritical in his faith as a Sicilian widow lighting a candle before a statue of the virgin."[23] That creates a challenge for those who lead lives of religious practice and are therefore more conscious, in a secular society, of the fundamental presuppositions they have had to make. So they will need to engage a robust dialogue not only with other spiritual traditions but also with the surrounding secular society, in order to make it more conscious of its own "absolute presuppositions" and the grounds, or lack thereof, for making them. This will no doubt also involve questioning prevailing assumptions, including potential confusion between the *process* of secularization and the *ideology* of secularism.

So the kind of educational contract I have called a "new ecumenism" eventually needs to include dialogue with the "faith" of unbelief. But it also needs urgently to deepen the traditional dialogue between spiritual traditions themselves, so that each may appreciate better what they have in common, but also where they are different and complementary, and what each has to teach the others. Because conversation, understanding, fellowship, and commitment to a common standard of truth imply learning. And learning doesn't involve agreement only, but respectful questioning and challenge too. That's an essential part of the educational contract.

✳

The obvious place to start is the learning that needs to occur, urgently, within and between the Western religious traditions themselves, and especially between Christianity and Judaism, on the one hand, and Islam, on the other. For reasons underlined by the headlines, there may be no greater need in the world today than this dialogue between the Western faiths. Finding the ways and forms for it to occur, or occur more frequently and audibly, should be a priority.[24]

In such a "family" dialogue between religious traditions which share common roots, all the participants can help the others to deepen, expand, and remain true to the authentic spiritual insights of their own particular traditions, and of their common heritage. The non-Islamic partners in such a dialogue can, for example, legitimately support their Islamic brothers and sisters in asserting the rich intellectual and spiritual tradition of Islam and the ways in which it is betrayed by extremists, who exploit religious feelings for purposes that have nothing to do with real religious values and who employ violent means that directly contradict them. Non-Muslims can and should encourage responsible Islamic leaders who speak out forcefully about true Islamic values.[25] They can support them in reminding others that the *Quran* authorizes only defensive violence, in response to external attacks: that in fact it condemns "aggression" and "coercion," declares that there "shall be no compulsion in religion," and directs the faithful to call others "to the path of your Lord with wisdom and kindly exhortation. Reason with them in the most courteous manner." And non-Muslims and Muslims alike can recall the *Quran*'s wonderful words of peace and understanding between persons of different faith: "God is our Lord and your Lord. We have our own works and you have yours. Let there be no argument between us. God will bring us all together, for to him we shall return."[26]

The non-Islamic partners in dialogue can and should insist that important Western values of freedom, tolerance, equality, democracy, human rights, and social progress are not only compatible with spiritual wisdom but are actually rooted in its revelations, from which they emerged, and without which they may not survive. They will find – perhaps to their surprise – that most Muslims around the world largely agree with them.[27] To turn one's back on the claims of these values in the name of other, supposedly religious values is to undermine them both.

But learning is a two-way street. Non-Islamic Westerners shouldn't assume learning can or should be all one-way. The confrontation with an assertive Islam is an important learning opportunity for the West, too. It can help other Westerners to see themselves in a new light, by holding up a mirror to our own spiritual dilemmas and weaknesses. When even young Muslims raised in Europe or North America reject much of what they see around them in our Western societies, we should not be content simply to condemn extreme acts. We should also reflect. Are we actually worthy of respect? Have our ideas led to a society and a way of life of which we can be genuinely proud?

Obviously our answer will be largely "Yes." But at the beginning of the twenty-first century, it would be hard to give an unequivocal "Yes." Muslim youth remind us, uncomfortably, of something we would rather not face: that societies in which, for example, pornography has recently become not only commonplace but pervasive and unavoidable – and even children now listen regularly to popular songs celebrating masturbation, fellatio, anal sex, and the degradation of women – are not societies of which we can be deeply proud.[28] Something has gone wrong. Some spiritual and ethical mooring has been lost. We know it, in our hearts, but are so comfortable in our individual lives that we want to ignore the problem. Timothy Garton Ash (b. 1955), a British scholar of international relations, has commented recently, "The idea that these young British Muslims might actually be putting their fingers on some things that are wrong with our modern, progressive, liberal, secular society; the idea that rational persons might freely choose to live in a different, outwardly more restricted way; these hardly feature in every day progressive discourse. But they should. Articulate British Muslims are not merely telling us non-Muslim Brits a lot about themselves. They are also telling us something about ourselves."[29]

If we in the West really took seriously "the broad critique of materialism, hedonism, and individualism of many devout Muslims," Terry Eagleton suggests, "Western civilization would most certainly be altered for the good."[30] Even the debate about "censorship" and freedom of expression – occasioned by Muslim outrage about Western depictions of the Prophet – should have reminded many Westerners of something they had almost completely forgotten. The opposite of the virtues of self-assertion are tyranny, oppression, dictatorship, totalitarianism, or (as we now say) the abuse of "human rights," and everyone knows that these are very bad things. But having largely forgotten the existence of the virtues of reverence, few remember that their opposite is irreverence, or "impiety." Irreverence can also be a bad thing. Evidence of how bad a thing it can be is all around us, in our changing environment, in our prisons, on our streets, in our schools, in our homes, in our all-pervasive electronic media. The world of much modern popular culture, as Susan Neiman remarks, is a world "never graced by a shadow of reverence. There's so much trash – sometimes masquerading as a satire of trash – on the airwaves that it's hard to say what's worse: The blunting violence that's called action? The lackadaisical transformation of sex to commodity? The shows that invite people to degrade themselves for a few dollars or minutes of fame? All of them chip away at human dignity."[31]

Western amnesia and surprise about accusations of impiety demonstrate the degree to which we have lost any lively awareness of the place of the sacred in human life. A society in which "nothing is sacred" is not a society in which you would want to live. Rediscovering and re-exploring the sacred is going to be one of the most important challenges for Western societies in the years to come. So the contemporary encounter with Islam might well play the same role as the "encounters" we observed in chapter 6, when individual persons come face-to-face with an otherness of the spirit that is just as real as the otherness of the material world. Just as these encounters can break through the walls of individual self-sufficiency, and open hearts and minds to new or forgotten realities, perhaps the encounter with Islam might do the same for the non-Islamic and largely secular West, helping it to learn again the virtues of reverence.

✳

Relearning the meaning of reverence is also something we can do in a broader dialogue between the Western and Eastern traditions. In chapter 4, we began to see how the world's great religious traditions complement and complete each other. It's almost as if the human paradox explored in chapter 1 can also be discovered in the spiritual life of humanity writ large. If the Western traditions embody, on the whole, the virtues of self-assertion, the Eastern traditions may be said to stand for the virtues of reverence. And just as life, if it is to be complete, must make room for both sides of the human paradox, spiritual life needs the insights and contributions of all its many connecting streams.

So we need to listen to what the Eastern traditions have to tell us. But first we must learn to appreciate again, by contrast, the distinctive insights of Western spirituality, which are the ultimate source of most of the features of our societies of which we are justifiably proud.

As we saw in chapter 9, there is implicit agreement among all spiritual traditions that whatever lies behind the universe, and within us, has at least the characteristics of being, oneness, and truth. To these basic three, however, the Western spiritual traditions add two more. And these two are among the West's most important contributions to the spiritual heritage of humankind. The first is the concept of the "good." It's not just that things *are*, and are therefore *one*, and therefore *true*. They are also *good*. This revelation, coming first from the Zoroastrian and Israelite traditions, has infused not only Christianity and Islam, but also philosophical traditions, beginning with the pre-Socratic Greeks. No one can prove it, in a purely intellectual or experimental way. It is a true, spiritual "revelation." But everyone can experience its truth. And once it has entered the conversation of humankind, it has transforming power. A world that is truly good, where good is not only possible, but is, so to speak, its natural element – the thing toward which the world yearns and tends – is a potentially very different world than one in which things are just what they are, and remain so, forever.

Especially when this idea is linked to the other great revelation of the Western spiritual traditions: a revelation that whatever mystery lies behind the universe has not only the characteristics of being, oneness, truth, and goodness, but also those of love. It *is* Love. This revelation – a truly radical one that even Western philosophy hesitated to proclaim until infused by revelation – has another important corollary, to say the least. Because, if the force that is behind the universe has the characteristics not just of being, unity, truth, and goodness, but also those of love, it must be personal, even if not subjective. So it is not just the impersonal *Good* of the philosophers, but the loving *God* of Abraham, Isaac, and Jacob.[32]

This is an even more potent idea than the previous one, because it is the "idea" that releases all the potential of the Good. By itself, the Good has a paradoxical effect, contrary to what you might expect. The Good has a nice, positive, enabling sound about it, doesn't it? So you would expect it to be an idea that would just naturally make people happy, peaceful, and constructive. In practice, however, that turns out not to be true. Instead, on its own, the idea of the Good reinforces two negative and destructive human feelings, the feelings of fear and guilt.

Though this sounds illogical at first, it makes perfect sense when you think about it for a moment. As soon as you proclaim anything to be good, let alone the Good, you can't help feeling anxious emotions related to the ways in which it appears to be fragile, threatened, or frequently absent from the world. If you truly value something, you naturally fear to lose it, or not to find it, or not to be worthy of it. And the more valuable it is, the more you fear these things. "Fear is a response to value," remarks Martha Nussbaum.[33] A very natural response, as the Hebrew Psalms illustrate so vividly. And so is guilt. Because you can't help noticing how very far from good many of your actions are, how far they fall short of the ideal.

A world without fear would be a world without value. That's one of the reasons (there are others) why so many religious traditions speak, quite appropriately, and centrally, about the "fear of God." But a world in which *only* the concept of the "good" appears – without the redeeming power of love – turns out to be a very dark world, ruled either by the iron law of necessity, by the arbitrary forces of fate and fortune, or by the capricious forces of chance, contingency, and accident, as the ancient poets and playwrights of Greece and Rome show.[34]

This is the problem that the revelation of a loving God helps to solve. "Acceptance by something that is less than personal could never overcome personal self-rejection," says German/American theologian Paul

Tillich (1886–1965). "A wall to which I confess cannot forgive me."[35] A power behind the human universe that is not just good but also loving wipes away the very fear and guilt that good itself created, or reinforced. We are loved and forgiven despite our shortcomings. And this releases us and empowers us to love in turn, and to make the good come to life in our world.

This idea is even more transforming than the idea of the good. Or rather, as I just mentioned, it is the key that has unlocked all the transforming potential of the good. God "sees us and seeks us," says Iris Murdoch, "Good does not."[36] History is no longer a vicious circle; it is a story with a purpose and a direction, a story in which the devout seek to transform themselves and their world so that God's will may be done on earth as it is in heaven. By releasing and fuelling energies of betterment, mercy, and reform, the idea of a loving and forgiving God, who calls on human beings to manifest his love in the world, has transformed the West, and continues to transform the world, even though it does so now in a largely secularized form.

The distinctive features of the Western religious experience are connected to the proclamation of a transcendent God, a God who is not only *inside* this world but somehow *outside* it too, beyond time and space. And from this fruitful idea flow, as we saw in chapter 4, many of the distinctive accomplishments of the West, including its philosophy, its scientific traditions, its ideas of freedom and democracy, its respect for the individual and human rights, and its constant pursuit of social betterment and progress. These are accomplishments of which we can be proud in themselves, but also as the products of our own distinctive religious and spiritual traditions. Isaac Newton, for example, got his idea of scientific "laws" (and even some of the laws themselves) from the French mathematician and philosopher, René Descartes (1596–1650), who himself was strongly influenced by the religious concept of divine law as developed by Augustine and Thomas Aquinas.[37] The reverence for human reason that played such a large part in Western achievements is itself a reflection of our religious values. "[W]hat we consider the rational," as Marcel Gauchet says, has "spiritual origins" – even if reason, in its modern form, rebels against such values.[38] These are things we have brought to the rest of the world, and we must continue to do so, as much from a spiritual as from a secular point of view.

✳

But what about learning in the other direction? We have already seen, in chapter 4, the riches of the Eastern religious traditions in psychological insight and depth, their deep understanding of the inner journey that is such an important part of spiritual life. The remarkable techniques of meditation and inner exploration that are such an important feature of the Eastern traditions have become popular in the West since the 1960s. Western control of the external environment is equalled and exceeded by Eastern mastery of the internal, psychic landscape. As C.G. Jung said, "what we have to show in the way of spiritual insight and psychological technique must seem, when compared with yoga, just as backward as eastern astrology and medicine when compared with western science."[39] Another great strength of Eastern religious traditions has been the close connection between the mind and the body. The techniques of yoga aim to discipline the body, through stretching, breathing, and other physical exercises, as the surest route to disciplining the mind and the spirit.

But these and other such features of Eastern spirituality are simply various manifestations of the Eastern emphasis on wholeness: its refusal to separate the physical and material from the spiritual, its reverence for the spirit in all things. In the Eastern spiritual traditions, we find that linking of the body with the psyche, the feelings, and the conscious mind, that emphasis on "oneness" and connectedness that, in chapter 3, I identified as the essence of spirituality. If the strength of the Western spiritual tradition, and thus of Western culture as a whole, has been the partial separation of the world from God – so that the world and humankind stepped forward, out of an undifferentiated unity, to became distinct objects of study and control – the great strength of the Eastern traditions is that they never made the separation. A Buddhist text, for example, specifically rejects as an "illusion," from a spiritual point of view, the exclusive focus on material and efficient "causes" ("the link of causes and effects") that is the essence of Western science: "do not seize on them as truth!" it warns.[40]

The strength of the Western traditions is analytic fragmentation, the ability to break things down into individual, discrete units, including individual human beings, with their individual rights and freedoms. The strength of the Eastern traditions is the opposite, the ability to see these same things, instead, as parts of a larger whole.

The Eastern emphasis on wholeness results in, among other things, an altogether different attitude to the natural world. At its most extreme, among the Jain sect of India, this spirit expresses itself as a refusal to kill or harm any living thing. "All breathing, existing, living, sentient creatures should not be slain, nor treated with violence, nor abused, nor tormented, nor driven away," says a Jain text. "This is the pure, unchangeable, eternal law, which the enlightened ones have proclaimed."[41] Jains are said to wear cloth face masks to prevent inhaling and killing insects, to refrain from drinking water at night to avoid drowning them, and to sweep the path in front of their steps so as not step on any live creature. A more typical version of this Eastern outlook is embodied in the Chinese Tao, in which the principles of the *yin* and the *yang* are intended to convey a sense of the inner spiritual harmony running through and uniting all things. The objective of the followers of the Tao – the Way – is to live in and through this universal harmony. The way of the Tao involves "a general attitude to the universal laws of nature, which is one not merely of resignation nor even acquiescence, but a lyrical, almost ecstatic acceptance."[42]

This vision of the interconnection of all things is something the West desperately needs to relearn – and already is beginning to relearn, sometimes without recognizing it. The Taoist vision of "totality as an harmonious perfection in movement," for example, is startlingly close to the most advanced thinking of modern physics, in which reality is viewed as "one totality," an "Undivided Wholeness in Flowing Movement."[43] And this insight is urgently needed by the West, and indeed by the world, to meet what has become our greatest challenge, a challenge profoundly spiritual in character, a challenge I will examine in the next chapter.

# Rediscovering Reverence:
# The Environmental Imperative

Humankind as a whole is currently facing one of the greatest challenges we have ever faced, the crisis of global climate change. This environmental crisis is also a spiritual one. It has both spiritual roots and spiritual consequences. For that reason, spiritual values and outlooks may also have a role to play in solving it. But whether they do or not, it seems likely that, as a result of this momentous challenge, and of our response to it, the spiritual outlook of the West will eventually be transformed.

*

Before we explore the spiritual sources and consequences of global climate change, let's review some of the realities of our current situation. For more or less the last 10,000 years, earth's overall temperature has been about 14°C. At this stable, moderate temperature, humankind has been able to flourish and establish high civilizations, including the religious traditions we have been exploring in this book. But our earth is currently absorbing more energy from the sun than it is able to radiate back into space. That means the world is very gradually heating up, and, if this trend continues uninterrupted, as it may well do, the consequences for the earth, and for humanity, will be catastrophic.

The reason for this gradual process of "global warming," as almost everybody knows by now, is that the earth's atmosphere lets in the sun's warming light without letting all of it escape back into space. Up to a point, this "greenhouse effect" is desirable, and helps to explain why the earth is a green and habitable place, unlike any other planet we know of in the universe, so far. But too much of a good thing can sometimes be a bad thing. And that's what we are now beginning to suffer from, in this area as in some others.

The problem is the growing accumulation of "greenhouse gases," the gases in the earth's atmosphere that prevent some energy from radiating back out into space. There are several of these gases, but the most important one is carbon dioxide, or $CO_2$, which is the direct or indirect cause of eighty per cent of all global warming. $CO_2$ has been collecting in the earth's atmosphere over the past two hundred years because of the burning of carbon-rich "fossil fuels," especially coal, but also petroleum oil and natural gas. Since the beginning of the industrial revolution at the end of the eighteenth century, the earth's climate has experienced an overall rise in temperature of about 0.63°C. This increase is mainly due to an increase of $CO_2$ in the atmosphere, from about three parts per 10,000 to almost four.

Because the changes were small and gradual at first, it took a long time for this process to be noticed. Even as recently as the 1950s, the warming of the overall global climate had not been detected, nor linked to its source in the burning of fossil fuels. But beginning in the 1970s, scientists began to record the gradual heating of the planet, and to link this process to its main sources. Thirty years later there is no longer any serious scientific doubt about either fact. The United Nations' Intergovernmental Panel on Climate Change (IPCC) now says the scientific evidence about the warming of the global climate is "unequivocal," and that most of the increase in global temperature is "very likely" due to human-generated greenhouse gases.[1]

Nor is there much doubt about the catastrophic effects on the planet and on the human race if this trend continues, because we are already beginning to see the effects of global climate change. One we all notice is the growing instability of weather patterns, the increase in droughts and in devastating storms and hurricanes. We may not as easily notice the effect on animals and plants. Climate change is contributing to the trend by which over half the species on the planet may become extinct by the end of the century.

Another dramatic impact of global climate change is on the Arctic and Antarctic icecaps. Both are already beginning to melt, setting in train a series of further consequences. The Inuit people of Canada could be the first community dislocated by climate change, because their habitat and way of life are already being destroyed by the melting of the Arctic ice. But the melting of the polar icecaps will have further grave consequences, the most obvious of which would be the rising of sea levels around the world.

Jim Hansen (b. 1941), one of the world's leading climatologists, has estimated that, if we go on as we now are, without significant changes to our way of life, global temperature could rise as much as 5°F during this century, and the resulting accelerated melting of the polar icecaps means that sea level could eventually rise as much as eighty feet (as happened when the world experienced similar temperatures in the past). This would devastate the major coastal cities of the U.S, including New York and Washington, perhaps submerge almost the whole of the state of Florida, and displace hundreds of millions of people in other parts of the world, including China, India, and Bangladesh.[2]

Global warming would also have a profound impact on ocean currents, which in turn would have horrendous results for global weather patterns and rainfall. In the Atlantic, the continued melting of the Arctic icecap would eventually interrupt the Gulf Stream (as has already happened in earth's distant past) bringing to a halt the flow of warm water that makes western Europe habitable, and turning it into a semi-arctic wasteland. While changes to Atlantic currents turn northern Europe and north-eastern North America semi-arctic, similar changes to ocean circulation in the Pacific would alter rainfall patterns, and turn most of the rest of North America and Australia into a desert.

These kinds of severe climate changes could have grave consequences for civilization in a very near future, starting within the lifetimes of children being born today, or their children. The potential changes to temperature, rainfall, and water levels – let alone the destruction wrought by the severe storms and hurricanes we are already beginning to see – might well be too much for some countries and even entire regions to handle. The mass migrations of displaced populations, food and water shortages and starvation, the spreading of diseases, and so on, could even overwhelm our current national and international systems, institutions, and ways of life. As the European Union's two top foreign policy officials said in a 2008 report, the result may be "a vicious circle of degradation, migration, and conflicts over territory and borders that threatens the political stability of countries and regions."[3]

Such a vicious circle might lead in either of two directions: to chaos and barbarism, a new dark age or, which might amount to the same, a new age of authoritarian regimes, capable of imposing the discipline needed to survive and to wage war on those who threaten from without. In a world of nuclear weapons, this could simply be another kind of endgame. Elizabeth Kolbert (b. 1961), a prize-winning American author on climate change, has commented: "It may seem impossible to imagine that a technologically advanced society could choose, in essence, to destroy itself, but that is what we are now in the process of doing."[4] In a similar vein, Tim Flannery (b. 1956), an Australian biologist and author of a best-selling book on climate change, has written: "[H]uman health, water and food security are now under threat from the modest amount of climate change that has already occurred. If humans pursue a business-as-usual course for the first half of this century, I believe the collapse of civilization due to climate change becomes inevitable."[5]

This possibility should give us more than enough motivation to do something about it. Scientists suggest we would need to cut our $CO_2$ emissions by about seventy per cent from 1990 levels, by 2050, if we want to stabilize $CO_2$ levels at slightly less than twice their pre-industrial level. They think this would lead to stabilizing overall global temperature by 2100 at about 1.1°C higher than current levels. They warn that a rise of 2°C from the pre-industrial average is probably the maximum the world could absorb without really disastrous consequences. Since we have already used up 0.63°C of this total, we don't have much margin or time in which to manoeuvre. The Intergovernmental Panel on Climate Change (IPCC) argues that, if timely action is now taken, it is still technically possible to reduce carbon emissions sufficiently to limit global warming to 2°C, and to do so with only a minimal impact on economic growth, perhaps slowing average annual global GDP growth by less than 0.12% up to 2050.[6]

Obviously this kind of timely action is needed to assure the survival of the human race and of the kinds of decent civilizations humankind has gradually evolved, during the last ten thousand years of relatively stable global climate.

But my concern here is not to pursue the actions that governments must take. Instead, I want to explore the spiritual roots and consequences of the global environmental crisis in which we find ourselves. From a spiritual point of view, the roots of our current environmental crisis go all the way back to the process of "mythic dissociation," beginning around 3000 to 2000 BCE, that we explored in chapter 4. You will recall that, through this process, Western religious traditions began to evolve a distinctive outlook in which God or the gods are to be found *outside* the world (or "transcendent"), as well as within it (or "immanent"). This evolving spiritual outlook, as we saw, had profound implications and consequences for Western culture, even for the emergence of modern science. Because God or the gods were now to be found "outside" the world, the world itself and all the things in it acquired a new status of their own, somehow separate and distinct from the spiritual ground in which they are set. They emerged from that background, and were gradually seen in a new light, with an autonomy and reality of their own.

The implications of this outlook first became apparent for human beings themselves, as we saw in chapter 4. Separated now from the sacred background, they stepped forth onto the stage of life with a dignity and importance of their own; and their powers – especially the power of reason – acquired a novel respect and place in human culture. The new status of human beings and of reason was evident in the civilizations of Greece and Rome with their rich currents of secular philosophical thought, and where individual persons began to acquire rights and freedoms, and traditions of self-government, under law, as free citizens of a political community. But these impulses were also reinforced by ideas and values coming from the Jewish and Christian traditions – including the special value of human beings in the eyes of God. The fertile marriage between the Greek, Roman, and Judaeo-Christian traditions, and the Western civilizations that emerged from them, gave pride of place, for the first time in human history, to what I have been calling the virtues of self-assertion.

For that reason, they also prepared the way for a new attitude to nature. Because God or the gods were to be found outside the world, the natural world could now be separated from the spiritual world and looked at objectively, that is to say, as an object, not as an emanation or expression of spirit. And because humans had acquired a new importance in the scheme of things, together with their powers of reason, nature was revealed to them in its neutral "otherness" as a field for their exploration, rational understanding, and control.[7] As a result, Greek and Roman civilizations witnessed important initial developments in biology, medicine, mathematics, and engineering. When these traditions were combined with the Judaeo-Christian understanding that God had given humankind the earth for its delight and had made "man" its ruler, the stage was set for humans to exercise the virtues of self-assertion not just in relation to each other, but to assert themselves against nature too. The stage was also set for the emergence of modern science and technology, the technology that has brought us to our current crisis, and on which we will also depend, in part, to get ourselves out of it.

＊

An important symbolic turning point historians of thought often point to – to illustrate the beginning of the modern, Western outlook, based on the virtues of self-assertion – is the *Oration on the Dignity of Man*, composed by the young Italian philosopher Giovanni Pico della Mirandola (1463–1494), about 1487.[8] In his *Oration*, Pico set himself to describe the exceptional position that humans occupy in the universe, unconstrained by any of the limits that apply to other creatures, and free to shape themselves as they wish. Almost at the beginning of his work, Pico imagines a conversation between God and Adam, in which God gives him license to do with himself as he desires, and judges best:

> Neither a fixed abode nor a form that is thine alone nor any function peculiar to thyself have we given thee, Adam, to the end that according to thy judgement thou mayest have and possess what abode, what form, what functions thou thyself shalt desire. The nature of all other beings is limited and constrained within the bounds prescribed by Us. Thou, *constrained by no limits, in accordance with thine own free will*, in whose hand We have placed thee, shalt ordain for thyself the limits of thy nature. We have set thee at the world's centre that thou mayest from thence more easily observe whatever is in the world. We have made thee neither of heaven nor of earth, neither mortal nor immortal, so that with freedom of choice and with honor, as though the maker and molder of thyself, thou mayest fashion thyself in whatever shape thou shalt prefer.[9]

*Constrained by no limits!* While it's important not to read Pico through a modern lens, or think him more modern than he really was, it's hard not hear in these words the stirrings of the modern outlook, in which the virtues of self-assertion have come to occupy such an overwhelming place. As a Renaissance Platonist, still very much influenced by medieval scholastic philosophy, Pico's declaration of "free will" is largely about man's relationship to himself, not to nature. Nevertheless, even here, man is already set "at the world's centre," with all that implies, including for the study of nature itself.

What it might imply was made clear within little more than a hundred years after Pico's *Oration*. While he was not himself a scientist, the English philosopher and statesman, Francis Bacon, is often considered the first modern philosopher of science. In his writings he developed the scientific method, according to which nature is studied experimentally, "put to the question" rather like a prisoner on the rack.[10] In setting out these new principles of scientific method, Bacon made very clear the spirit and ambition which lay behind them, a spirit, like Pico's, "constrained by no limits." His purpose, he said, was to "lay more firmly the foundations, and extend more widely the limits, of the power and greatness of man."[11] Writing in the great age of discovery and of European expansion over the globe, Bacon compared the ambition of the new science to those who seek "power" (as he had done) within their own country, or those, like the new imperial conquerors, whose goal was to "extend the power of their country and its dominion among men." To Bacon, the ambition of the new age of science was even "more noble" than either of these: it was to "to establish and extend the power of the human race itself over the universe." It was, in fact, to establish "the empire of man over things."[12]

In these words we already hear the unmistakable spirit of the modern world. Within the next generation it was quickly echoed by René Descartes, often considered the initiator of modern philosophy and of the modern outlook. Descartes celebrated not only man's "free will" as Pico had done, but also, like Bacon, the potential of the new science to extend the power of man over nature. Descartes' first and most famous work, the celebrated *Discours de la méthode*, published in 1637, was actually titled a "Discourse on the Method of Rightly Conducting the Reason and Seeking for Truth in the Sciences." In it he argued that the "very useful" knowledge to be derived from physics and the other new, experimental sciences – including about the "laws of nature" – would make men "the masters and possessors of nature."[13]

These were the assumptions embraced by the scientists and thinkers of the seventeenth and eighteenth centuries who fashioned our modern world. At its heart, this modern world has always harboured two closely related ideas: the ideal of freedom and of free-will on the one hand, and on the other, the domination and subjection of nature through science and technology. These two ideas have been held together through the last three centuries by a common mental stance toward the world, by a common moral outlook, and by a common spiritual background.

The mental stance is the stance of disengaged reason, standing back from the world, viewing it objectively. The moral outlook is that of the virtues of self-assertion, which express themselves both in the drive for liberation and freedom from constraint, and in the drive to master nature and subject it to our control. The spiritual background to both of these was the religious traditions in which the sacred is found *outside* this world, not just in it, traditions which allowed both human beings and nature to be seen as "objective" realities, in their own right. The risk in this modern blend of ideas and outlooks is that it becomes harder to see the world itself as sacred, and requiring respect or even veneration. In fact, they risk banishing the sacred from the world altogether.

✳

Of course even the West has never been altogether of one mind about these various outlooks derived from the Enlightenment, far from it. In fact, there have been repeated revolts against them, beginning in the eighteenth century itself.

The Romantic movement at the beginning of the nineteenth century was the most important revolt of all, and the one from which all the later revolts have drawn much of their impetus and assumptions. Dissatisfied with what they saw as an atomistic, mechanistic, reductionist world view, the Romantic poets, thinkers, and artists argued instead for a more organic view: one more respectfully attuned to nature, to community, and to the human heart. In some ways, the history of Western culture over the last two centuries can be seen as an argument between these two points of view.[14] The modern environmental movement, for example – which is one of the most important forms of resistance to the virtues of self-assertion, one of the major exceptions to their dominance in the contemporary world – finds its roots in nineteenth-century outlooks spawned by the Romantic movement.

But the problem with the Romantic revolt against eighteenth-century rationalism, like so many similar resistance movements, including the "modernist" protests of the twentieth century, is that, as a whole, it actually ended up by reinforcing some of the most central elements of the very stance against which it claimed to rebel, especially the virtues of self-assertion. In the 1830 preface to his hit play, *Hernani*, French writer Victor Hugo (1802–1885) famously declared that Romanticism was simply "liberalism in literature."[15] While this judgment overlooked many

currents in England and Germany, Hugo's insight that the Romantic revolt actually carried forward the assertive thrust of the Enlightenment in
a different form was essentially sound. Instead of genuinely transforming
the way we relate to each other and to the natural world by turning us
*outward*, it provided what Charles Taylor has called "the basis for a
new and fuller individuation ... an even more radical subjectivism" by
turning us even more *inward*.[16]

But perhaps not far enough. With a few important exceptions,
Romanticism as a whole stopped short, at the particular self. It did not
go far enough inward to rediscover the eternal self. To put this in Hindu
terminology, it did not go far enough inward to discover *Atman* and, by
so doing, come out the other side, to *Brahman*. The idea of being expressed by the Romantics and their anti-Enlightenment successors was
not the decentring, unselfing experience of the *Upanishads* or of Thomas
Aquinas but rather "the gratifying experience of the self as an entity."[17]
At one extreme of these outlooks, even forming habits can be considered a kind of "failure," because the end is not some kind of living wisdom but rather the intensity or "ecstasy" of momentary experience.[18]
At the other extreme is what Friedrich Nietzsche called the "will to
power."[19] As a result, Romanticism and the later anti-Enlightenment
could provide little of a brake on the assertive human virtues unleashed
in the seventeenth and eighteenth centuries, including the ambition to
become the "masters and possessors of nature," *constrained by no limits*. In fact, they probably reinforced them

✳

This is the spiritual background – the spiritual roots – of the global environmental crisis in which we now find ourselves. Having exploited
nature and her resources to build up greater technological and industrial power than Bacon or Descartes could ever have dreamt of, we now
discover that self-assertion unconstrained by reverence has brought us
to the verge of global self-destruction. As Tim Flannery remarks, "It is a
reductionist world view that has brought the present state of climate
change upon us."[20]

To get out of this crisis alive, humankind may have to develop a less
reductionist world view than the one the West has been gradually building up for the last five hundred years or so. This is much easier to say
than to do, because that view is complex and pervasive. But one of the

things it may entail is rediscovering reverence and hence learning, all over again, to live within limits, perhaps even – at least as far as the environment is concerned – some very strict limits. Because if we are able to solve the climate change crisis – a very big if – there will be other, similar challenges right behind it.

Global warming is, by any measure, the biggest issue facing the human race today, and nothing should distract attention from solving it. Because, unless we do, there is no future ahead for us. But it's still only the leading edge of the environmental and ecological challenges we face. Another is the sheer rate at which human beings – especially those of us in the West – are consuming the world's resources. Scientists calculate that 1986 was the last year in which human beings were consuming an amount of resources roughly equal to what the world can produce. Ever since then we've been living in deficit, running down our asset base. It's estimated that by 2050, at the current rate of consumption, we may be using up resources equivalent to *two earths*, not just one. Obviously this isn't sustainable. Even if we are able to find a way out of the crisis of climate change, as the IPCC says we can, we may still have to live within limits.

This will be hard to do. Because the very idea of limits is fundamentally at odds with the virtues of self-assertion which are at the core of modern, Western culture, obscuring or hiding all others. The modern idea of freedom, the central, organizing principle of modern life, means something rather different from earlier notions of freedom. It means, as Pico saw, freedom from constraint.

I say the "idea" of limits is at odds with the virtues of self-assertion, because that's where the problem lies. Not in reality, but in our minds. In reality, in everyday life, as we saw in chapter 2, we go on living by very different virtues as well, and we know, intuitively, how to blend and reconcile these other virtues with the virtues of self-assertion. Or, rather, the other way around: in our daily lives we know how to blend and reconcile the virtues of self-assertion with the other virtues which are the ground and pre-condition for them. The *sine qua non*. But because we have lost a language for these other, prior virtues, they have little or no place in our culture and receive little public support. Those who continue to cultivate them do so almost heroically, in defiance of public taste and received opinion. They therefore do so privately, almost stealthily, like a rather eccentric "life-style" choice, a "hobby" among countless others, like bird-watching or a taste for jazz.[21]

These prior, background virtues the global climate crisis may require us to rediscover are what, in chapter 2, I called the virtues of reverence. As we saw in that chapter, the virtues of reverence are the habits of feeling and behaviour associated with the connectedness of things. They reflect the reality, and our own experience, that all individual things, ourselves included, are part of some larger whole. They are the feelings and behaviours arising from the recognition that we are part of a larger reality we did not create and do not control, but toward which we have duties and obligations: duties and obligations that are connected, in the end, with our own well-being, even our survival. The virtues of reverence can be contrasted with the virtues of self-assertion, which are the habits of feeling and behaviour associated with the opposite impulse: the impulse of every individual thing, ourselves included, toward their own self-preservation, self-gratification, self-expansion, self-development, empowerment and, in the case of humans, self-expression.

The starkness of the global climate crisis reveals to us in a flash – a revelation – what the last five hundred years of Western expansion have often obscured: why the virtues of reverence must, in the end, take priority over, or come before, the virtues of self-assertion. Because self-assertion can only take place within a larger whole. And our first obligation is, therefore, to ensure the well-being of that larger whole, without which self-assertion is pointless, or impossible, or suicidal – literally, it turns out, as well as spiritually and psychologically.

To survive the global climate crisis, it will therefore be very helpful, or even essential, to rediscover the virtues and practices of reverence our culture has so very largely forgotten, or covered up, or fallen silent about. In part, this may mean rediscovering the spiritual resources and practices buried within our Western culture, especially the Jewish, Christian, and Islamic spiritual traditions and practices. Now, more than ever, "the fate of the world depends on the conduct of man," as Italian poet and Jewish mystic Moses Luzatto (1707–1746), put it in his *Mesillat Yesharim* (Way of the Upright): "if he controls himself ... and makes use of the world only to the degree that it helps him in serving His creator, he raises himself to a higher level of existence, and the world rises with him."[22]

Rediscovering the spiritual resources of the West is certainly worthwhile, and overdue, but it will also be an ambiguous encounter. The ambiguity in our traditions goes right back to that ancient turning point of "mythic dissociation" I described in chapter 4. Because Western religious traditions are based on the idea of a "transcendent" God, who is outside this world as well as within it, they have always been somewhat ambiguous about man's relationship to nature. On the one hand, the three great Western traditions, all rooted in the Book of Genesis, proclaim the natural world to be "good," a reflection of God's handiwork, and therefore an expression of his goodness, and to be respected as such. But, at the same time, the Genesis myth also states that God gave man "dominion" over the earth and its creatures, and authorized him to "subdue it."[23] In fact, in 1690, only a little more than fifty years after Descartes' *Discourse*, the English philosopher John Locke (1632–1704) used these very biblical passages as the starting point for developing his influential theory of private property within an economic system based on the exploitation of nature.[24] Together with those of Bacon and Descartes, these ideas furnished the intellectual foundation of the Enlightenment, and of our modern world.[25]

So the Western spiritual traditions always harboured an assertive or instrumental attitude to the natural world, as well as a reverential one. In its scientific and technological outlooks, as in so many other ways, our modern culture builds upon tendencies already implicit in the spiritual traditions from which it developed. Bacon, Descartes, and Locke were all avowedly religious men, and they saw no contradiction between their professions of Christian faith and "putting nature to the question" on the interrogation rack.

So, as far as nature and the global environment themselves are concerned, relearning the virtues of reverence from our own Western religious traditions may be an important first step. But because of the ambiguity we find there, we may also need help, as we saw at the end of the last chapter, from other spiritual traditions, in which "mythic dissociation" never occurred, and the world never became separated from the ground of its own being. North American aboriginal spiritual traditions, for example, never ceased seeing the natural world as a spirit world, one that needed to be treated with the respect and reverence due to a spiritual being. And the Eastern spiritual traditions, as we saw, can also instruct the West in the recovery of a perception of wholeness they have never lost.

✳

We would certainly be greatly helped in meeting the challenge of climate change if we were able to mobilize the virtues of reverence that lie buried within our own Western traditions. Given the gravity of our global situation, you might even say it is urgent for us to do so.

But it may not work that way. In fact, it's just as likely to work the other way around. "We cannot will back a faith that has been lost," said William Barrett (1913–1992), an American philosopher. "We shall have to live back into that way of being in whose ambience the religious once drew breath. We shall have to find ourselves within nature before God is able to find us."[26] In other words, instead of relearning the practices and values of reverence in order to solve the problem of climate change – or the wider environmental crisis beyond it – our encounters with these challenging realities may well lead us back, indirectly, to the virtues of reverence.

Spiritual outlooks are usually related in some way to the social and cultural circumstances in which they arise, or by which they are nourished. In saying this, I obviously don't mean to suggest that spiritual outlooks are just a self-serving rationalization of material circumstances, as Karl Marx claimed. The process is much more complex than that, and clearly a two-way street: spiritual outlooks and other ideas can shape material circumstances just as much as the reverse. But, however the process works, it's clear that social and material conditions make a difference to the way ideas and outlooks rise and spread. It's no coincidence, for example, that the precedent Francis Bacon used to justify his optimism about the limitless potential of science and technology to establish "the empire of man over things" was Europe's initial experience of global expansion and conquest in the sixteenth and seventeenth centuries. From the European point of view, the world looked like a boundless frontier of land and resources simply waiting for the taking. This extraordinary (or heinous, depending on your point of view) experience of world conquest and occupation naturally spawned an outlook, a mood of "limitless" expansion and exploitation. In the words of a recent history of the ensuing "great land rush" of European colonialism, from the seventeenth to the twentieth century, this outlook exhibited "a disregard for moral, customary, or judicious restraints on dreams of unlimited material possibilities. This was [the] modern."[27]

A world without limits is a world ripe for the virtues of self-assertion. So these centuries were a natural seed-bed for the flowering both of science and technology, and of ideals of freedom and of liberation from constraint – and also, it must be said, equally assertive programs of "improvement" and "reform,'" though they were often reforms directed to removing constraints on freedom of action.

It looks as if the twenty-first century, by contrast, will be one in which we must learn again to live within some kinds of limits: limits which must be respected if we are to survive. And the experience of living within limits, and in a spirit of respect for the larger whole on which we depend, is almost certain to reshape our way of relating to the world, our moral and spiritual outlooks, just as the great age of expansion fostered the virtues of self-assertion that shaped the modern world. When all the signposts around you are pointing in the same direction, you eventually turn your head to look in that same direction, whether you want to or not.

Once you start down one of these paths, as I observed in chapter 3, it may take you much farther than you expected to go. When Christian poet John Milton (1608–1674) wrote *Areopagitica* or when John Stuart Mill wrote *On Liberty* – both in favour of freedom of speech and against censorship – neither probably foresaw where the virtues of self-assertion, unbalanced by any sense of reverence, might lead: to the reality of the modern Internet. In the same way, once we begin to govern our decisions and our conduct by respect for the larger whole, we will find we are already on the slope toward reverence. As a result, the forward journey may well take us on a voyage of discovery something like the one you already took, from chapter 1 to chapter 4, from the human paradox and the virtues of reverence to the meaning of religious practice and religious life.

Once you recognize that in the global environment, "everything is connected to and influences everything else," as Tim Flannery puts it, you are already half way to seeing the world as sacred once again, because that is one of the things that "sacred" means.[28] In the 1970s, when the ecological and environmental movements were beginning to gather steam, Gregory Bateson (1904–1980), a British anthropologist and cyberneticist, noted that humankind was gradually working itself back toward a sense of the "sacred unity of the biosphere": "We are beginning to play with ideas of ecology, and although we immediately trivialize these ideas into commerce or politics, there is at least an impulse still in the human breast *to unify and thereby sanctify* the total natural world, of which we are."[29]

The "sacred" is what we encounter when we recognize that we are part of a larger unity, something larger than ourselves, something we did not create and do not control, and toward which we have obligations and duties. And the habits of feeling and behaviour that are both nourished in us by this encounter, and also its source, are what, in this book, I have called the virtues of reverence.

As the global climate crisis reintroduces us, willingly or unwillingly, to the virtues of reverence, there are two grave temptations we shall have to avoid. I will call these the temptation of one-sidedness, and the temptation of pantheism.

The temptation of "one-sidedness" is the perennial temptation to mistake some portion of the good for the whole. Just as, over the last three centuries, we have been increasingly tempted to think the virtues of self-assertion were everything and the virtues of reverence nothing, so now, when the global climate crisis finally breaks upon our consciousness – especially if we delay action long enough to create a really desperate urgency – we may find ourselves tempted to think the reverse. This would be just as foolish, and destructive.

As I said in chapter 1, just because something is good doesn't make it the whole story. The virtues of self-assertion are real virtues. That's why I called them virtues, and not something else. They are good. The habits of feeling and behaviour associated with the virtues of self-assertion are one half of what it means to be human, and we can no more do without them than we can do without the virtues of reverence. The way in which they have been nurtured in Western civilization is one of the things of which the West can be most proud, and perhaps our greatest contribution to the civilization of the world. When I referred to the "rationalism" of the Enlightenment, the description was not pejorative. As I said in the Introduction, reason is one of the highest expressions of the human spirit, and nothing that is fully human can fail to meet its test. Anything that threatens it, threatens the good.

Of course reason detached from the virtues of reverence can do much harm. But so can any good. It is no argument against a good – though many people have thought it so – that some harm can or has come of it. That's true of all good things, if they are taken to extreme, or if they are not balanced by other goods, as Leibniz pointed out. Much harm and evil have been done over the centuries, and continue to be done today, in the name of piety and religion. That was and still is one of the strongest arguments against them. But it is a false argument, just as false as it would be if used in reverse against reason and science, simply because they have brought us to the verge of self-destruction.

Science and technology may have created the problem of global warming, but we will also depend on them to get us out of it. We need them now, more than ever, to make the careful calculations and devise the controls that can stabilize $CO_2$ emissions, and save the planet. If they succeed, it will only be the latest in a long series of such acts of mercy, healing, and compassion that science and technology have performed, to the incalculable benefit of humankind. Science is a "prerequisite of all human dignity."[30]

The danger of "one-sidedness" gives us yet another reason to revisit Hegel's formula I already quoted in chapter 1, that "life is the union of union and non-union." The extreme case of global warming helps us to see another dimension of what he was getting at. The virtues of reverence are the virtues of "union": the habits of human feeling and behaviour associated with a deep awareness of the unity and connectedness of all things. The virtues of self-assertion are the virtues of "non-union": the habits of feeling and behaviour associated with the impulse to freedom, expansion, and self-development. Both are necessary to life, even to biological life, and especially to human life. But only the impulse to union, by definition, can provide a ground to link and nurture them both. That's why, both logically and in reality – in our real lives, even if we no longer have eyes to see it, or the words to express it – the virtues of reverence must take priority over the virtues of self-assertion; why they must come first. Because they establish the frame. Self-assertion can only take place within a larger frame. Without that larger frame – without, at the extreme limit, a habitable world – they both die.[31] But without the virtues of self-assertion, we do not have anything worthy to be called life. Without both sides of the human paradox, it would not be a human world.

This will be very important to have much in mind as the world grapples with global climate change. If our inaction and delay create a really grave global crisis, there might be a mood of panic, and the world might be tempted by a new authoritarianism, argued to be necessary to save the world. Based on recent experience, such arguments would stand a very good chance of being successful. Following the 9/11 terrorist attacks on New York and Washington in 2001, the citizens of great and proud democracies showed themselves willing to throw away, overnight, liberties it had taken them a thousand years to acquire. How much more would they be willing to do so if they realize the danger they face is no longer a remote danger of terrorist attacks but a danger of total global collapse?

As we move forward into this new world, where the virtues of reverence must again take their rightful place, one of our biggest challenges and duties, in the West, will be to safeguard also the virtues of self-assertion, especially the heritage of our Enlightenment.[32] What is needed now is not the rejection of the achievements of the Western Enlightenment but rather a new *dual Enlightenment*, one in which the virtues of reverence are once again accorded a place equal to the virtues of self-assertion. After all, what the Buddha achieved under the Bodhi-tree is called "enlightenment" too. So what we can and should aim for is "a culture where both kinds of enlightenment [are] respected and cultivated together."[33]

This may not be as difficult as it seems. In fact it may involve recovering neglected elements of the Western Enlightenment itself. Susan Neiman argues that the moderate Enlightenment emphasized some of the key virtues of reverence – hope, gratitude, justice, and reverence itself – just as much as reason, freedom, and the other virtues of self-assertion.[34] In any case, the Enlightenment ideals of human reason, of rights and liberties, of democracy, of reform and improvement, and of freedom under law, grew directly out of important elements in the Western spiritual traditions from which they emerged. That's the "good' side of the ambiguity in those traditions I mentioned earlier. Our shortcomings are just the flip side of our spiritual strengths. And the strengths are what we have to contribute to the spiritual capital of humankind. We owe it to the world to ensure they are not lost. It would profit us nothing, after all, to save the world, and lose our own soul.

✳

The other great temptation will be the temptation of pantheism. "Pantheism" is the worship of nature, and it is a perennial temptation on the human pathway. It will certainly be a temptation this time around, because the crisis of climate change will require us to adopt a deeply reverential attitude to the natural world on which our survival depends. In fact, we can see the pantheist temptation already at work in thinkers like Gregory Bateson or British scientist James Lovelock (b. 1919). In his influential 1979 book, *Gaia: A New Look at Life on Earth*,

Lovelock proposed that we should think of the earth and its surrounding atmosphere like one great organism, in which everything is connected, and works together to maintain a certain environment.[35] Lovelock called this planetary organism "Gaia" after the ancient Greek earth goddess, no doubt for the express reason of encouraging respectful, even reverential attitudes on the part of his readers. The title of his 2000 autobiography, *Homage to Gaia*, made this even more explicit.

While these are helpful images, especially when changing mental outlooks is critical to our survival, the danger would be in taking them literally. The worship of nature has always proven a dead-end for human beings. Pantheism is the worship of matter or, at best, biological life, and this state of mind is just as reductionist, and just as harmful, in the end, as seeking "the empire of man over things." In fact, they may even work together, as they sometimes did in the eighteenth century, for example.[36] It was against this potent combination that Samuel Taylor Coleridge composed some of his greatest poems, including *Dejection: An Ode* (1802), the fourth section of which declares that:

> ... we receive but what we give,
> And in our life alone does Nature live:
>     Ours is her wedding garment, ours her shroud!
> And would we aught behold, of higher worth,
> Than that inanimate cold world allowed
> To the poor loveless ever-anxious crowd,
>     Ah! From the soul itself must issue forth
> A light, a glory, a fair luminous cloud
>     Enveloping the Earth –
> And from the soul itself must there be sent
>     A sweet and potent voice, of its own birth,
> Of all sweet sounds the life and element!

The natural world is not sacred by itself; "sacred" is a human concept. The natural world is sacred because it is *seen* by humankind as being so. And in *seeing* it as sacred, human beings, when they are wise, use it not as an idol, an end in itself, or even as a mirror, but rather as a window: a window to something that can be found within us, but also beyond us, and beyond nature, something that is truly worthy of our reverence.

The revelation of the great religious traditions is that the natural world is sacred as the creation, or expression, or image, of a spirit which is, in the end, much more like us at our best than like unconscious matter or life. That is to say, a spirit that is moral, loving, merciful, and just. These are qualities that cannot be found in the natural world. They are hard enough to find in the human world. And as soon as we begin to worship the natural world for its own sake, or for ours, we will find that these qualities have fled from our world, even if it survives.

✳

Since the natural world is a window *through* which human beings can look to discover something important, including about themselves, the environmental crisis can also be an occasion to rediscover a different but equally important "ecology." The external environment can help us reframe the internal one.

Over the last three centuries, as the virtues of self-assertion assumed a larger and larger place in Western culture, members of Western societies have sometimes been tempted to take an attitude to their own internal psychic landscape that mirrored our attitude to the natural one. We have been tempted to think we can do anything we like, without paying a spiritual price, just as we thought we could do what we felt like doing to the natural world without paying an environmental price.

Neither was true. Just as we know now that every gram of $CO_2$ emitted by an automobile tailpipe or a coal-fired electrical plant lingers in the atmosphere for fifty years, contributing its part to the greenhouse effect, we may be ripe for learning that each one of our actions also has a similar psychic and spiritual cost. We are part of the natural world and cannot abuse ourselves or each other with impunity any more than we can abuse the world of which we are a part. Despite a long tradition of Western thought that confuses the laws of our spiritual nature with criminal laws (something we may be punished *for*),[37] they are really much more like the laws of physical nature Descartes extrapolated from them. They are not *laws-for* but rather, as W.H. Auden observed, *laws-of*:

> laws, that is to say, which [man] is free to *defy* but no more to *break* than he can break the law of gravity by jumping out of the window, or the laws of biochemistry by getting drunk, and the consequences for defying them must be as inevitable and as intrinsically related to their nature as a broken leg or a hangover ... In the case of physical

laws, we learn very soon the painful consequences of defying them, though even this certain knowledge does not prevent some of us from destroying ourselves with alcohol or drugs. But in the case of spiritual laws, where the consequences of defiance are not perceptible to the senses and take effect only gradually, we are all too inclined to behave, either like madmen who imagine they are magicians who can fly, or like suicides who smash themselves up out of despair or, more often, out of spite.[38]

We are the stewards of the internal as well as the external environment. We find our true fulfilment when we look beyond ourselves, when we are loyal to an otherness we find within ourselves yet which is more than ourselves.[39] We cannot betray it without betraying ourselves. In fact, we become most fully ourselves when we strive toward it. And that toward which we strive is what makes us at once most noble, and yet most fully human. We are ends as well as matter – "final" causes as well as material causes – and we cannot ignore those ends without cost.

There is an ecology of the spirit, too.

# 13

# A Secular World?

The sub-title of this book is "The Meaning of Faith in a Secular World." I've been talking a lot about faith. But what's a secular world? And just how secular is our world, after all?

Debate about these questions has spawned a large academic industry. But its conclusions are inevitably influenced by its assumptions. For example, here's one definition from a leading scholar: "[S]ecularization primarily refers to the beliefs of people. The core of what we mean when we talk of this society being more 'secular' than that is that the lives of fewer people in the former than in the latter are influenced by religious beliefs."[1]

Now obviously, from the point of view developed in this book so far, this definition leaves a lot to be desired. In fact, it seems to be based on exactly the confusion between faith and belief I've been trying to help untangle. Such confusion is understandable because, as we have seen, it has been developing in Western societies for hundreds of years. But it has probably contributed significantly to the very secularization a definition like this tries to capture.

Charles Taylor's definition is much more satisfactory. He suggests that the "heart" of secularization is that modern life has led to a decline in what he calls the "transformation perspective." He defines this perspective in contrast to an "immanence perspective" which (as we already saw in chapter 1, and again in chapter 10) "sees our highest goal in terms of a certain kind of human flourishing, in the context of mutuality, pursuing each his/her own happiness on the basis of assured life and liberty, in a society of mutual benefit." The "transformation perspective" aims instead at "a transformation of human beings that takes them beyond or outside what is normally understood as human flourishing, even in a context of reasonable mutuality (that is, where we work for each other's flourishing)."[2] It is the decline of this second perspective, in favour of the first, which makes ours a secular world.

But Taylor's "two solicitations" by which the human "situation" is defined[3] seem to be a specific instance of what, in this book, I have called the human paradox. So a fairly simple way to define a secular world – a definition that would fit with the concepts used in this book – would be to say that a secular society is one in which the virtues of self-assertion take priority over the virtues of reverence. The *degree* to which they take priority is the measure of how much it is a secular society. In an entirely secular society, the virtues of reverence would become almost completely invisible, unnoticed, and unremarked, even if they continued to operate (as they can't help doing) in practice.

✳

Clearly, following this kind of definition, Western societies are now, at the beginning of the twentieth-first century, predominantly secular societies. In fact, the words "secular" and "modern" are sometimes used interchangeably. For many people, modern means secular, and becoming secular is what it means to become modern.

The influential description of modern economic and social life given by the German sociologist Max Weber (1864–1920) more or less makes this equation. For Weber, "modern" societies are those based on rational calculation of usefulness and cost derived from an essentially instrumental or utilitarian view of the world. In this kind of world, reverence and the sacred are replaced by science and technology; rational calculation of efficiency and self-interest replaces tradition, loyalty, and commitment; individualism, and mobility (of all kinds, including money) replace community; and institutions no longer have a primarily symbolic or expressive role but a mainly utilitarian one.[4]

This makes a huge difference, even to the way people "see" the world they're living in. It becomes a completely different world. In a non-secular society, a society based on the virtues of reverence, everything in the world is seen as having spiritual or religious meaning; as being a sign of the sacred. In this kind of society, people naturally see things, even ordinary, everyday things, through a spiritual lens. As a result, they also see different things. The spontaneous language for interpreting the world is a spiritual language.

In a secular society, the reverse occurs. In this kind of society, even the spiritual or religious are interpreted in secular terms, as the expression merely of material, physical, psychological, or social needs and "forces." In a non-secular society even sexuality (perhaps especially sexuality) is interpreted in spiritual terms, as Augustine did. In a secular society, even the religious can be interpreted as merely an expression of sexuality, as Sigmund Freud did.

Consider, for example, the case of a late-Renaissance Italian painter like Caravaggio (1571–1610), a contemporary of Francis Bacon. To modern eyes, even many of Caravaggio's explicitly religious paintings, such as the *Ecstasy of Saint Francis*, have a strongly erotic flavour to them. So many modern eyes are tempted to see the erotic element as the "true" story about them, and the religious frame as merely a cover or excuse, a metaphor for sexuality. But this way of seeing them is profoundly anachronistic and misleading. Because for Caravaggio and his contemporaries, not yet living in a secular world, it was probably the other way around. As Ingrid Rowland, an American art historian, has observed, "sex was still only a metaphor for a sensation they called piety, a sensation they often felt was the most real experience in their lives."[5]

Modern culture reverses this equation. Spiritual experience and ideas are not the real story. They are only a metaphor, perhaps a cover, for something else. Spiritual values can and do live on, in the lives and actions of human beings, because without them human beings would not be human. But they do so on the margins, tolerated only as long as they do not get in the way, or make any real or public claims. They operate in a hidden way, hidden even from many of those who rely on them to provide the inner energy for projects of improvement and reform. If spiritual perceptions ever enter public or intellectual debate, they continually suffer from what lawyers call a "reverse onus": that is to say, they carry the burden of proof. The secular frame is assumed to be the "natural" one, and other ways of seeing the world have continually to justify themselves, or make their case all over again, starting usually from zero.

So most of us, in the West, live in pretty secular societies, though the *degree* to which they are secular varies from country to country, and even within the same country, from region to region. We live in what Stephen Carter has called a "culture of disbelief."[6] It is supported from many sources which combine, from various directions, to maintain a prevailing secular outlook. The modern idea of what is "natural," for example, is shaped by our secular culture, and by the virtues of self-assertion it expresses.[7] So its inevitable use as a basic reference point – as a value, or (what I earlier called) an "absolute presupposition" – in any modern discussion, biases the argument from the start.

I am very far from thinking that the idea of the secular is a bad one, or that secular societies are undesirable. On the contrary. The idea of the secular, like the virtues of self-assertion from which it grows, is one of the important contributions of Western culture to world civilization. For historical reasons, and because of the distinctive character of the Western spiritual tradition (including the "ambiguity," discussed in the last chapter), Christianity almost always made a distinction between the secular, which is the business of civil authority and the citizens as a whole, and the spiritual, which is the business of the church or the churches. One of Jesus' best-known sayings ("Render unto Caesar the things which are Caesar's, and unto God the things that are God's" – a saying that appears in three of the four Gospels) appears to endorse this distinction, which was made official Christian doctrine by Pope Gelasius (d. 496) in 494.[8] So for the Christian, "there is such a thing as a relatively autonomous area of secular culture."[9] Even where the secular and the spiritual have been linked, as they almost always were until modern times, "Christianity always kept the two spheres distinct."[10] And in secular matters Christians believe "the temporal power should be obeyed before the spiritual," as Thomas Aquinas put it.[11]

The wisdom of this distinction is surely illustrated in the contemporary world by the drawbacks and oppressions of "theocratic" government, whether explicitly religious, or a secular form of "theocratic" government, as in communist or fascist countries. A clear distinction between the secular and the spiritual, between religious life and civil government and public business, seems to be one of the conditions of good government and a civil society.[12] And this distinction is one of the important contributions of Western culture to the world.

The issue then, if there is one, is an issue not of kind but of degree. An appropriate distinction between secular and spiritual does not automatically require us to fall into the arms of an ideology – a new "faith" – called secularism.

I was reminded of just how thoroughly secular some of our Western societies have become by a public ceremony of mourning and remembrance held on Parliament Hill in Ottawa, Canada's capital, to honour those who perished in the 9/11 terrorist attacks in 2001. In this solemn ceremony – in the very circumstances where the consolations and insights of religious practice have perhaps their greatest contribution to make – there was not a single non-secular element. No prayers. No references to any religious views about life or death. No invocation of a deity, or even of a Great Spirit. No reference to spiritual values or experience, or to anything beyond, or even inside this life, that might give it a larger, an eternal meaning. Nothing. A great, secular void.

✳

But does the fact that we Westerners live in secular societies mean that we also live in a secular *world*?

There are at least two ways to pursue this important question. One would be to ask whether the present is actually as secular as we think. Another would be to ask whether the past was really as different as we think. I will consider them in that order.

As far as the present is concerned, the world as a whole seems very far from secular. The strength of Islam even among many young people raised in secular societies, and its increasing impact would almost suffice, by themselves, to give the lie to that notion. They would also appear to call into question the assumption that the process of secularization is inevitable, built right into the process of modernization from which it is largely indistinguishable, and that the secular vision of the world is bound to flourish once obstacles to it have been removed. The evidence from Eastern traditions also seems to cast into doubt any too easy assumption that a secular world is natural or inevitable. The renewed influence of the Hindu tradition in India also suggests the continuing power of religious traditions in the contemporary world.

Even Christianity is growing energetically in the Third World, especially in its Pentecostal forms. Christians in Africa, Asia, and South America now outnumber Christians in the North and West, and are making their presence felt in all the churches. In the Anglican Communion, for example, the non-North American churches have virtually expelled the North American churches for their disregard of traditional Anglican principles and solidarity.

So, from a global perspective, we seem to be living in anything but a secular world.

And even in the West, despite the official secularism of many states, and the secularism of intellectual and media elites and opinion leaders, a great many ordinary people go on seeking a spiritual dimension to their lives, often in traditional forms. The continuing strength of religious practice in the US, despite its officially secular status, is well known. Over nine out of ten Americans believe in God, and some four out of five pray regularly.[13] About forty per cent attend religious services at least once a week, and Americans give more money and time to religious organizations than to all other volunteer organizations combined.[14] In fact, the strength of religious practice in the US is often decried elsewhere, because of the odd way it is sometimes blended with nationalism, populism, libertarianism, authoritarianism, xenophobia, and militarism, a strange mixture that has given rise to the label of the "religious right."

But even in Canada, a more moderate and (now) more secular country – where historically it has been more accurate to speak of a "religious left" – some eighty-one per cent of the population still believes in the existence of God or a higher being; seventy-three per cent believe God cares about them personally; and nearly fifty per cent believe they have experienced the presence of God. About eighty per cent of Canadians identify themselves as members of a religious group, and about seventy-four per cent of Canadians pray.[15] Formal religious membership has actually increased over the past twenty years, and remains by far the largest voluntary activity.[16]

It's hard to know exactly what to make of figures like these, or how to interpret them. They do not call into question the overwhelming power of secular frameworks and assumptions. Even following these practices, most respondents would probably feel confusion, perplexity, and possibly even guilt, because they can't justify their practices in a rational manner, or explain them in ways that would satisfy the criteria of a secular society. Especially if they are asked to do so, as the surrounding secular society would probably expect, on the basis of their so-called "beliefs." So they practice them half-apologetically, without any expectation that their religious life should play a role in their professional or public ones, as citizens.

But at the very least, such responses suggest the need to qualify the official picture. The presence and power of spiritual practice may also be felt by those who respond negatively to this kind of survey but who nevertheless seek out the many secular forms of spirituality in which modern society abounds. Or by the great many (possibly the majority,

despite what they tell pollsters) who live in a "middle space" of "undefined spirituality" I noted in chapter 3: "shying away from materialism,
or from a narrow view of the morality of mutual benefit, and yet not
wanting to return to the strong claims of the transformation view, with
its far-reaching claims about the power of God in our lives."[17] Religious
or spiritual impulses may even be felt, more deeply and subtly, in the
motivations even non-religious people still feel toward goodness, their
continuing capacity for guilt, and their sincere desire for improvement,
reform and social benevolence.

✳

So the modern *world* is not necessarily a secular one, even if our Western
societies and official Western thought are. But what about the past? Was
it really as different from our present condition as we think?

Clearly, as we saw in the example of Caravaggio, there is a big difference, for most people. When the virtues of reverence predominate,
everything can be seen through a spiritual lens. When the virtues of self-
assertion set the agenda, even the spiritual must be seen through a profane lens. In the modern world (as this book itself demonstrates), the
question for any religious person is: why? In a pre-modern world, the
question, for most people, would have been the opposite: why not?

Obviously this makes a big difference, at the level of everyday life, for
most people, and for public affairs. But when we look specifically at
religious experience in its highest representatives, I'm not so sure.

If I consider the religious thinkers I know best – Christian writers
such as Blaise Pascal, Thomas Aquinas, Augustine of Hippo, and Paul of
Tarsus, for example – they do not seem to stand in any different relationship to ultimate things than I do. They seem to have the same questions, the same dilemmas, the same ignorance, the same mysteries, and
the same awareness of the need for fundamental, difficult choices affect-
ing the meaning and direction of our lives – what modern thinkers (as
we saw in chapters 6 and 8) call "existential" choices – as we do.

This is least surprising, perhaps, in the cases of Augustine and Pascal,
who stand more than a thousand years apart, at the beginning and at
the end of the Christian era. Augustine was well aware of the alternatives to a religious life and to Christianity, because it was his enormous
intellectual labour that helped to create that religious tradition in the first
place. He was raised in a pagan society and trained in the intellectual

traditions of pagan antiquity. He had to make a painful, wrenching choice, a choice he described so memorably in his *Confessions*, which became one of the greatest classics of Christian spirituality.

Pascal stands at the other end of the Christian era, acutely aware of the impending breakdown of the Christian consensus, a breakdown heralded, implicitly, by the thought of his contemporary, René Descartes. Many of the reflections in his great *Pensées* are devoted to justifying Christian and religious insights, refuting thinkers like Descartes, or giving advice to young persons on how to choose a life path correctly in such an uncertain world.

Aquinas stands almost at the mid-point between these two. Perhaps partly for that reason, his writing has a more serene tone than theirs, though this may also reflect, equally, his own even temperament. But when we look at the substance of his thought, it seems to be just as concerned to explain the value of and reasons for a religious life as the other two. How could it have been otherwise? He spent his life meditating not just on the Bible and on other Christian sources, but on the great ancient thinkers, especially Aristotle and Plato. He was also part of a rich medieval dialogue that included Islamic scholars such as Avicenna (Abu Ali al Hosain ibn Abdallah ibn Sina) and Averroes (Mohammad ibn Roshd), as well as the great Jewish philosopher, Maimonides (Moses ben Maimon), of whom he always spoke with the deepest respect. So he was daily aware of the possibility of other ways of seeing the world than his, both religious and non-religious. He felt acutely as any other thinker the need to show why one would choose a life of religious practice over another, what this kind of "decision" means in an uncertain world, and what would be lost, if it were not made.[18]

If we go even farther back, to Paul or to the Jewish scriptures, the very same voices can be heard, voices that in their way are just as contemporary as you and I. In chapters 7 and 8 we saw how the Psalms, for example, present, as starkly as any modern text, the existential dilemma human beings encounter, confronting a potentially meaningless and hostile world, and the agonizing decisions that must be made in the face of this. In the Book of Deuteronomy, when we read the memorable words I quoted in chapter 9 – "See, I have set before you this day life and good, and death and evil ... therefore choose life" – we recognize a challenge and a choice that are as fresh and as alive as we are.

Perhaps this is all that twentieth-century theologians meant, in talking about "demythologizing" the scriptures. Hidden within the language of a writer like Paul about "sin," "faith," "flesh," and "spirit," for example, is an utterly relevant and contemporary message about the choice that confronts every human being: the choice about how to lead a life worth living, about where to look for help in making such a choice, and about the paradox of losing your life to save it.[19] But any great Christian writer, indeed any great religious writer, for the last two thousand years – certainly those mentioned above – could have told them that.

✳

In the end, the world is what it always was.

Cultures change, and social consensus changes. As a result, we may be less supported, or more supported, in "seeing" the world in a certain way, or in leading a certain kind of life, or in following the practices, religious and otherwise, that support both. Some practices and values will be more spontaneous, or less spontaneous, than others. "A mode once well-established in a particular culture may later wane," as Margaret Donaldson remarks. "It will not be lost entirely from the consciousness of certain individuals but it may lose prevalence, it may cease to flourish. Dark Ages may come."[20]

There is more than one kind of Dark Age. We are accustomed to think of the early medieval period of European history as such a Dark Age. But what if we ourselves were now living in one? An age in which the virtues of reverence have been temporarily eclipsed, to our great harm, just as the virtues of self-assertion were eclipsed in that earlier era.

Whether we can see it or not, the world is just as it always was, both secular and non-secular. Just as it was to the authors of Deuteronomy and the Psalms, to Paul, to Augustine and Thomas Aquinas, to Avicenna, Averroes, and Maimonides, and to Blaise Pascal. It has always taken personal insight – the insight that is sometimes called revelation, or "epiphany" – to "see" it as one or the other. "The capacity to see is a high and lofty power," said the Rabbi Nahman of Bratslav (1772–1810), a leading figure in the Jewish pietist movement known as Hasidism. "[Man's] eyes are always seeing but they do not know what they are seeing."[21] On his deathbed, the Taoist sage Chuang-Tzu (4th century BCE?) told his students: "The person who uses only the vision of the eyes is conditioned purely by what he sees. But it's the intuition of the spirit that perceives reality."[22] When the Buddha had achieved enlightenment and apprehended the four holy truths, he said it was "as if my organ of spiritual vision had been opened."[23] This kind of seeing, said Plotinus, is scarcely "vision" at all: "It is a seeing of a quite different kind, a self-transcendence, a simplification, self-abandonment, a striving for union ... This is the way one sees in the sanctuary. Anyone who tries to see in any other way will see nothing."[24]

As Paul said, this is seeing "with the eyes of your heart."[25] This kind of seeing often takes a choice or decision, a decision (as a Buddhist text puts it) "to bring within the range of vision that which was outside it."[26] It was through this kind of decision that Gautama Shakyamuni became the Buddha. The decision can be explicit, as it was for Shakyamuni when he left his father's palace to seek enlightenment, or it can be implicit.

In a pre-modern world, the decision to see the world in essentially spiritual terms would have been implicit for most people, taken for them by the surrounding culture. Seeing the world as secular, as determined largely by material or "efficient" causes, took a conscious mental effort, the kind of effort Francis Bacon argued for in his *New Organon*. In a modern, secular culture it is the reverse. In our culture, the decision to see the world as ruled by efficient causes and by the virtues of self-assertion is implicit, taken for most of us by the surrounding culture. But this is just as much a matter of "faith," as the pre-modern condition. It is what the Hindu tradition calls *shraddha*, an initial, unconscious decision to view the world in a certain way. It is only after this initial option or orientation that our conscious mind goes to work on it. As R.G. Collingwood explained: "Reason builds on a foundation of faith, and moves within a system whose general nature must be determined by faith before reason can deal with it in detail."[27]

In modern secular culture, therefore, the decision to see the world through a spiritual lens must normally be conscious and deliberate; as conscious as Francis Bacon's decision had to be to see it the other way around. And seeing the world this way transforms it. It is a different world. Because we can now see new things we couldn't see before. "[R]everence is not simply a virtue for which we may expect full marks in heaven, or a device for bolstering up the social establishment," said English writer Owen Barfield (1898–1997). "It is an organ of perception for a whole range of qualities that are as imperceptible without it as another whole range is imperceptible without an ear for music."[28]

There are three consolations to be noted about the need for a decision to see the world with a reverent heart, as well as a warning. The first consolation is that, precisely because of this requirement, a secular world can actually be a gain for true spirituality. As Karl Rahner points out, our secular condition helps reveal again the true nature of faith as a kind of action. This spiritual reality can be obscured in a religious culture when individuals are "indoctrinated about God" in a manner "contrary to the ultimate nature of faith" which "requires a personal decision."[29] But a secular culture lays bare again for us the true nature of religious life.

The second consolation is that this decision is no different than the one humankind has faced for thousands of years. In making it, we stand in much the same place as the authors of the Taoist and Buddhist texts or of the *Upanishads*, the *Bhagavad Gita*, Deuteronomy, and the Psalms; the same place as Jeremiah, Ezekiel, Paul, Augustine, and Muhammad, as Aquinas, Avicenna, Averroes, and Maimonides, and as Blaise Pascal. What they have to say about it is as alive and as relevant as when they wrote.

The third consolation is that in this arena, religious traditions are on their own home turf: the mystery that surrounds and inhabits human life. On this field of mystery, their methods and insights are of equal or greater value than those of science and reason, which have nothing much to say about these kinds of mysteries unless they do so reverently. Without reverence, their writ runs out where mystery begins. Because this kind of mystery is not a problem to be "solved," but rather, a deep well to draw on, "an inexhaustible source of soluble problems."[30]

The warning brings us full circle, to where this book began. It's about the nature of "seeing," and how it is we come to "see," in one way or another. Because this is not primarily the mental, intellectual, disembodied or abstract task our modern world would assume. That usually comes later, as Collingwood suggested, and is a reflection on something else: a reflection on – or *of* – the experience of action. The way we see the world, and therefore the meaning things have for us, come not just from our eyes or our minds but – as Plotinus reminds us – from our stance in the world, the way we act within it. If we do not have the experience of performing spiritual actions, there will be nothing to reflect on, or to be reflected. The world will be a different place. So the fundamental question, for all of us, is not, in the first instance, about what we *think* but about what we will *do*.

# 14

# The Question

The question, for all of us, is: how shall I lead my life?

This is not an academic question. It is not an abstract or intellectual one. It's personal, immediate, and urgent. It's the old joke about the meaning of life. But it's no joke, when your own life is at stake. It's the question that keeps us awake at night. Or gnaws away at the back of our minds, no matter how comfortable or successful we are. And it's a question most of us have to answer, somehow.

You can try to hide from the question, and simply immerse yourself in the comforts of everyday life.[1] This option is appealing because Western industrial societies provide so many rich opportunities for consumption and distraction, and because our modern culture attaches such a high value to "the affirmation of ordinary life."[2] But it may take a lot of consumer goods, and a great deal of deliberate busyness and pleasure, to dull the mind completely, and shut out the nagging question about the point of it all: the question that keeps disturbing your peace.[3] As Samuel Taylor Coleridge remarked, such a person "may *sleep to death* in the lethargy of carnal presumption and impenitency; but a true, lively, solid peace he cannot have."[4]

Most of us, most of the time, aspire to lead lives of integrity. But integrity, as I noted earlier, is inseparably connected to its root meaning of "wholeness." You can't have "integrity," if some part of you or your life is in flagrant contradiction with some other part. That means you need to think about *yourself* as a whole, and your *life* as a whole.[5]

Thinking about your *life* as a whole means thinking about it as a story: the story of where you came from and where you're going. Not just what you want to *do*, but who you want to *be*. Not just in your career, or your working life, but in your real life, including its inevitable end, in death – and the light this inevitable conclusion will throw, and already does throw, on everything that precedes it. It means thinking about your life as an ongoing "journey," as we saw in chapter 7. Thinking about your life in this way means thinking about it reverently, the way Whitehead said we should think about time, as we saw in chapter 2: as a unity, with the past and the future joined in the present. Thinking about it not just as a series of momentary, fragmented experiences, no matter how intense, but rather as a wholeness, shaped by time and will – the very qualities necessary to make a great marriage, or great friendships, or good communities.

Thinking about *yourself* as a whole means giving due attention to your whole nature. One side of it will probably take care of itself, or at least will not fail to get ample support from your surrounding culture and society. Developing, promoting, empowering, exploring, enriching, expressing, enjoying and asserting your own "self," your own individual ego, is the essence of what it means to be "modern" – as a glance at the magazine rack in your local supermarket will tell you – because these virtues of self-assertion are the concrete expression of the organizing principle of modern life: the principle of freedom. Or, rather, a certain "expressive" idea of freedom is the conceptual form we give to the eternal virtues of self-assertion, at the beginning of the twenty-first century. But there are at least two types of freedom. There is the freedom to do whatever we want, just for the hell of it, as Augustine noted. And there is the freedom to acknowledge something, or some things, other than, and perhaps more important than, ourselves – our families, our community, our world, and so on – in service to which we may actually find our true fulfilment. There is a service which is perfect freedom.

Recognizing this means that – to be a whole person, and to lead a whole life – you need to nurture not only the virtues of self-assertion but also the virtues of reverence which make up the other side of what, in chapter 1, I called the human paradox. Failing to nurture this side of your self is a denial of half of your humanity. Living without the virtues of reverence would be only half a life. You can't get away with it anyway, in practice, as we saw in chapter 2. We go on living the virtues of reverence, in some degree or other, whether we recognize it or not. So the only question for you is whether you will nurture them consciously or not, or just let them go on operating underground without your help.

Leaving aside the environmental imperative we discussed in chapter 12, and the potential loss of our benevolent public culture in a purely secular society,[6] there are lots of personal reasons for cultivating the virtues of reverence. Those we have already considered in this book include the search for meaning and dignity, and for human fullness or fulfilment. Another theme of traditional spiritual wisdom is the warning that life doesn't always go smoothly. Most of us experience failure, suffering, and sorrow, much of the time. And even those who don't, for a while, will eventually experience, like the rest of us, illness, betrayal, pain, disappointment, failure, humiliation, abandonment, loneliness, fear, physical decline, and eventually, death. The last is certain. In these circumstances, the virtues of self-assertion, by themselves, will probably not sustain you, though they are a precious help. You will also need a very different kind of help.

And that's one of the things the major religious traditions talk about a lot. The first of the four Buddhist "Holy Truths," for example, is the universal reality of suffering. Most Buddhist teaching is therefore about how best to live in a world that is "carried away in distress on the flooded river of suffering, which the foam of disease over-sprays, which has old age for its surge and rushes along with the violent rush of death."[7] One of the chapters in the *Quran*, "The Spider," observes that those who live without a strong religious foundation "may be compared to the spider which builds a cobweb for itself. Surely the spider's is the frailest of all dwellings." Whereas the person who "surrenders himself to God and leads a righteous life stands on the firmest ground."[8] Some of the most famous stories and sayings attributed to Jesus are about this same spiritual problem: about the man who built his house on sand, for example, only to find it washed away by the storms of life. Or about working for the food that endures rather than for the food that perishes. Or about not storing up riches in the wrong place, where moths and rust corrupt.[9] Not the least of reasons for nurturing the virtues of reverence is storing up riches in the *right* place, to prepare for those storms, and those moths.

✳

As we saw in chapter 3, a great many people today seek comfort and nourishment in many forms of secular or non-religious spirituality. They define themselves as spiritual but not religious. They recognize they have spiritual needs, but they try to meet them from non-religious sources, especially nature and art. This is one of our many inheritances from the Romantic movement of the nineteenth century, which high-lighted nature and art as sources that could provide an antidote to the dehumanizing rationalism of the Enlightenment.

Valuable as they are, however, it is at least open to question whether they can ever be enough, by themselves, without something more to give them meaning.[10] Seeking spirituality outside a religious frame of refer-ence is certainly worthwhile, as far as it goes. The problem is it may not go far enough. And it may miss the point. Non-religious spiritualities often miss the essence of spirituality, which is spiritual habits, spiritual exercise, spiritual discipline, spiritual behaviour, and action in the world. In fact that's exactly why people prefer the non-religious kinds of spiri-tuality. Because they're easier. They make fewer real demands. They don't make you change your routines, or your habits, or yourself, or your world. They don't require a turning of the heart, the inner "trans-formation" Thomas Aquinas called "faith."[11] Religious life is too hard, it's too demanding – mentally and otherwise – it's too inconvenient. It's too tiring. I'd rather sleep in, or go skiing, or go bird-watching, or go for a walk in the park. Or have another cup of coffee.

These kinds of attitudes fit well both with the culture of comfort and convenience in contemporary societies – the culture of self-assertion and expressive individualism, sometimes called a culture of "narcis-sism"[12] – and with the "affirmation of ordinary life" which is such an important part of modern values.

To be fair, however, these attitudes are also supported, and rational-ized, by a genuine confusion about the nature of authentic religious life. The confusion stems, in part, from the misleading language of "reli-gion" that has grown up in Western culture over the last five hundred years, a confusion I have tried to unravel in this book, especially in chapter 5. As a result of this confusion, most people in Western societies – and probably almost all non-religious people – think that so-called "religion" is about belief, that faith and belief are the same thing (as the definition of secularization I quoted at the beginning of the last chapter simply took for granted). Since they're not sure about the beliefs, they assume a religious life can't be for them, even if they feel the need of something more in their lives. And they probably also think that doubt and faith are incompatible. Since they start with some real doubts, they figure that rules them out, too.

I hope that by now I have been able to help you distinguish faith from belief. Religious belief can only become plausible in the context of an ongoing life of religious practice and reverence, a life of faith. Faith is something you *do* before it can become something you think, or possess. And doubting is one of the main things you do, as the Psalms clearly show us. I will come back to this. But for the moment I'd like to continue thinking – in the spirit of the distinction I've just reiterated, between action and belief – about how you get over the hump of "unbelief," so you can discover the real nature of religious life.

This is something to which Blaise Pascal gave a lot of thought. And his answer has become known to history as Pascal's "wager." You might think Pascal had something rather crass in mind: a kind of crude wager on the probabilities of an after-life. In reality, he was expressing something much closer to the distinction between faith and belief. Rational "proofs," he knew, convince only the rational "mind," which is not the heart of the matter. "Custom" and habit are the real and "strongest" demonstration of the value of a religious life. So the first step is to develop religious "habits," and the "soul" follows "naturally."[13] So he advised the person who hungers after an authentic spiritual life, to begin "by *doing* everything *as if* they believed."[14] In his great dialogue, the *Phaedo*, Plato called this "the risk of believing." And, he declared, "the risk is noble."[15] Similarly, a rabbinical teaching in the Jewish tradition suggests people who have lost touch with God can find him again by *doing* what he wants them to do, that is to say, by keeping his 'law': "Since they then would have been occupied with it, the light which is in it would have restored them to the right path."[16]

✳

As if. That seems to be one of the important clues about how to initiate a religious life. It's related to the insight that what we *do* has at least as much influence on what we can *see*, and therefore on what we think, and on what we are, as the reverse. That our deeds determine us as much as we determine our deeds, as George Eliot put it.

This is a very old insight that underlies much of Eastern spirituality. The techniques of yoga, for example, are based on the premise that the best way to work on your mind and spirit is not necessarily to start there, but to start with the body instead. If you can regulate your muscles, breathing, bodily rhythms, and awareness, gradually your mind will begin to clear, or to recede, and your spirit will come to the fore. Our actions determine us – even what we can perceive, or think – as much as we determine them.

This ancient insight is one of the principles underlying all ritual, religious or otherwise. It's why ritual – or *Li* – is so central to eastern traditions of reverence like that of Confucius: by performing a ceremony or playing a role – which may be artificial at first – we can become something other than "ourselves," and better. The heart of the Confucian tradition is that through regular, careful observance of ritual, we can "overcome" the self and achieve "benevolence." [17]

The same insight has also been recognized by modern psychology, as it has struggled to develop ways we can make ourselves less vulnerable to the potentially destructive forces of the psyche, and develop "better" desires. Psychologist Bruno Bettelheim (1903–1990) was a prisoner in the Nazi concentration camps of Dachau and Buchenwald before the Second World War, where he gradually became aware of a striking fact. The prisoners who stood up well to their treatment became better men, while those who didn't became worse. His experience in the Nazi camps taught Bettelheim "that how a man *acts* can alter what he *is*." [18] As we already saw in chapter 7, acting *as if* is often a critical step to bring about deep inner change. The "without," as Karl Rahner puts it, "can actually bring the 'within' into being." [19]

Many of us already have some experience of acting *as if* in the way we take up new roles in life. How do we become anything, except by acting *as if* we were...? As if we were a camp counsellor, or a prefect, or a skier, or a coach, or a salesperson, or a waiter, or a teacher, or a manager, or an architect, or a doctor, or a professor, or a father, or a leader. Sometimes we don't feel very authentic in these roles at first. In fact, very often, we feel like "impostors." We're amazed, maybe even embarrassed, when other people take us seriously, and start to respect our authority or seek us out as experts. Some people have a lot of difficulty getting over this "impostor syndrome."

Beginning to act "as if" you were a Jew, or a Muslim, or a Buddhist, or a Christian isn't very different from how we act in any of our other roles in life. And, even more than most other roles, it's the only way to find out what it's really like to be that kind of a person, or to lead that kind of a spiritual life: the only way to find out what it really means. In the Buddhist scriptures, the *Dharma* – the Buddhist word for the spiritual force behind and in everything, like the Chinese Tao – is likened to a taste: the word of the Buddha is said to have the taste of peace, the taste of freedom, the taste of Nirvana, and so on. "It is, of course, a peculiarity of tastes that they are not easily described," remarks the Buddhist scholar, Edward Conze (1904–1979), "and must elude those who refuse actually to taste them for themselves."[20] Since faith is a kind of *doing*, or practice, you have to *do* or practice some of the things it entails, in order to find out what it's all about. Taste and see.[21] There's no other way. It's only afterward, as a result of "experience, prayer, and practice," that "what was initially a mere leap of faith comes to be more and more clear and undeniable."[22]

Let's assume you've reached this point in your search. You have probably already begun to explore one or more of the enormous variety of ways in which spirituality can be experienced and cultivated today. You may have explored the potential of exercise and begun to get your body into shape. You may also have begun to regulate your diet, conscious of how what you eat can affect your mind and spirit. You may have experimented with yoga and meditation, or read some of the popular books on "spirituality." You may have given time to benevolent, community, or environmental causes. Or you may not have done any of these, but simply seek spiritual nourishment in art, or music, or nature. But you have also begun to feel that none of these are enough, by themselves. That there must be something more. That you want to go further, or higher. You may even have begun to suspect that all this activity could be self-defeating if it remains nothing more than the cultivation and manipulation of your own modern "self."

How should you continue your spiritual journey? There are lots of people who will be only too eager to attract you to their particular brand of spirituality. But in the spiritual "marketplace," as in others, the right counsel is "buyer beware." In fact one of the oldest warnings, in various religious traditions, as I noted in chapter 3, is the warning about "false prophets." That's because the spiritual dimension is such a powerful force in the human psyche that it can easily be perverted by shallow, misguided, unscrupulous, or evil persons, with enormous potential danger to the victims. The continuing appeal of cults and other ersatz "religions" testifies to the enormous spiritual vacuum and hunger felt by many modern people, despite (or perhaps because of) the rationalist bias of our times. It also shows how important is the choice of a future path for your own spiritual journey, and how careful you should be.

For these reasons, the best place – perhaps the only really promising place – to continue your own spiritual journey is in one of the world's great religious traditions.[23] One strength of a well-established, historic religious tradition – continuing the "market" metaphor I used, rather facetiously, above – is "quality assurance." Since the danger of falling into the hands of "false prophets" is so great, the wisest course is to choose a form of religious practice that has had a long time to prove itself, where many of the potential errors or false paths have already been identified, and weeded out. Catholics use the word *magisterium* for the body of teaching and insight built up by the Catholic Church over two thousand years. The main (or Sunni) tradition of Islam uses the word *ijma* for this same established "consensus" of the tradition. One of the advantages of a *magisterium* or *ijma* – or their equivalent in any longstanding religious tradition – is to help ensure genuine religious insight is effectively sorted out from falsehood, and that what remains is of real value. "Over the centuries," Stephen Carter observes, "the religious traditions, like traditions of other kinds, tend to abandon what is useless and preserve what is useful."[24] In a form of activity like religious practice, which is not based "upon principles demonstrative and scientific" but rather on "observation and experience," Samuel Johnson remarked (in a different context), "no other test can be applied than length of duration and continuance of esteem. What mankind have long possessed they have often examined and compared; and if they persist to value the possession, it is because frequent comparisons have confirmed opinion in its favour."[25]

Whatever form it takes, in the various religious traditions, a magisterium is useful not just to weed out "false prophets" but also to build up riches: intellectual, cultural, and spiritual. An historic faith has had enough time for the greatest minds of the ages – minds like those of Paul, Augustine, Aquinas, Maimonides, and Pascal – to contribute the insights of their genius. Equally or even more important, it has been able to amass a wealth of spiritual practices, including ritual, liturgy, sacraments, poetry, and music, the resources that are essential to give depth, richness, meaning, and power to a religious spirituality, and are at its heart. As Elaine Pagels said (in chapter 6), we could make all this up, out of our own experience. But we don't have to. And we could never do so with the rigour, richness and depth a great tradition offers us.[26] Anglican Christians, for example, can draw on a rich liturgical and musical heritage, cherished spiritual treasures the Anglican tradition has built up over some five hundred years: from Thomas Cranmer, Orlando Gibbons, William Byrd, George Herbert, and Henry Purcell in the sixteenth and seventeenth centuries to Charles Villiers Stanford, Ralph Vaughan Williams, Robert Bridges, Healey Willan, Herbert Howells, Herbert O'Driscoll, and John Rutter in the twentieth and twenty-first. It has been said that the liturgy, poetry, and music of Anglicanism at its best can "create a world of wonder in which it is very easy to fall in love with God."[27] Every other religious tradition offers similar examples.

A great religious tradition of this kind has also been able to maintain continuity with what, in chapter 6, I called the "encounter," the initial experience or revelation that gave birth to it in the first place. World-changing spiritual events like the Buddha's encounter with Mara, the Lord of Desire, Death, and Duty, that led to his enlightenment under the Bodhi-tree. Or the day in Sinai when the six hundred and thirteen commandments of the Torah were transmitted by God to Moses and the whole people of Israel. Or the night in a cave on Mt Hira, when Muhammad was assaulted by an invisible presence, commanding him to recite the first verses of what was to become the *Quran*. Or that day on the road to Emmaus when Jesus' former disciples had a stunning encounter with a stranger.

Maintaining a link with these primal encounters – the moments when a mysterious power seems to break through the surface of ordinary human existence – is normally an important feature of religious traditions, something that distinguishes them from other forms of human activity.[28] By maintaining the link with these events, the great religious traditions tap into the sources of vital power they reveal or represent. Rabbinical teaching holds, for example, that whenever a person is studying the Torah, he or she can say, "It is as though I received the Torah at Sinai on *this* day."[29]

Another way to sum all this up is to say that the strength of a great religious tradition is precisely that it *is* a tradition. In a book like this one, for individual readers, it's inevitable to focus on individual experience. But if the necessary human impulse to reverence springs from the reality of oneness and connectedness – the reality of union that underlies and binds all our non-union – then it must express itself in the same way: through connectedness and participation in something larger than our individual selves. This takes at least two forms, which can be called "horizontal" and "vertical."[30]

By "horizontal," I mean participation in a community of persons who are on a similar spiritual journey today, both a community of "corporate worship" and a quest community, "a group activity of searching," a "common pilgrimage."[31] As we saw in chapter 2, it's in communities such as the family that we learn, or don't learn, virtues like those of reverence, and encounter what they reveal to us.[32]

By "vertical," I mean participation in another kind of community, a "community of memory": the community of all those through the centuries who have made the same journey, and have had the same encounters with the otherness of the spirit.[33] Our stories intersect with their stories. Our own encounters are often encounters with *their* encounters. These "second-hand" encounters are the source of most of the strengths of an authentic religious tradition I just mentioned. They also provide both support and authority. The support comes from the way a deep tradition helps us to put its insights to work. We could not embody, sustain, or transmit its truth on our own, without being supported by the empowering presence these second-hand encounters make available to us, and by the wealth of story and example we are moved to re-enact or, rather, reinvent in our own lives. If our own lives are best lived as a unified story, they should also be seen as parts of an even bigger story, the ongoing story of a tradition that helps us understand the "future possibilities which the past has made available to the present."[34]

The authority of such a tradition also challenges us by establishing practices and values that place demands on us, demands that call upon us to transcend and transform our own egos. The practices and symbols we encounter within a religious tradition are "at once an inspiration *and* a judgment of oneself."[35] Without the second part, without religious demands, spirituality would remain little more than a self-regarding "therapy," reinforcing the very problem it claims to cure, locking us deeper in the prison of the modern self.

✳

Which of the world's great religious traditions is the right one for you, to undertake your own spiritual journey? For some people, the right one will turn out to be different than their own cultural background. Since the 1960s, many people in the West have been attracted to various Eastern religious traditions, especially Buddhism, because they emphasize the spiritual exercises with which the Western traditions were never as well endowed, and which have now largely been forgotten. To Westerners, the Eastern traditions don't seem burdened down with the emphasis on "beliefs" that is an ambiguous legacy of Western rationalism. As a result, participation in Eastern practices seems to offer escape from the experience of guilt that is a necessary part of the Western traditions, rooted in "mythic dissociation." To many in the West the Eastern religious traditions appear more like alternative therapies than "religion," and are therefore much more compatible with the culture of self-assertion and expressive individualism. The escape from guilt may be paid for, however, by an increase in anxiety if the experience of the Eastern traditions is only skin deep, and doesn't involve a genuine encounter with what those traditions call the "eternal self," the absence of which only makes the problem of the particular self more acute.[36]

Even if they don't go as far as to embrace an Eastern religious tradition, some people in the West find they can pursue their own spiritual quest more rewardingly in another Western tradition, or in another denomination. A strength of Islam and Judaism, for example, is the way they continue (as traditions of "practice" rather than of creeds and dogmas) to emphasize the everyday reverence which encourages religious observance to be built into the daily cycle of life in the family and the community. For some people from a Christian background, these qualities may offer a richer and more promising way forward.

But most people will be best able to pursue an adult spiritual journey in the religious tradition of their own culture. There are many reasons for this. There is a very close link between religion and culture. Encounters and revelations occur within a culture, and they often carry something of that cultural flavour with them. Religious experience also expresses itself through cultural means such as stories, myths, symbols, art, music, and poetry, and these will be more readily understandable and meaningful to people who are rooted in the same or a related culture.

Fundamentally, this is a question of what might be called "resonance." Resonance is the quality possessed by a piano or a violin that makes them vibrate in harmony when certain notes are played. The same thing happens in human beings when certain cultural notes are played. For someone raised in a Christian culture, for example, certain words and symbols will have a deep resonance that those from other traditions may never have, in equal degree. Take, for example, the relationship between the English language and the Authorized (or King James) Version of the Bible and the Anglican Book of Common Prayer. The

English language is shot through with the cadence and rhetoric of these two masterpieces of the language. So English-speakers from a Christian background are already culturally "programmed," through these and many other influences, to respond intuitively to certain kinds of religious language and symbols, if their minds and ears are not closed to doing so.

Another way to put this question of resonance is to relate it to what I called an "encounter." The reason these resources have resonance for you is that you have already had some encounters with them within your own tradition. You have probably already had a glimpse of that tradition's "inner spiritual power,"[37] even if you turned away from it in the past, because it seemed incompatible with what you took to be the demands of adult rationality, or simply with your own desires. You may now be ready to rediscover that power, and explore its source.

Yet another way to put this is to link back to the ongoing "conversation" from which this book – like our own lives – began. The reason you may have had some of these encounters is that you are already part of an ongoing conversation. Pursuing your spiritual quest within your own tradition is also a way of finding yourself, by linking up again with the conversation that made you what you are. Rejoining the conversation of your tradition is one of the things that can help give meaning to a life. It's one of the deepest things that "meaning" can mean.[38]

✳

Rejoining the spiritual conversation of your tradition means listening again to its stories, myths, symbols, art, music, and poetry, but with a new mind. This may involve shedding many assumptions about "religion" that Western culture has been gradually building up for five hundred years or so, beginning around the time of Pico della Mirandola. Contrary to our settled assumption since the eighteenth century, "religion" is not, primarily, a form of thought, or a set of propositions, but a form of action or practice.[39] Faith, as Terry Eagleton says, is "performative rather than propositional."[40] Before it can become something you think or say or agree to, it has to be something you do. The relationship between ideas and practice is by no means a one-way street. They both influence each other. But in more areas of life than we normally recognize, the practice actually "carries" the understanding, that is to say the understanding is embedded in and implicitly – even unconsciously – justified by the practice.[41] The beliefs of unbelief, for example – what I earlier called its "absolute presuppositions" – are carried by the practices of self-assertion, just as the practices of reverence shape those that are carried by a religious life.[42] It's partly because the practices of self-assertion are so pervasive in modern life that secular presuppositions seem so much more self-evident to people today, and are simply taken for granted.[43]

The priority of practice in religious life is, if anything, even greater, because of the way it includes but goes beyond human reason. We can think of religious practices as a kind of language in which ideas of fundamental importance for human beings are expressed. And because of the difficulty of expressing these ideas in other ways, the practices may well be the best or even the only way to express them.[44] In a religious life, the thought normally comes afterward, if it comes at all. It is, literally, an afterthought. It is a form of reflection on – or *of* – the action or practice or experience.[45] "[P]erformance," as Bernard Lonergan says, "must precede reflection on performance."[46] The reflection is important. Even very important, especially in some traditions, like Christianity. But it's not at the heart of what it means to lead a religious life.

To sum up: *a religious life is a life of reverent practice, individual and collective actions that, by their very reverence, bring the seeker continuously or repeatedly into the presence of a sacred mystery or power, always hoping and seeking to participate in the mystery and to be empowered by its presence – empowered for reverent and transforming action in the world and within themselves.*

The pilgrimage of religious life takes the form of a rhythm of religious observance through which the faithful seek to come into the presence of the sacred: monthly, weekly, daily, possibly even hourly. These regular observances take place in larger cycles of a year or more, and together they constitute the great rhythm of religious life. This rhythmic pattern of religious habit is like the beating of a heart, or the breathing of the lungs. The rhythm at the heart of life. Life begins in rhythm – the rhythms of in and out, back and forth, permanence and change, part and whole, union and non-union, the rhythms in which biological life arises, which *are* biological life – and it ends in rhythm: that is to say, it finds its "end," its goal, its fulfilment, in the rhythms of a reverent life, lived in harmony with the whole.

A life of religious practice is fundamentally a life of regular habits: both habits of feeling that express themselves as habits of behaviour, and habits of behaviour (internal, mental behaviour, and external behaviour, in the world) that nurture habits of feeling. To be the best that we can be, human beings seem to require "some practical ritual and moral 'structure' that orders our freedom and binds our choices into something like habits of the heart."[47]

Those who go regularly to churches or temples or synagogues aren't going there to recite a "creed," or to subscribe to some "beliefs," or to give assent to a set of propositions. Creeds exist, of course, in some religious traditions. But where they do (which is only in the Christian churches), they are actually a response to doubt, as I said in chapter 9. Giving excessive importance to "the letter of a written confession," as Friedrich Schleiermacher observed, is actually a form of "unbelief."[48] Creeds are a rather clumsy attempt by the assertive, rational intellect to give a rational form to the mystery that reverence experiences in quite another way. Leszhek Kolakowski puts it like this: "To be sure, it is not impossible to assent to certain 'statements' belonging to the doctrinal side of religion and to accept them as true in the same sense as we accept without question many pieces of information, factual or theoretical. Such acts of assent simply do not belong to what we usually call religious belief; these 'statements' lie fallow, as it were, and have no significance as instruments of communion with the Sacred; our brain stores countless fragments of vitrified knowledge, connected to nothing, serving no purpose, having no value in our life, and there is no reason why some of them should not be theological in content. With religious faith they have little to do."[49]

If creeds have any significance in a real religious life (as opposed to theology), it is mainly through the reverent feelings, attitudes, and experience that accompany their recitation, and the behaviours this kind of reverent recitation both embodies and causes. "We use language with God, not to manifest our thoughts to him," Thomas Aquinas said, "but to induce reverence in ourselves and others."[50] From this point of view a creed, if there is one, or something like it, in your tradition, is a resource for your spiritual journey, not an end to it. A well or spring, not a stagnant water barrel. Its mysteries will probably never be plumbed or exhausted, and certainly never fully "explained." But in exploring them, your mind and spirit can be prodded along their journey. "A creed is not an imprisoning wall," said the American writer Vida Scudder (1861–1954), "it is a gate, opening on a limitless country."[51]

People do not go to church or to a synagogue, mosque, or temple, in order to be made more ethical, more moral, as many eighteenth-century thinkers assumed, though that is normally one of the results. And they do not do it for motives of psychological hygiene, as many twentieth-century thinkers assumed, though that too is one of the usual outcomes. They do it, instead, out of an unquenchable desire to come into the presence of a sacred mystery, to participate in it, and to be empowered by the experience. As Paul put it, "The kingdom of God depends not on talk but on power."[52]

✳

This is, of course, a form of self-assertion. But all action is self-assertion, by definition. To act is to assert yourself. As the Lord Krishna explains to the young prince Arjuna in the Hindu *Bhagavad Gita*, "Even to maintain your body, Arjuna, you are forced to act."[53] Hence reverence is not an *alternative* to self-assertion. It is a *kind* of self-assertion. The virtues of reverence are not a separate kind of action, to be found over *there*, as it were, and the virtues of self-assertion over *here*. They are both *here*. Reverence is a quality added to actions of self-assertion which, depending on the degree of its presence, gradually turns them into their opposite.

Reverence refers to the context for action. All action takes place within a context. "We are always in situations," as Karl Jaspers said.[54] Reverence is an attitude or spirit we can adopt toward the whole situation or context in which we find ourselves. So reverence is the spirit – the attitude, feeling, or purpose – that accompanies some actions, some acts of self-assertion, and transforms them into acts of reverence also. Reverence is the habit of feeling and behaviour that expresses awareness and acceptance of our place in this larger whole, or oneness.

The virtues of reverence are added to, and modify, the virtues of self-assertion. There can be virtues of self-assertion with only very little reverence, but no virtues of reverence at all without self-assertion.[55] As Krishna explains again to Arjuna, "He who knows that the way of renunciation and the way of action are one, he verily knows."[56] The Tao calls this marriage of reverence with self-assertion "action-less action," or *wu-wei*.[57] The Arabic word *jihād*, which is often translated in English as "holy war," actually means what, in this book, I have called self-assertion, but in its highest form: the self-assertion that turns into its opposite.[58] A famous Islamic *hadīth* (or sacred saying) proclaims one of the most profound paradoxes at the heart of this book: "The most excellent self-assertion (*jihād*) is that of the conquest of self."[59] The highest acts of self-assertion are acts of reverence. And the highest acts of reverence are heroic acts of self-assertion.[60]

That's what we mean when we talk about someone being a "saint" or, in the Eastern and Jewish traditions, a "sage": think of Brébeuf, Albert Schweitzer, Dietrich Bonhoeffer, Mother Teresa, or Jean Vanier. These are people empowered to perform heroic feats of reverent self-assertion. Even non-action, from this point of view, can be a kind of heroic action. The person who refuses to save herself, in order to save others. Or who endures ferocious torments or temptations, without being moved. It was Gautama Shakyamuni's heroic non-action, in the face of the repeated onslaughts from Mara, the Lord of Desire, Death, and Duty, that turned him into the Buddha.

When it's a question of ultimate ends such as religious reverence encounters, as Thomas Aquinas said, there's "no virtuous moderation, no reasonable mean; the more extreme our activity, the better we are."[61] Of course, this means heroic acts of reverence, humility, service, and selflessness. "These are the things for which no limit is prescribed," a Jewish daily prayer book says.[62] Not the assertive heroism of power and domination.[63] It means a love that, in Charles Taylor's words, "goes way beyond any possible mutuality, a self-giving not bounded by some measure of fairness."[64] And without the possibility of this kind of heroic goodness, the rest of us will behold nothing by which to be inspired, nor, in the end, may we even be safe. As the American writer Vicki Hearne (1946–2001) noted, "the great literature of the heroic tells us that the quest and the hearth are the same thing, that genuine safety demands the genuine heroic, or at least that they must be mated if life is to be fecund of meaning."[65]

By themselves, the virtues of self-assertion are empty.[66] Self-assertion for what? Freedom to do what? Equality for what? The answer can't come from self-assertion itself. To have any value content, freedom must have some context, goal, or objective. So the "unattached will" can't serve as "a prime source of value" for us.[67] In fact the best image for the virtues of self-assertion on their own (as I suggested in chapter 8) is perhaps the Hindu symbol of the demon of pure hunger eating itself up, which the god Shiva is said to have ordered to be placed over the doors of all his temples.

Actually, as the Hindu symbol suggests, the problem is deeper than emptiness. In fact, all evil actually comes, ultimately, from self-assertion. From the assertion of our own egos, from the sheer desire to be ourselves.[68] This may be another part of what Christians call "original sin," and it is the great insight at the heart of most of the Eastern religious traditions. "The reason we have a lot of trouble," says the *Tao Te Ching*, "is that we have selves."[69] That's why most of the Eastern traditions aim to achieve salvation or Nirvana through serene detachment, or even the extinction of the ego and its merger with the greater Whole. Buddhist monks, and indeed monks (or the equivalent) from all religious traditions, have as their goal to overcome self-assertion through heroic acts of reverent self-assertion.

Value can only come from the context, from the revelation of a concrete relationship to others, to otherness, and to the whole.[70] We find, paradoxically, that we ourselves are most fulfilled when we can bow our heads to something larger than ourselves, something we did not create and do not control, but which somehow commands our allegiance and our love, something toward which we have duties and obligations. "[C]omplete freedom and complete union do not cancel each other out," says N.T. Wright, "but rather celebrate each other and make each other whole."[71] We are at our best when we are on our knees.

That's why so many people keep going to their temples, churches, synagogues, or mosques when all the pressures and prejudices of a secular society are against it. Not *because* of their beliefs. Rather, in spite of the *difficulty* of belief. The awe they experience in the presence of the sacred empowers them, filling them again with the confidence, strength, and peace of mind required for the highest and most demanding tasks of life. Through and in their acts of reverence, they find life and the world as a whole do have meaning, after all, and that they are connected to a source of sustaining, mysterious power that can help them to make that meaning a reality in their lives and in their world. As Samuel Johnson said, "he who, with proper fervour and humility, prostrates himself before God, will always rise with an increase of holy confidence."[72]

✳

What does this perennial human experience tell us about reality? Can reverence be toward nothing? What is at the centre of our reverence? Does the human instinct for reverence point us to something that would be worthy of our reverence? What *would* be worthy of it?

The ongoing religious quest of humankind, has been to discover something truly worthy of our ineradicable impulse to reverence. The revelations of all religious experience are revelations of what it must be like. As we saw in chapter 4, those revelations have evolved over the last few thousand years, as humankind has gradually refined its intuitions about what would be truly worthy of our deepest reverence.

The Western traditions (as we saw in chapter 11) take a different tack on this than the Eastern traditions. While all agree (as I noted in chapter 9) that whatever is behind the universe – "the ground of everything that is"[73] – must, have the qualities of being, unity, and truth, none of the Western traditions embrace what sometimes appears to be assumed by many Eastern traditions: that this reality is an undifferentiated mixture of goodness and evil, of blessing and sorrow, from which wisdom teaches one to escape, through what the Tao calls "freedom from attachment" or the *Bhagavad Gita* calls "an attitude of detachment," or even, as in the Buddhist tradition, through the complete extinction of the ego.[74] Instead, Western traditions declare this oneness to be also good and loving. For if things, as a whole, are really part of a oneness, if they work together, "all things must work together for good," as Paul put it, in his great letter to the Romans.[75]

For the Western mind, this is the proper description of a mystery that would be truly worthy of our reverence.

Obviously, this is a "projection" of human ideas and hopes, as Ludwig Feuerbach rightly claimed.[76] But is that *all* it is? To stop where Feuerbach did would be to fall into the perennial error of mistaking "the causes, the conditions and the occasions of our becoming conscious of certain truths and realities for the truths and realities themselves."[77] Paul himself declared (as I recalled in chapters 5 and 9) that faith is a form of hope, and that it is by hope that we are saved. While the revelation of a mystery that is both good and loving may well be a projection of human hopes, the experience of Western spirituality is that those hopes are somehow fulfilled, even in the hoping itself.[78] The spirit encountered within is not encountered *only* there. There is an otherness of the spirit that is just as "real" as the otherness of the material world. Northrop Frye has described such experience this way: "God, Word, Spirit, Father and the like ... are, at first, the objective counterparts of subjective psychic elements in the human complex, and as long as they are that they could be called pure projections. But as the subject-object cleavage becomes increasingly unsatisfactory, subject and object merge in an intermediate verbal world, where a Word not our own, though also our own, proclaims and a Spirit not our own, though also our own, responds."[79]

Frye describes this experience as occurring in an "intermediate *verbal* world." But words are only one of the means through which the creative energies of humankind turn hope and trust into substantive realities that dissolve the separation between subject and object.[80] In the kind of unselfing love affirmed by all three Western traditions, for example, "the person who is loving is simultaneously affirming the Otherness of that which is loved and their deep involvement with that Other. This takes us way beyond the objective/subjective divide."[81] The subject/object cleavage is itself a product of self-assertion. As we saw in Chapter 4, it is self-assertion – the "self-assertive spontaneity" of the ego in the form of rational consciousness – that makes us encounter the world as separate object. In the world as it is revealed by the virtues of reverence, a world of self-*giving* rather than self-*seeking*, this distinction disappears.[82] In this deeper kind of experience, we encounter instead "a *relationship* where giving and receiving merge."[83] We encounter (as Yury Zhivago did) the power behind and before even the words and sentences we speak, "concealed behind our talk as its ground" – "a spiritual reality, an otherness of a creative power not ourselves."[84]

But this kind of reality will always remain a mystery. Because it is both too close to us – as close as our own being, and therefore invisible to us – and as large as all reality, of which we are too small a part to comprehend the totality. The deepest wisdom of humankind has always been that the right attitude to adopt to this kind of mystery is a spirit of the most profound reverence, a spirit that, paradoxically, ends by making human beings at once most noble and most human. Yet another mystery: that the highest form of freedom turns out to be a kind of surrender. In fact, that is the literal meaning of *islam* in Arabic: surrender.[85]

We must "surrender completely before the mystery of existence." But when we do, "when we let go completely, we do not fall."[86] By losing ourselves, the great mystery at the heart of religious experience declares, we somehow find ourselves. As C.G. Jung said, "Being a part, man cannot grasp the whole. He is at its mercy. He may assent to it, or rebel against it; but he is caught up in it and enclosed within it ... If he possesses a grain of wisdom, he will lay down his arms and name the unknown by the more unknown, *ignotum per ignotus* – that is by the name of God. That is a confession of his subjection, his imperfection, and his dependence; but at the same time a testimony to his freedom to choose between truth and error."[87]

Actually, the name we give this reality is not the most important thing. *Tao*, *Dharma*, *Atman*, and *Brahman* are good words, too. What *is* important is what we do about it. Faith, as Northrop Frye concludes, is not developed "by clogging the air with questions of the 'Does God really exist?' type and answering them with equal nonsense, but in working, in words and other media, toward a peace that passes understanding ... a peace infinite in both its source and goal."[88] The answer to the question "Who is God?" says Karl Rahner, "is love your neighbour ... so that you genuinely transcend yourself in a properly incomprehensible unselfishness, and then you will know what is meant by God, even if you were never to hear the word, the name, 'God'."[89]

✳

If you are one of the people for whom life is more than a chance collision of atoms, and who do encounter (as I suspect most do) an "inwardness infinitely interested in existing," you probably have also recognized the limits of the virtues of self-assertion.[90] You already sense the need to develop and nurture also the virtues of reverence. Not just for the planet, or for your family and community, though they won't survive the loss of these virtues either. But also for yourself. Because without them, you will only be half a person.

There are many secular ways today to nourish and support these virtues in your life. You have probably already begun to explore some of them. But, as you yourself may have already begun to recognize, they will only take you so far. If you want to go beyond what they can offer, you will need to begin a spiritual journey or quest within one of the world's great religious traditions, one that can offer you real depth, riches, and rigour.

You may think you need to have some kind of prior "conversion" experience or belief. But one of the main points of this book is that that's another illusion of our modern culture. If some encounter (of the kind I discussed in chapter 6) has already awakened in you a yearning, a hunger, an awareness, or a need, what you require is more such encounters. It's a mistake to think you need to have discovered something called "faith" before you can seek them out. On the contrary, faith, properly understood, is the name for the search itself. And the best way to seek them is through sincere acts of religious practice that will bring you again – and again – into the presence of the sacred. Not empty gestures, but sincere acts of searching that are part of an honest quest or pilgrimage. If two people are standing in exactly the same place, one may experience the sacred and the other may not, because one is looking for it, and the other isn't. "Wherever you turn your eyes the world can shine like transfiguration," writes Marilynne Robinson. "You don't have to bring a thing to it, except a little willingness to see."[91]

The place to start on such a spiritual journey is therefore not with religious beliefs, but rather by beginning to develop some religious habits. John of the Cross said that faith is an "obscure habit of union," that is to say (in the language of this book) a habit of reverence.[92] American writer Ari L. Goldman (b. 1949) makes a comparison between religious practice and physical exercise. No one expects to stay in shape, much less to run in the Boston Marathon, without regular exercise. So no one should expect to have a spiritual life without the same kind of regular practice and discipline. "The way I see it," says Goldman, "we're all exercising."[93] When we talk about religious "practice," we use the word in two ways: the doing *of* an action, here and now; but also practicing *for* the action, developing your spiritual muscles and reflexes for the long-distance run of your whole life, through regular "exercise."

A life of religious practice is therefore, fundamentally, a life of regular religious habits. One of these, in many traditions, is regular participation in the rituals and ceremonies of the tradition. If you're lucky, or wise, your chosen tradition will have a rich heritage of worship – the activity of acknowledging ultimate worth – a deep wealth of ritual, music, song, poetry, and story that will make your participation in such regular exercises of reverence joyful, meaningful and nourishing, perhaps even thrilling. If it doesn't, you may want to look around.

But this is only the starting point.[94] You will soon need to go beyond regular participation in the practices and rituals in at least two ways. First, by undertaking your own private exercises of prayer, meditation, and reading.[95] If you have made it to this point in this book, you will certainly enjoy digging into the spiritual classics of your own tradition, some of which I hope may already have been mentioned here. But the second way you will need to go beyond the rituals – and even beyond the private prayers, reading, and meditations of your tradition – is in your own outlook and behaviour: to use a spatial image once again, in the turning of your own heart. The inner transformation that enlightens the mind and warms the heart. This is, in the end, where it all leads. The other practices are only preparation and support for this.

The only thing you need to bring to the journey is a spirit of reverence, hope, and trust. It's important to remember that the original meaning of the Latin word *credo*, which we now translate as "I believe," was apparently "I trust."[96] So you need to start by trusting, not believing. The kind of trust I'm talking about is not trust in specific people, or institutions – being human, they will always be fallible – but rather in the greater realities they are meant to serve. As we also saw in chapter 5, this kind of trust can be called fundamental, ultimate, or "primal trust," the kind that provides a foundation for a whole life.[97]

If a life of religious practice is a life of religious habits, the habits are both of feeling and behaviour. Remember what we saw in chapter 1: virtues have an inside and an outside. The outside is a habit of behaviour; the inside is a habit of feeling that accompanies the behaviour. These work together. If you start with the behaviour, you will almost certainly begin to develop habits of feeling, too.[98] But it's a two-way street. Habits of feeling also shape behaviours. So you should start, as far as you can, with two of the most important behaviours and feelings, which are trust and hope. Trust and hope work together too. Hope creates trust, and trust nourishes hope. And together, as Thomas Aquinas said, they lead to love.[99]

This may sound too easy but it isn't easy at all, for at least three reasons. First of all, it's not "natural" (at least not in the modern sense of the word), and it's not reasonable. No process of rational thought can lead you to these three virtues.[100] None of the lists of traditional, reasonable virtues – those the ancient philosophers recommended – contained them. Thomas Aquinas called them the theological, heroic, or divine virtues.[101] And, as Charles Taylor notes, they were one of the things left behind on the road to the modern world.[102] Recovering these virtues means giving an entirely new spin to the modern virtues of self-assertion, by rediscovering what self-assertion can mean when it is allied to the spirit of reverence. This will involve reaching back, as William Barrett suggested, "beyond post-Kantian German philosophy to an older meaning of the will: to the meaning that *voluntas* had for some medieval philosophers, which goes back to St Augustine and beyond him to the *Eros* of Plato. Perhaps the will, at its deepest, does not connote self-assertion and dominance, but love and acquiescence; not the will to power but the will to prayer."[103]

Cultivating the virtues of trust, hope, and love will also not be easy, because neither they nor anything else can make life smooth sailing. It will still be full of pain, loneliness, disappointment, and sorrow. In fact, a religious life may even add something to that load at times, because it brings its own share of hard moments, as we have already seen: the inevitable moments of doubt and despair, the dark nights of the soul. No religious tradition can promise to rid you of any of this, and none do. In fact, religious practice is, in part, a response to these very facts of life, which the modern search for "happiness" prefers to bury. "Religion," Susan Neiman remarks "is one kind of attempt to solve the problem of evil."[104] What most religious traditions offer is not a promise that you will not encounter sorrow, pain, or fear but rather a promise that you will not be alone when you do. That you will be comforted.[105]

To get an idea of just how far this kind of promise can go, think of the worst possible thing that could happen to you. What is it? Whatever you have thought of, there's something worse still. And I already talked about it, in chapter 12. The worst possible thing that could happen to you would be the end of the world itself. But this is a possibility the three Western religious traditions have already thought about. In fact, they have been thinking about it for thousands of years. And their answer is that even in this, the worst possible of all evils, love would still be there, in the heart of it. God is our refuge and strength, a very present help in trouble, the Psalms declare to us. Therefore will we not fear, *though the earth itself be removed,* and though the mountains be carried into the midst of the sea. Even in this, the very worst possible scenario from the climate change we have brought upon ourselves, the Lord of hosts would still be with us, the Psalms promise; the God of Jacob would still be our refuge.[106]

The third reason beginning a real spiritual journey will not be easy for you is that there is a cost. Yes, there is comfort to be gained. Yes, there is a peace that passes all understanding. Yes, there is trust, and hope. But they come at a price. The price is in your own actions, the transformation of your own will, the turning of your own heart.

To underscore this price, what it entails, and what it purchases, let's end with someone who has been a regular companion throughout this book. One of the sermons Samuel Johnson composed for his clergyman friends is about trust. In that great sermon, Johnson declared that "peace was to be attained by trust in God, and by that only." But trust in God, he explained, is not to be obtained by mental thought, by comforting ourselves with sentimental ideas about God's inherent goodness, but rather through our own behaviour, our own actions, our own practices. "Trust in God, that trust to which perfect peace is promised, is to be obtained only by repentance, obedience and supplication, not by nourishing in our hearts a confused idea of the goodness of God ... He that hopes to find peace by trusting God, must obey him ... *this constant and devout practice, is both the effect, and cause, of confidence in God* ... by recollecting his promises, [the seeker] will confirm himself in the hope of obtaining what he desires, and if, to secure these promises he steadily practices the duties on which they depend, he will soon find his mind stayed on God, and be kept in perfect peace, because he trusteth in him."[107]

Trust in God, and the peace that it offers, Johnson reminds us once again, are obtained by what we *do* before they can become the way we *think*. Our *practice* is both cause and effect, at the same time.[108]

And they who truly and sincerely thirst after God, and seek him with their whole heart, may find that he meets them half way. They may find that he is already present in the thirst, and is to be found in the search itself, even in the very thought of searching. Going through this vale of tears, they will be able to use it for a well. And, if they do, they will then find that the river of God is full of water. They will be like a tree sending out its roots by the stream: it does not fear when the drought comes, and it does not cease to bear fruit. And if they persevere to the end, they may also find what is promised, that those who put their trust in the Lord are even as the mount Zion, which may not be removed, but stands fast, forever.[109]

# Notes

## EPIGRAPHS AND PREFACE

1 "The Dialectic of Mind: Some Thoughts on Reason and Civility," *Journal of Canadian Studies* 6, no. 3 (February 1971), 1–2, 63–4. See also: "The Virtues of Reverence," 12, no. 1 (February 1977), 1–2, 92–5; "Liberalism and Censorship," 13, no. 4 (Winter 1978–79), 1–2, 120–2; "The Educational Contract," 14, no. 2 (Summer 1979) 1–2, 142–5; "The Other Daemon," 14, no. 4 (Winter 1979–80), 1–2, 151–2; "Two Solitudes," 15, no. 1 (Spring 1980), 1–2, 123–4.

2 Again, see the *Journal of Canadian Studies* for the following essays: "Mr. Stanfield's Failure," 9, no. 1 (February 1974) 1–2, 66–7; "The Sympathy of the Whole," 12, no. 2 (Spring 1977), 1–2, 93; and "The Meaning of Monarchy," 12, no. 4 (Summer 1977), 1–2, 115–17.

3 Samuel Taylor Coleridge, *Coleridge's Notebooks*, ed. Seamus Perry (Oxford: Oxford University Press, 2002), 125.

4 Étienne Gilson, *L'Esprit de la philosophie médiévale* (Paris: Vrin, 1943, 1989), 62.

5 T.H. White, *The Once and Future King*, (London: HarperCollins, 1996), 508.

6 Robertson Davies, *The Manticore* (Toronto: Macmillan, 1972), 185.

## INTRODUCTION

1 In this book the word "Western" (with a capital) will be used normally in a cultural sense to refer to cultures with roots in western Europe which can now also be found in North America and Australasia, among other places. However, when the word is used specifically in discussion of the religious

traditions, it will also include Islam which, for reasons discussed in chapter 4, is clearly part of the religious world of the West rather than of the East.

2 "Without reason we perish; but reason does not go all the way down ... [I]t is only if reason can draw on energies and resources deeper, more tenacious, and less fragile than itself that it is capable of prevailing." Terry Eagleton, *Reason, Faith, and Revolution: Reflections on the God Debate* (New Haven: Yale University Press, 2009), 109–10.

3 Iris Murdoch calls this "a proof by morality and love, not by logic." *Metaphysics as a Guide to Morals* (London: Vintage, 1992, 2003), 509. Similarly, N.T. Wright refers to an "epistemology of love," a knowing that is a "form of love," in *Surprised by Hope: Rethinking Heaven, the Resurrection, and the Mission of the Church* (New York: HarperCollins, 2008), 239.

## CHAPTER ONE

1 Hans-Georg Gadamer, *Truth and Method* (New York: Continuum, 2002), 463.

2 Hugh Hood, *Reservoir Ravine* (Ottawa: Oberon Press, 1979), 195–6.

3 In philosophical language, this can be called the "transcendental condition of interlocution." Charles Taylor, *Sources of the Self: The Making of the Modern Identity* (Cambridge, Mass: Harvard University Press, 1989), 39.

4 *Exodus* 20:12; *Deuteronomy* 5:16; *Genesis* 2:24; *Matthew* 19:5.

5 Francis Bacon, *Of the Dignity and Advancement of Learning*, cited in Michael Bilig, Susan Condor, Derek Edwards, Mike Gane, David Middleton, and Alan Radley, *Ideological Dilemmas: A Social Psychology of Everyday Thinking* (London: Sage Publications, 1988), 15–16. For another modern list of paired proverbs, see Robert E. Quinn, *Beyond Rational Management: Mastering the Paradoxes and Competing Demands of High Performance* (San Francisco: Jossey-Bass, 1988), 30.

6 James Q. Wilson, *The Moral Sense* (New York: The Free Press, 1993), 234.

7 Susanne K. Langer, *Mind: An Essay on Human Feeling*, Vol. 1 (Baltimore: Johns Hopkins University Press, 1967), 354.

8 "Only in the continuous encounter with other persons does the person become and remain a person." Paul Tillich, *The Courage to Be* (New Haven: Yale University Press, 1952), 91.

9 Irvin D. Yalom, *Love's Executioner* (New York: HarperCollins, 1990), 7.

10 Marcel Gauchet, *The Disenchantment of the World: A Political History of Religion*, translated by Oscar Bruge (Princeton: Princeton University Press, 1997), 11–12.

11  Hans-Georg Gadamer, *Dialogue and Dialectic: Eight Hermeneutical Studies on Plato* (New Haven: Yale University Press, 1980). The problem of the one and the many (and other related dualities) goes back at least to the pre-Socratic Greek philosophers known as the Pythagoreans. See Aristotle, *Metaphysics*, Book I, Chapter 5, 985b 23–986a 30, translated by W.D. Ross, in Richard McKeon, ed., *The Basic Works of Aristotle* (New York: Random House, 1941, 1968), 698–9; G.S. Kirk and J.E. Raven, *The Presocratic Philosophers* (Cambridge: Cambridge University Press, 1964), 236–62.

12  G.W.F. Hegel, *Early Theological Writings*, translated by T.M. Knox and Richard Kroner (Chicago: University of Chicago Press, 1948), 312, cited in Emil J. Fackenheim, *The Religious Dimension of Hegel's Thought* (Boston: Beacon Press, 1967), 26. This formula has been called Hegel's whole future philosophical system "in a nutshell." Although his youthful formula seems to me both clearer and more useful, Hegel's own mature formula for expressing this dialectic was: "The Absolute is the identity of Identity and Non-Identity," or "the identity of the Identical and the non-Identical." Ibid, 247. Charles Taylor has called this "perhaps the central and most 'mind-blowing' idea of the Hegelian system." Charles Taylor, *Hegel* (Cambridge: Cambridge University Press, 1975), 49. One of Hegel's distant precursors was the Roman neo-Platonic philosopher Plotinus, who observed that "the perceptible is ... identity and difference." Plotinus, *Enneads*, V, 9, 10, in Elmer O'Brien, ed., *The Essential Plotinus* (New York: Mentor Books, 1964), 54. On this "polar structure of being," see also Tillich, *The Courage to Be*, 86–90; and Martin Buber, *I and Thou*, second edition, translated by Ronald Gregor Smith (New York: Charles Scribner's Sons, 1958), 3, 62–5, 77, 95–6, 100–1, 116.

13  Thomas Hobbes, *Leviathan*, Part I, Chapter 11 (Indianapolis and New York: Bobbs-Merrill, 1958), 86; Baruch Spinoza, *Ethics*, Third Part, Propositions VI and VII, in John Wild, ed., *Spinoza Selections* (New York: Charles Scribner's Sons, 1930), 215–16; G.W.F. Hegel, "The Spirit of Christianity and its Fate," in *Early Theological Writings*, 186, cited in Taylor, *Hegel*, 58; T.H. Green, *Lectures on the Principles of Political Obligation* (London: Longmans, Green, 1927), 10; J.S. Mill, *On Liberty* (Harmondsworth: Penguin Books, 1974), 127; Paul Tillich, *The Courage to Be*, especially 18–31.

14  Aristotle defined a virtue (depending on the translation) as a "state of character" or a "disposition" in his *Nicomachean Ethics*, Book II, Chapters 5–6, 1106a, 10–25 as translated by W.D. Ross, in McKeon, ed., *The Basic Works of Aristotle*, 957, and by J.A.K. Thomson, as revised by Hugh Tredennick

(London: Penguin Books, 2004), 39–40. Thomas Aquinas defined a virtue as "a good habit" in his *Summa Theologica*, Ia-2ae. lv. 3, in St Thomas Aquinas, *Philosophical Texts*, selected and translated by Thomas Gilby (London: Oxford University Press, 1951, 1956), 301. Bernard Williams defines a virtue as "an ethically admirable disposition of character ... [virtues] involve characteristic patterns of desire and motivation" in *Ethics and the Limits of Philosophy* (Cambridge, Mass.: Harvard University Press, 1985), 9. Alasdair MacIntyre defines a virtue as "an acquired human quality the possession and exercise of which tends to enable us to achieve those goods that are internal to practices and the lack of which effectively prevents us from achieving any such goods." *After Virtue*, second edition (Notre Dame: University of Notre Dame Press, 1984), 191. Finally, N.T. Wright defines virtue as "what happens when wise and courageous choices have become 'second nature.'" *After You Believe: Why Christian Character Matters* (New York: HarperCollins, 2010), 21.

15 Aristotle, *The Nicomachean Ethics*, Book II, Chapter 3, 1104b 5–1105a 17; Chapter 5, 1105b 20–1106a 15; Chapters 8 and 9, 1108b 10–1109b 27; Book X, Chapter 9, 1179b 20–31, translated by Thomson, revised by Tredennick, 35–7, 46–9, 278.

16 Robert N. Bellah, Richard Madsen, William M. Sullivan, Ann Swidler, and Steven M. Tipton, *Habits of the Heart*, updated edition with a new introduction (Berkeley and Los Angeles: University of California Press, 1985, 1996), 111.

17 Taylor, *Sources of the Self*, 395.

18 Bellah et al., *Habits of the Heart*, 127; Charles Taylor, *A Secular Age* (Cambridge and London: The Belknap Press of Harvard University Press, 2007), 171.

19 Michael Ignatieff, *The Rights Revolution* (Toronto: Anansi, 2000); Taylor, *Sources of the Self*, 305. That the language of "rights" is now almost the only language in which social goods can be discussed was nicely illustrated by the recent declaration of Antonio Tajani, the European Union's commissioner for enterprise and industry: "Travelling for tourism is a right." Bojan Pancevski, "Tourism a Human Right, EU Decides," *Ottawa Citizen*, 19 April, 2010, 1–2.

20 Alexis de Tocqueville, *L'ancien régime et la Révolution* (Paris: Gallimard, 1967), 203.

21 C.B. Macpherson, *The Political Theory of Possessive Individualism: Hobbes to Locke* (Oxford: Oxford University Press, 1962). Robert Bellah and his colleagues use the term "utilitarian individualism" to describe the contemporary expression of this outlook, but Macpherson's historical term seems to me more readily comprehensible to the ordinary reader. See Bellah et al., *Habits of the Heart*, 27.

22 Charles Taylor developed the term "expressivism" under the influence of Isaiah Berlin's term "expressionism," originally used to describe the influence of Herder on the post-Enlightenment. Taylor alters the noun to avoid confusion with the twentieth-century artistic movement also called "expressionism." *Hegel*, 13.

23 Christopher Lasch, *The Culture of Narcissism: American Life in an Age of Diminishing Expectations* (New York: W.W. Norton, 1978).

24 Bellah et al., *Habits of the Heart*, 333–4. See also 27, 33–5, 47.

25 Taylor, *A Secular Age*, 473–5.

## CHAPTER TWO

1 "Young men should always show their elders the respect due to their age by rising at their approach, and giving up their seats to them, and similar courtesies." Aristotle, *The Nicomachean Ethics*, Book IX, Chapter 2, 1165a 25–30, translated by J.A.K. Thomson, revised by Hugh Tredennick (London: Penguin Classics, 2004), 233.

2 Marcel Gauchet, *The Disenchantment of the World: A Political History of Religion*, translated by Oscar Bruge (Princeton: Princeton University Press, 1997), 178.

3 The use of the word "reverence" in this way, to express family virtues, among others, seems well established in the history of the English language. See, for example, John Locke, *Some Thoughts Concerning Education* (1692) in *On Politics and Education* (Roslyn, NY: Walter J. Black, 1947), 287, 291.

4 From a letter of Nahmanides to his son, in Israel Abrahams, *Hebrew Ethical Wills* (Philadelphia: Jewish Publication Society, 1948), 95–8, in Arthur Hertzberg, ed., *Judaism* (New York: Washington Square Press, 1963), 186.

5 Susan Neiman calls these "two moral paradigms" the "two Abrahams," based on two contrasting stories about the biblical Abraham: Abraham at Mount Moriah and Abraham at Sodom; the Abraham who "submits" and the Abraham who "questions." *Moral Clarity: A Guide for Grown-Up Idealists* (Orlando: Harcourt, 2008), 12–13. Deirdre McCloskey calls these two families of virtues the "P and S" virtues. "P" stands for a list of virtues or "modes of being" all beginning with the letter "P," especially "profane" and "prudence." "S" stands for a similar list, especially "sacred" and "solidarity." But because of the literary device of only including words beginning with these two letters, the lists are necessarily incomplete lists of the virtues of self-assertion and of reverence. The "P" list lacks courage, for example. And the "S" list lacks justice, and even reverence itself. Deirdre N. McCloskey,

*The Bourgeois Virtues: Ethics for an Age of Commerce* (Chicago: University of Chicago Press, 2006), 408.

6  Martha Nussbaum, *Upheavals of Thought: The Intelligence of the Emotions* (Cambridge: Cambridge University Press, 2001), 54.

7  "Wonder and awe are akin, but distinct: wonder is outward-moving, exuberant, whereas awe is linked with bending or making oneself small. In wonder I want to leap or run, in awe to kneel." Ibid, note 53.

8  Pascal, *Pensées* (Paris: Garnier-Flammarion), 139, 145. "Qu'est-ce qu'un homme dans l'infini? ... Le silence éternel de ces espaces infinis m'effraie." My translation.

9  Michael Frayn, *The Human Touch: Our Part in the Creation of the Universe* (London: Faber and Faber, 2006), 113.

10  Samuel Johnson, *The Rambler* 41 (7 August, 1750), in G.B. Hill, ed., *Select Essays of Dr. Johnson*, Vol. 1 (London: J.M. Dent and Co., 1889), 56. See also Frayn, *The Human Touch*, 135–7.

11  Samuel Johnson, quoted in James Boswell, *The Journal of a Tour to the Hebrides*, cited in W. Jackson Bate, *Samuel Johnson* (New York: Harcourt Brace, 1975), 473.

12  "[L]e présent est gros de l'avenir." G.W. Leibniz, *Essais de Théodicée* (Paris: Garnier-Flammarion, 1969), 329; *Principes de la nature et de la grâce fondés en raison – Principes de la philosophie ou Monadologie*, ed. André Robinet (Paris: Presses Universitaires de France, 1954, 1986), 53.

13  Ernst Cassirer, *An Essay on Man* (New York: Bantam Books, 1970), 54–5.

14  Alfred North Whitehead, *The Aims of Education* (New York: The Free Press, 1967), 14. Karl Jaspers calls this "eternity in time." "On My Philosophy," translated by Felix Kaufmann, in Walter Kaufmann, ed., *Existentialism from Dostoevsky to Sartre* (Cleveland: World Publishing Company, 1956), 154. See also 139, 193.

15  Maureen Mancuso, Michael M. Atkinson, André Blais, Ian Greene, and Neil Nevitte, *A Question of Ethics: Canadians Speak Out*, revised edition (Toronto: Oxford University Press, 1998, 2006), 44. Charles Taylor cites similar French data from studies by Jean-Louis Schlegel and Sylvette Denèfle in *A Secular Age* (Cambridge and London: The Belknap Press of Harvard University Press, 2007), 824, n23.

16  Karl Rahner, *The Practice of Faith: A Handbook of Contemporary Spirituality* (New York: Crossroad, 1983), 58. "The solidarity expressed in cheerfully greeting a neighbour is a kind of love. The fleeting solidarity of the deal agreed is a kind of justice. The solidarity of the sports fan is a kind of faith." McCloskey, *The Bourgeois Virtues*, 128.

17 Paul Woodruff, *Reverence: Renewing a Forgotten Virtue* (New York: Oxford University Press, 2001), 36–7.

18 Lionel Trilling, *Sincerity and Authenticity* (Cambridge, Mass.: Harvard University Press, 1972), 41.

## CHAPTER THREE

1 While I have used the word "beginning" here, it should be understood primarily in a conceptual or a "logical" sense. From a purely historical or anthropological perspective, the process may well have worked in the opposite direction, or in all directions simultaneously. But the logical chain I am exploring would have been there, from the beginning. As Aristotle notes: "[W]hat is last in the order of analysis seems to be first in the order of becoming." *Nicomachean Ethics*, Book III, Chapter 3, 1112b 20–5, translated by W.D. Ross, in Richard McKeon, ed., *The Basic Works of Aristotle* (New York: Random House, 1941, 1968), 970.

2 Confucius, *The Analects*, 1.2, translated by D.C. Lau (London: Penguin Books, 1979), 59; Aristotle, *The Nicomachean Ethics*, Book II, translated by J.A.K. Thomson, revised by Hugh Tredennick (London: Penguin Classics, 2004), 31–49; James Q. Wilson, *The Moral Sense* (New York: The Free Press, 1993), 243–4.

3 Confucius, *The Analects*, 9.11, quoted in Paul Woodruff, *Reverence: Renewing a Forgotten Virtue* (New York: Oxford University Press, 2001), 146.

4 Although he normally refrains from talking about it, Confucius is quite explicit that "Heaven is the author of the virtue that is in me," and the Way he taught was the "Way of Heaven." Confucius, *The Analects*, 7.23, translated by Lau, 89.

5 Karl Rahner, *The Practice of Faith: A Handbook of Contemporary Spirituality* (New York: Crossroad, 1983), 57.

6 The great medieval Christian thinker, Bernard de Clairvaux, described these two directions of the spiritual journey: "I ascended above what was highest in me ... I descended to my lowest depths ... I looked to the outside ... I looked within." Bernard of Clairvaux, *Sermons on the Song of Songs*, in Bernard McGinn, ed., *The Essential Writings of Christian Mysticism* (New York: Modern Library, 2006), 223. Bernard may have had in mind Plotinus' much earlier description of the spiritual journey "outside everything else and inside myself." Plotinus, *Enneads*, IV, 8, 1, in Elmer O'Brien, ed., *The Essential Plotinus* (New York: Mentor Books, 1964), 62.

7 Charles Taylor, *Sources of the Self: The Making of the Modern Identity* (Cambridge, Mass.: Harvard University Press, 1989), 6.

8  Bernard Lonergan, "Variations in Fundamental Theology," a 1973 lecture at
   Trinity College of the University of Toronto, cited in Frederick E. Crowe,
   "Editors' Preface" in Bernard Lonergan, *Verbum: Word and Idea*, eds.
   Frederick E. Crowe and Robert M. Doran, *Collected Works of Bernard
   Lonergan*, Vol. 2 (Toronto: University of Toronto Press, 1997), viii.
9  Karl Jaspers calls this limitless horizon *within* which humans exist the
   "Encompassing" or the "Comprehensive" (depending on the translation).
   *Reason and Existenz*, translated by William Earle, in Walter Kaufmann, ed.,
   *Existentialism from Dostoevsky to Sartre* (Cleveland: World Publishing
   Company, 1956), 184–6; *Way to Wisdom*, translated by Ralph Manheim
   (New Haven: Yale University Press, 1960), 28–38.
10 Rahner, *The Practice of Faith*, 3, 6, 42.
11 Karl Jaspers calls this limitless horizon of the *internal* human landscape the
   "Encompassing which we are." *Reason and Existenz*, in Kaufmann, ed.,
   *Existentialism*, 186–91.
12 R.G. Collingwood, *The New Leviathan* (London: Oxford University Press,
   1942, 1966), 18–39.
13 Susanne K. Langer, *Mind: An Essay on Human Feeling*, Vol. 1 (Baltimore:
   Johns Hopkins University Press, 1967), 149.
14 Hans-Georg Gadamer, *Dialogue and Dialectic: Eight Hermeneutical Studies
   on Plato*, translated and with an introduction by P. Christopher Smith (New
   Haven and London: Yale University Press, 1980), 88.
15 *Chāndogya Upanishad*, Chapters 8–16, in *The Upanishads*, translated and
   edited by Valerie J. Roebuck (London: Penguin Books, 2003), 176–80.
16 The image of "deeper" is a notoriously ambiguous one and may yield different conclusions depending on the perspective from which it is used. For
   Augustine, influenced by Greek traditions of rationalism, the deepest inner
   core of humankind was reason itself. Denys Turner, *The Darkness of God:
   Negativity in Christian Mysticism* (Cambridge: Cambridge University Press,
   1995), 94. This view (a highly defensible one, depending on the perspective)
   was very influential in the Christian tradition, and yielded some of the problems which are discussed in chapter 5, including an eventual split between a
   dominant religious emphasis on belief, doctrine, and theology on the one
   hand, and a marginalized spirituality described as "piety" or "mysticism" on
   the other.
17 Martin Buber, *I and Thou*, second edition, translated by Ronald Gregor
   Smith (New York: Charles Scribner's Sons, 1958), 39. In order to avoid misunderstanding, I should point out that Buber does *not* mean it is "his whole
   being" with which man "enters into relation." Rather, entering into "relation"

with something or someone *else* is the primal act, and the spiritual person performs this primal act "with his whole being."

18 Paul Tillich, *The Courage to Be* (New Haven: Yale University Press, 1952), 82, 123–4. Similarly, Coleridge said that "the Spirit is an Energy not a Soul." Marginal note on a copy of *Aids to Reflection*, cited in Owen Barfield, *What Coleridge Thought* (Middletown: Wesleyan University Press, 1971), 147. N.T. Wright suggests that, in the New Testament, the word "soul" refers "not to a disembodied entity hidden within the outer shell of the disposable body but rather to what we would call the whole person or personality, seen as being confronted by God." N.T. Wright, *Surprised by Hope: Rethinking Heaven, the Resurrection, and the Mission of the Church* (New York: HarperCollins, 2008), 28.

19 Aristotle, *The Nicomachean Ethics*, Book II, Chapter 6, 1106a 15–20, translated by Thomson, revised by Tredennick, 39–40.

20 Aristotle, *Physics*, Book 2, Chapter 3, 194b 20–195a, 20, translated by R.P. Hardie and R.K. Gaye; *Metaphysics*, Book 1, Chapter 2, 983a 25–983b 5; Book V, Chapter 1, 1013a 20–35; Book VIII, Chapter 4, 1044a 30–1044b, translated by W.D. Ross, in Richard McKeon, ed., *The Basic Works of Aristotle* (New York: The Modern Library, 1941), 240–1, 693, 752, 817. On the four types of cause, see also Thomas Aquinas, Commentary, V *Metaphysics, lect.* 2 in St Thomas Aquinas, *Philosophical Texts*, selected and translated by Thomas Gilby (London: Oxford University Press, 1951, 1956), 43–6.

21 Ewert Cousins and G. Wakefield, quoted in Bernard McGinn, "The Letter and the Spirit: Spirituality as an Academic Discipline" in Elizabeth A. Dreyer and Mark S. Burrows, eds., *Minding the Spirit: The Study of Christian Spirituality* (Baltimore: Johns Hopkins University Press, 2005), 32.

22 Evelyn Underhill, *Mysticism: A Study of the Nature and Development of Man's Spiritual Consciousness* (1911), quoted in Richard H. Schmidt, ed., *Glorious Companions: Five Centuries of Anglican Spirituality* (Grand Rapids: Wm. B. Eerdmans, 2002), 243. Underhill's term was "mysticism" rather than "spirituality," but the intent was clearly the same, as the title indicates.

23 In spirituality, "vitality and intentionality are united." Tillich, *The Courage to Be*, 84. This is where, as Karl Jaspers puts it, "for the first time there is both impulse and goal." *Reason and Existenz*, in Kaufmann, ed., *Existentialism*, 194.

24 Thomas McFarland, *Originality and Imagination* (Baltimore: Johns Hopkins University Press, 1985), 199.

25 Terry Eagleton, *Reason, Faith, and Revolution: Reflections on the God Debate* (New Haven: Yale University Press, 2009), 83.

26  Susanne K. Langer, *Feeling and Form* (New York: Scribner's, 1953), 405.

27  The two terms of this contrast are from Charles Norris Cochrane, *Christianity and Classical Culture* (New York: Oxford University Press, 1976), 29. But he used them in the *opposite* direction: to describe the evolution from the pagan to the Christian empire of Rome.

28  Margaret Donaldson, *Human Minds: An Exploration* (New York: Allen Lane, 1993)

29  W.H. Auden, *Forewords and Afterwords* (New York: Vintage Books, 1974), 28.

30  Leszek Kolakowski, *Religion* (New York: Oxford University Press, 1983), 195. If we were to put this dilemma, prematurely, into religious language, we could say, with Blaise Pascal, that it is a very long way from the knowledge to the love of God. *Pensées* (Paris: Garnier-Flammarion, 1973), 241. "Qu'il y a loin de la connaissance de Dieu à l'aimer!"

31  David Smail, *Illusion and Reality: The Meaning of Anxiety* (London: J.M. Dent, 1984), 141–6.

32  Charles Taylor, *A Secular Age* (Cambridge and London: The Belknap Press of Harvard University Press, 2007), 360.

33  On "general" and "specific" spirituality, see the comments of von Balthasar, Aumann, and Principe quoted in McGinn, "The Letter and the Spirit," 31.

34  Mary Froelich defines spirituality as "the human spirit fully in act." This means "the core dimension of the human person radically engaged with reality (both contingent and transcendent). It refers to human persons being, living, acting according to their fullest intrinsic potential – thus, ultimately, in the fullness of interpersonal, communal, and mystical relationship." "Spiritual Discipline, Discipline of Spirituality: Revisiting Questions of Definition and Method," in Dreyer and Burrows, eds., *Minding the Spirit*, 71.

## CHAPTER FOUR

1  I may seem at first to be parting company here with contemporary neo-orthodox theologians, such as N.T. Wright, whose work I admire and am grateful to cite rather frequently in this book. Christian neo-orthodoxy sometimes appears to react against the rediscovery of *religio* (or "spirituality") as the foundation of religious life because this rediscovery risks veering toward a purely private spirituality, a modern "quietism," or a politically-correct relativism. (N.T. Wright, *Surprised by Hope: Rethinking Heaven, the Resurrection, and the Mission of the Church* (New York: HarperCollins, 2008), 235–7.) Neo-orthodoxy therefore re-emphasizes, instead, fidelity to the message of the scriptures. This is fine, as far as it goes. But this book asks:

how can the scriptures gain a hearing or acquire any deep authority and meaning except within a prior practice of reverence or authentic encounters with the spirit? The neo-orthodox view can seem to suggest that you practice the virtues "*after* you believe." (N.T. Wright, *After You Believe: Why Christian Character Matters* [New York: HarperCollins, 2010], 2–7.) This obviously isn't wrong. It may even be entirely true for those – relatively few, I think – who experience a sudden "conversion." But for everyone else it seems to me half-backwards. It is only through the practice of the virtues themselves – especially what I call here the virtues of reverence – that most people can come to whatever it is we mean by "belief." And what *does* religious "belief" mean, in practice, if not the practice of these virtues? What does scriptural revelation lead us to if not to the very same virtues, to this kind of *life*? Even a "conversion" would wither quickly away (as they often do) unless it became rooted in *habits* of reverence. This is where the two views come together. Although we sometimes seem to get there from different directions, Bishop Wright and I end up nevertheless at the same place: in a common emphasis on transformative *action* (both personal and societal) in the "here and now" – "the transforming, shaping and marking of a life and its habits" – instead of on (or, rather, as an expression of) our ineradicable hope for some kind of future life. (Ibid, 7.)

2  C.G. Jung, "The Difference between Eastern and Western Thinking," translated by R.F.C. Hull, in Joseph Campbell, ed. *The Portable Jung* (New York, Viking Press, 1971), 495.

3  Mircea Eliade, *A History of Religious Ideas*, Vol. 1, translated by Willard R. Trask, *From the Stone Age to the Eleusinian Mysteries* (Chicago: University of Chicago Press, 1978), xiii. Emphasis added.

4  Karl Jaspers, *Way to Wisdom*, translated by Ralph Manheim (New Haven: Yale University Press, 1960), 99–103.

5  Charles Taylor, *A Secular Age* (Cambridge and London: The Belknap Press of Harvard University Press, 2007), 366–72; Marcel Gauchet, *The Disenchantment of the World: A Political History of Religion*, translated by Oscar Bruge (Princeton: Princeton University Press, 1997); Susanne K. Langer, *Mind: An Essay on Human Feeling*, Vol. II (Baltimore: Johns Hopkins University Press, 1972), 301–14; William H. McNeill, *Keeping Together in Time: Dance and Drill in Human History* (Cambridge, Mass.: Harvard University Press, 1995).

6  Robert M. Pirsig, *Zen and the Art of Motorcycle Maintenance* (New York: Bantam, 1975), 345.

7  *Buddhist Scriptures*, selected and edited by Edward Conze (Harmondsworth: Penguin Books, 1959, 1969), 113, 115.

8 Arthur Avalon (Sir Joseph Woodroffe), *The Serpent Power* (Madras: Ganesh and Co., 1913, 1924, 1931, etc.), 317–478, cited in Joseph Campbell, *Myths to Live By* (New York: Bantam Books, 1973), 109–16.

9 Ibid., 117.

10 *The Book of Chuang Tzu* in Mark Forstater, ed., *The Tao: Finding the Way of Balance and Harmony* (New York: Plume, 2003), 81.

11 Ibid, 178, 231, 95, 107.

12 Ibid, 178, 161.

13 Marcel Gauchet dates the "bifurcation" from around 3000 BCE; Joseph Campbell places the beginning of the process about 2000 BCE. Gauchet, *The Disenchantment of the World*, 10, 16; Joseph Campbell, *The Masks of God: Occidental Mythology* (Harmondsworth: Penguin Books, 1976), 72–5.

14 Campbell, *The Masks of God*, 72–5, 78, 106, 114.

15 Campbell, *Myths to Live By*, 74–5.

16 Ibid., 80.

17 Marcel Gauchet calls this the "fundamental paradox" of Western religious history: "the growth in the gods' power, which might reasonably be expected to be detrimental to humans, proves to be to their ultimate advantage." *The Disenchantment of the World*, 30.

18 In Marcel Gauchet's words, "as soon as the world was attributed to a separate subject, it became possible to separate humans from the cosmos." Ibid, 73.

19 Martin Buber, *I and Thou*, second edition, translated by Ronald Gregor Smith (New York: Charles Scribner's Sons, 1958), 18–23.

20 John S. Dunne, *The City of the Gods: A Study in Myth and Morality* (New York: Macmillan, 1965), 33.

21 Karen Armstrong, *The Case for God* (New York: Alfred A. Knopf, 2009), 73.

22 Aristotle, *The Nicomachean Ethics*, Book X, Chapter 7, 1177b 25–30, translated by J.A.K. Thomson, revised by Hugh Tredennick (London: Penguin Classics, 2004), 272.

23 Plato, *The Republic*, Book II, in *Great Dialogues of Plato*, translated by W.H.D. Rouse and edited by Eric H. Warmington and Philip G. Rouse (New York: New American Library, 1956), 175–8.

24 Plato, *Phaedrus*, in *Euthyphro, Apology, Crito, Phaedo, Phaedrus*, translated by H.N. Fowler, Loeb Classical Library, no.36 (London and Cambridge, Mass.: William Heinemann and Harvard University Press, 1914, 1966), 487–9.

25 Martha Nussbaum, *The Therapy of Desire: Theory and Practice in Hellenistic Ethics* (Princeton: Princeton University Press, 1994).

26 Eliade, *A History of Religious Ideas*, Volume 1, 304; Karen Armstrong, *The Great Transformation: The Beginnings of Our Religious Traditions* (New York: Alfred A. Knopf, 2006), 8.

27 Reza Aslan, *No god but God: The Origins, Evolution and Future of Islam* (New York: Random House, 2005), 150.

28 Elaine Pagels suggests this was a notion previously advocated only by the so-called "Johannine" Christians. *Beyond Belief* (New York: Random House, 2005), 62. Pagels may have overemphasized the role of the Gospel of John in asserting the divinity of Jesus, and underemphasized the much earlier role of Paul. It has been suggested that the idea of the Trinity is already fully implicit in the letter to the Galatians, one of the very earliest Christian documents. N.T. Wright, *Paul* (Minneapolis: Fortress Press, 2009), 98.

29 Saint Augustine, *City of God*, translated by Henry Bettenson (London: Penguin Books, 2003), 373–4.

30 *The Koran* 2:199–200, translated by N.J. Dawood (London: Penguin Books, 2003), 30. Emphasis added.

31 Karl Rahner, *The Practice of Faith: A Handbook of Contemporary Spirituality* (New York: Crossroad, 1983), 61.

32 Ibid, 178.

33 Wilfred Cantwell Smith, *The Faith of Other Men* (New York: Mentor Books, 1965), 17. Emphasis added.

### CHAPTER FIVE

1 In his otherwise admirable book, *Reverence: Renewing a Forgotten Virtue* (New York: Oxford University Press, 2001), Paul Woodruff, for example, frequently seems to assume that religious life is defined by creeds and beliefs. Michael Frayn, another thoughtful observer, also seems to equate religious faith with belief. *The Human Touch: Our Part in the Creation of the Universe* (London: Faber and Faber, 2006), 259–62. See also the comments of Steve Bruce at the beginning of chapter 13.

2 This is a shining example of what I noted at the end of the last chapter: that a religious tradition's strengths are sometimes its weaknesses, and its weaknesses sometimes reflect its strengths.

3 Maimonides notes that the early Christian Fathers, eager to convert the Hellenistic world of Asia Minor, were led to develop a "science of Dogmatics" modelled on the Greek thought of the communities they were addressing. *The Guide for the Perplexed*, translated by M. Friedländer (New York: Dover Publications, 1956), 109. Marcel Gauchet suggests the distinctive Christian emphasis on dogma also derives from the religious idea of the "Incarnation." As a "religion of Incarnation," Christianity necessarily became a "religion of interpretation." Only dogma could solve the "enigma" of the "unnatural union" of the human and divine in Christ. *The*

*Disenchantment of the World: A Political History of Religion*, translated by
Oscar Bruge (Princeton: Princeton University Press, 1979), 76–83. Diarmaid
MacCulloch seems to agree with both views: *Christianity: The First Three
Thousand Years* (New York: Viking, 2010), 30–1, 95–6, 141–3, 196, 211–28.

4  Wilfred Cantwell Smith, *The Faith of Other Men* (New York: Mentor Books,
1965), 55. Emphasis added.

5  Denys Turner, *The Darkness of God: Negativity in Christian Mysticism*
(Cambridge: Cambridge University Press, 1995), 216–25. The "organized
exploration" given the name of "theology" was itself an "invention" of the
Western Christian Church, "first given currency in the 1120s by the Paris
theologian Peter Abelard." MacCulloch, *Christianity*, 398.

6  Charles Taylor, *A Secular Age* (Cambridge and London: The Belknap Press
of Harvard University Press, 2007), 8–14, 293–4, 613–14. Diarmaid
MacCulloch suggests that, because of Empress Theodora's ninth-century
"Triumph of Orthodoxy" with its strong ensuing emphasis on art, music, and
liturgy, Eastern Orthodox Christianity displayed "much less inclination to
separate out the activity of biblical scholarship from meditation and the everyday practice of worship than is the case in the Western tradition."
*Christianity*, 455.

7  Marilynne Robinson, *The Death of Adam: Essays on Modern Thought* (New
York: Picador, 2005), 215–16; Alister McGrath, *Christianity's Dangerous
Idea: The Protestant Revolution – A History from the Sixteenth Century to
the Twenty-First* (New York: HarperCollins, 2007), 291–2.

8  John Bowden, ed., *Christianity: The Complete Guide* (Toronto: Novalis,
2005), 483.

9  John Calvin, *The Institutes of the Christian Religion*, in Alister E. McGrath,
ed., *Theology: The Basic Readings* (Oxford: Blackwell Publishing, 2008),
8–9; Alister E. McGrath, *Theology: The Basics*, second edition (Oxford:
Blackwell Publishing, 2008), 17–19; Bruce Gordon, *Calvin* (New Haven:
Yale University Press, 2009), 60. One of Martin Luther's favourite words for
faith, however, was the Latin word "fiducia" which means confidence or
trust. McGrath, *Theology: The Basics*, 10–13. The kind of knowledge Calvin
seems to have had in mind is knowledge of God's "benevolence towards us"
– his goodness, not just his existence – which allows McGrath to argue that
this knowledge is actually anchored in the kind of "encounter" I describe in
chapter 6.

10  McGrath, *Christianity's Dangerous Idea*, 102–3.

11  Patrick Collinson, "The Late Medieval Church and its Reformation:
1400–1600," in John McManners, ed. *The Oxford Illustrated History of*

*Christianity* (Oxford: Oxford University Press, 1990), 266, 263. John Calvin said that "doctrine is the soul of the Church." Calvin to Protector Somerset, 22 October 1548, cited in Gordon, *Calvin*, 255.

12 Paul Tillich, *The Courage to Be* (New Haven: Yale University Press, 1952), 132.

13 McGrath, *Christianity's Dangerous Idea*, 264.

14 As a case in point, Voltaire said that "deism is good sense not yet instructed by revelation; other religions are good sense perverted by superstition." *Philosophical Dictionary*, translated by Abner Kneeland, in Lewis White Beck, ed., *18th Century Philosophy* (New York: The Free Press, 1966), 190. "The Enlightenment theory of secularization and of the relation of religion and science is itself only understandable as a reaction to a particular religious tradition, one with a strong cognitive bias and a stress on orthodox belief." Robert N. Bellah, *Beyond Belief: Essays on Religion in a Post-Traditional World* (New York: Harper and Rowe, 1970), 238.

15 Wilfred Cantwell Smith, *The Meaning and End of Religion* (New York: Macmillan, 1963), 40.

16 Friedrich Schleiermacher, *On Religion: Speeches to Its Cultured Despisers*, translated by John Oman (New York: Harper and Row, 1958), 46–7.

17 Karen Armstrong points out that even the Evangelical, Methodist, Pentecostal, fundamentalist and other such movements that seem to revolt against these modern assumptions often serve to confirm them, both by what they affirm and by what they seek to resist. They are forms of religious positivism, seeking an "absolute certainty" (in emotional experience, speaking in tongues, biblical literalism, or something else) modelled, ironically, on the modern scientific ideal but alien to genuine spirituality, with its necessary emphasis on mystery and unknowing. *The Case for God* (New York: Alfred A. Knopf, 2009), especially 269–75. On experientialist "positivism," see also Turner, *The Darkness of God*, 249, 259, 262.

18 Tillich, *The Courage to Be*, 172. For examples of precisely this view, see Bertrand Russell's definition of faith as "a firm belief in something for which there is no evidence" in *Human Society in Ethics and Politics* (1954), cited in *Lapham's Quarterly* 3, no. 1, (Winter 2010), 213; or A.C. Grayling's definition of faith as "an attitude of belief independent of, and characteristically in the countervailing face of, evidence." In Mick Gordon and Chris Wilkinson, eds., *Conversations on Religion* (London: Continuum, 2008), 3.

19 McGrath, *Christianity's Dangerous Idea*, 429–30.

20 Luke 7:36–50.

21 Matthew 9:20–22.

22  Mark 10:46–52.

23  Mark 4:38–40.

24  Genesis 13:14–18.

25  Thomas Pangle, *Political Philosophy and the God of Abraham* (Baltimore: Johns Hopkins University Press, 2003), 142. Emphasis added.

26  *The Koran* 2:129–31, 60:4–5, translated by N.J. Dawood (London: Penguin Books, 2003), 22, 389–90. Emphasis added.

27  Romans 4:13.

28  Hebrews 11.

29  Saint Augustine, *City of God*, translated by Henry Bettenson (London: Penguin Books, 2003), 513.

30  Karl Jaspers, *Way to Wisdom*, translated by Ralph Manheim (New Haven: Yale University Press, 1960), 51. In other words, the same thing can be said about faith that Aristotle said about happiness (or "flourishing"): it is a "kind of activity; and an activity clearly is developed and is not a piece of property already in one's possession … [it] consists in living and being active." *The Nicomachean Ethics*, Book IX, Chapter 9, 1169b 29–31, translated by J.A.K. Thomson, revised by Hugh Tredennick (London: Penguin Books, 2004), 247.

31  Thomas Aquinas, *Summa Theologica*, 2a-2ae. lxxxi. 5, *ad* 3, in St Thomas Aquinas, *Philosophical Texts*, selected and translated by Thomas Gilby (London: Oxford University Press, 1951, 1956), 349. Emphasis added.

32  Friedrich Schleiermacher, *On Religion*, 60. "Feelings are a mere accompaniment to the … fact of the relation." Martin Buber, *I and Thou*, second edition, translated by Ronald Gregor Smith (New York: Charles Scribner's Sons, 1958), 81.

33  Karl Rahner, *The Practice of Faith: A Handbook of Contemporary Spirituality* (New York: Crossroad, 1983), 5–9. "Faith may be defined as fidelity to our own being – so far as such being is not and cannot become an object of the senses … and hence, by clear inference or implication, to being generally, as far as the same is not the object of the senses." Samuel Taylor Coleridge, *Essay on Faith*, cited in Owen Barfield, *What Coleridge Thought* (Middletown: Wesleyan University Press, 1971), 151.

34  Arthur Hertzberg, ed., *Judaism* (New York: Washington Square Press, 1963), xiv, xxii.

35  Adin Steinsaltz, *The Essential Talmud*, thirtieth anniversary edition (New York: Basic Books, 2006), 263.

36  Edward Conze, *Buddhism: A Short History* (Oxford: Oneworld Publications, 1993, 2008), 7.

37  Joseph Campbell, *Myths to Live By* (New York: Bantam Books, 1973), 104.

38 Mark 5: 35–6.

39 Thomas Aquinas, Disputations, XIV *de Veritate*, I, in *St Thomas Aquinas, Theological Texts*, selected and translated by Thomas Gilby (London: Oxford University Press, 1954), 195–7. Samuel Taylor Coleridge also said that faith is "a state and disposition of the will, or rather of the whole man, the I, or finite will, self-affirmed." *Notes on Donne*, cited in Owen Barfield, *What Coleridge Thought* (Middletown: Wesleyan University Press, 1971), 151. Karl Rahner variously describes this basic act of faith as the "act of unconditional acceptance of the meaningfulness of my existence," the "act of accepting existence in trust and hope," or "the act of letting oneself sink trustfully into the incomprehensible mystery." *The Practice of Faith*, 6.

40 Rahner, *The Practice of Faith*, 21–2, 31–2, 35, 56, 61, 120–4, 220, 232.

41 Augustine, *City of God*, 330. "Only when life is freely accepted in general as having a sheltering significance, in an ultimate primal trust, will man in his freedom be also prepared to carry out the conscious formulation of this primal trust in the direction of God." Rahner, *The Practice of Faith*, 61.

42 Rahner, *The Practice of Faith*, 62. See also William James, *The Varieties of Religious Experience* (New York: Collier Books, 1961), 42, 390.

43 William Temple, *Nature, Man and God* (London, 1934), 317, quoted in Smith, *The Meaning and End of Religion*, 321.

44 Rahner, *The Practice of Faith*, 14, 22, 59–60, 62–5.

45 Aquinas, *Summa Theologica*, 2a-2ae. lxxxi. I, *ad* I, in *Philosophical Texts*, 349–50. The first kind of religious acts, says Aquinas, are those "conducting to grace," and the second kind are those "coming from grace." *Summa Theologica*, 1a-2ae. cviii. 1, in *Theological Texts*, 154.

46 The image of spiritual "turning" is a richly biblical one. For just three among innumerable examples, see 2 Chronicles 36:13, Psalm 85:4 and James 1:17. As a result, the image of an inward "turning" is also a common one in traditional Christian spirituality. See, for example, Evagrius Ponticus, Bernard de Clairvaux, John Tauler, Johann Arndt, and Nicholas Cusanus in Bernard McGinn, ed., *The Essential Writings of Christian Mysticism* (New York: Modern Library, 2006), 107–9, 150, 279, 349, 436. For a modern Jewish use of the image, see Martin Buber, *I and Thou*, 57–61, 100–1, 119–20.

47 Thomas Aquinas, *Summa Theologica*, 2a-2ae. lxxxi. 5, in *Theological Texts*, 388.

48 Hertzberg, ed., *Judaism*, 183.

49 Letter of Maimonides to Hasdai Halevi, in F. Kobler, ed., *A Treasury of Jewish Letters* (Philadelphia: Jewish Publication Society, 1954), Vol.1, 197–8, quoted in ibid, 16.

50 Thomas Aquinas, Commentary, 2 *Corinthians*, ii, lect. 3, in *Theological Texts*, 184.

51 Hertzberg, ed., *Judaism*, 232.

52 Colossians 3:10–14; N.T. Wright, *After You Believe: Why Christian Character Matters* (New York: HarperCollins, 2010), 147.

53 Rahner, *The Practice of Faith*, especially 3–17.

## CHAPTER SIX

1 Martin Jay, *Songs of Experience: Modern American and European Variations on a Universal Theme* (Berkeley: University of California Press, 2005), 7.

2 "I said *he believes*, but that really means *he meets*." Martin Buber, *I and Thou*, second edition, translated by Ronald Gregor Smith (New York: Charles Scribner's Sons, 1958), 60.

3 "'Expérience' a toujours désigné le rapport à une présence, que ce rapport ait ou non la forme de la conscience." Jacques Derrida, *De la grammatologie*, quoted in Iris Murdoch, *Metaphysics as a Guide to Morals* (London: Vintage, 1992, 2003), 190–1.

4 "The awakening of ... primal trust does not take place effectively merely through words. It comes about through participation in the life of another person who, in his serenity and love, may be able to provide a fruitful model for this primal trust." Karl Rahner, *The Practice of Faith: A Handbook of Contemporary Spirituality* (New York: Crossroad, 1983), 61.

5 Adin Steinsaltz, *The Essential Talmud*, thirtieth anniversary edition (New York: Basic Books, 2006), 32.

6 George Steiner, *Lessons of the Masters* (Cambridge, Mass.: Harvard University Press, 2003).

7 Hugh Heclo, "The Spirit of Public Administration," *PS: Political Science and Politics*, December 2002, 694.

8 William Temple, *Nature, Man and God* (London, 1934), 321, quoted in Wilfred Cantwell Smith, *The Meaning and End of Religion* (New York: Macmillan, 1963), 321. Emphasis added.

9 Rahner, *The Practice of Faith*, 141–3.

10 Karl Rahner describes many different ways in which the spirit is encountered in the experience of daily life, in *The Practice of Faith*, especially 58, 63, 80–4, 114–15, 201, 242, 251, 263, 265, 293, 311.

11 Northrop Frye, *Words with Power* (New York: Harcourt Brace Jovanovich, 1990), 76.

12 Boris Pasternak, *Doctor Zhivago*, translated by Max Hayward and Manya Harari (London: Collins and Harvill Press, 1958), 391–2.

13 Hugh Hood, *Reservoir Ravine* (Ottawa: Oberon Press, 1979), 204–5.

14 Lionel Trilling, *Sincerity and Authenticity* (Cambridge, Mass.: Harvard University Press, 1972), 157.

15 Susan Neiman, *Evil in Modern Thought: An Alternative History of Philosophy* (Princeton: Princeton University Press, 2002), 317.

16 Iris Murdoch, *Metaphysics as a Guide to Morals* (London: Vintage, 1992, 2003), 408; Plotinus, *Enneads*, 1, 6, 5, in Elmer O'Brien, ed., *The Essential Plotinus* (New York: Mentor Books, 1964), 38.

17 Arthur Hertzberg, ed., *Judaism* (New York: Washington Square Press, 1963), 8.

18 Seneca, *Moral Epistles*, 41.1–2, quoted in Martha Nussbaum, *The Therapy of Desire: Theory and Practice in Hellenistic Ethics* (Princeton: Princeton University Press, 1994), 326.

19 "[A] reality which is always present … even though unrecognized." Karl Jaspers, *Reason and Existenz*, translated by William Earle, in Walter Kaufman, ed., *Existentialism from Dostoevsky to Sartre* (Cleveland: Meridian Books, 1956), 196. Bonaventure said that because we are accustomed to the "opaqueness" of beings or of visible things, our mind "appears to see nothing when it gazes on the light of the highest being. It cannot understand that this very darkness is the supreme illumination of our mind, just as when the eye sees pure light, it seems to see nothing." *The Soul's Journey into God*, 5, 4, in Denys Turner, *The Darkness of God: Negativity in Christian Mysticism* (Cambridge: Cambridge University Press, 1995), 128. Turner paraphrases Bonaventure: "'[B]eing' is the light in which we see 'beings'. Hence when the mind turns its gaze away from particular beings toward the light of 'being' in which it sees them, it sees nothing." *Faith, Reason and the Existence of God* (Cambridge: Cambridge University Press, 2004), 56.

20 Isaiah 45:15.

21 *Wen-tzu* in *The Taoist Classics*, The Collected Translations of Thomas Cleary, Vol. 1 (Boston: Shambhala, 2003), 164.

22 Frédérique Doyon, "La complainte du vide intérieur: Une anthropologue se penche sur le côté sombre de la chanson actuelle," *Le Devoir*, 23 March 2010, 1.

23 Jack Hodgins, *Broken Ground* (Toronto: McClelland and Stewart, 1998), 325.

24 Frederick Buechner, *Listening to Your Life* (New York: HarperSanFrancisco, 1992), 127–8.

25 2 Corinthians 12:2–4.

26 Turner, *The Darkness of God*, especially 226–73. The words quoted are on page 264.

27 "When nominalism removed the human relationship with God from the sphere of reason, it came close to the mysticism which flourished from the thirteenth century." Diarmaid MacCulloch, *Christianity: The First Three Thousand Years* (New York: Viking, 2010), 566.

28 Bernard McGinn, *The Presence of God: A History of Western Christian Mysticism*, Vol. 1 (New York: Crossroad, 1992), xvii, quoted in Turner, *The Darkness of God*, 262–3.

29 Pascal, *Pensées* (Paris: Garnier-Flammarion, 1973), 247–8. "Éternellement en joie pour un jour d'exercice sur la terre." My translation.

30 William James, *The Varieties of Religious Experience* (New York: Collier Books, 1961), 329.

31 "Religious belief can be very close to madness." MacCulloch, *Christianity*, 13.

32 Rahner, *The Practice of Faith*, 60.

33 James A. Weisheipl, *Frère Thomas Aquinas, sa vie, sa pensée, ses œuvres* (Paris: Cerf, 1993), 352–3, quoted in Benoît Garceau, ed., *L'Expérience de Dieu avec Thomas d'Aquin* (Montreal: Fides, 2001), 8. My translation.

34 Thomas Aquinas, *Summa Theologica*, 2a-2ae. lxxxv. 1, in St Thomas Aquinas, *Philosophical Texts*, selected and translated by Thomas Gilby (London: Oxford University Press, 1951, 1956), 56.

35 Bernard J.F. Lonergan, S.J., *Insight: A Study of Human Understanding* (New York and London: Philosophical Library and Dartman Longman and Todd, 1958, 1973), 625.

36 Matthew 11:28.

37 David Adams Richards, *God Is: My Search for Faith in a Secular World* (Toronto: Doubleday Canada, 2009), 31.

38 "[I]n the very moment of deepest need a hitherto undreamt-of movement forwards and outwards." Buber, *I and Thou*, 50.

39 Elaine Pagels, *Adam and Eve and the Serpent* (New York: Random House, 1988); *The Origin of Satan* (New York: Random House, 1995).

40 Elaine Pagels, *Beyond Belief* (New York: Random House, 2005), 3–5.

41 Ibid., 144–5. Emphasis in original.

42 Ernst Cassirer, *An Essay on Man* (New York: Bantam Books, 1970), 87.

43 Marilynne Robinson, *The Death of Adam: Essays on Modern Thought* (New York: Picador, 2005), 71. The English word "worship," like the word

"religion" itself, has secular roots. Its original secular use for acknowledging worth can be seen in the honorary title of address, "Your Worship," still used for mayors in some English-speaking countries. James F. White, *Introduction to Christian Worship*, third edition revised and expanded (Nashville: Abingdon Press, 2000), 27.

44 Susanne K. Langer, *Mind: An Essay on Human Feeling*, Vol. III (Baltimore: Johns Hopkins University Press, 1982), 142.

45 N.T. Wright, *After You Believe: Why Christian Character Matters* (New York: HarperCollins, 2010), 188.

46 Moses Maimonides, *The Guide for the Perplexed*, translated by M. Friedländer (New York: Dover Publications, 1956), 367, 356.

47 "It suffices him to be able to cross again and again the threshold of the holy place wherein he was not able to remain; the very fact that he must leave it again and again is inwardly bound up for him with the meaning and character of this life. There, on the threshold, the response, the spirit, is kindled ever new within him; here, in an unholy and needy country, this spark is to be proved." Buber, *I and Thou*, 52–3. N.T. Wright points out that there is "a to-and-fro in the Old Testament between the presence of God filling, and dwelling in, the Temple, and that same presence eventually filling, and dwelling in, the whole world." *After You Believe*, 84. See also *Surprised by Hope: Rethinking Heaven, the Resurrection, and the Mission of the Church* (New York: HarperCollins, 2008), 189–232.

48 Origen, the first great Christian theologian, explained: "by the very attitude with which he prays, [the person who prays sincerely] shows that he is placing himself before God and speaking to him as present, convinced that he is present and looking at him." Origen, *Prayer. Exhortation to Martyrdom*, translated and annotated by John J. O'Meara (New York: Paulist Press, 1954), in Bernard McGinn, ed., *The Essential Writings of Christian Mysticism* (New York: Modern Library, 2006), 82–3. Similarly, in his *Mishneh Torah* (Repetition of the Torah), a compendium of Jewish law, Maimonides said that to "achieve correct intention" in prayer, one must "free the mind of all thoughts and see oneself as standing before the divine Presence." Cited in Joel L. Kraemer, *Maimonides: The Life and World of One of Civilization's Greatest Minds* (New York: Doubleday, 2008), 336. "[I]f you hallow this life, you meet the living God." Buber, *I and Thou*, 79. See also Rahner, *The Practice of Faith*, 70, 83–4. On participation and empowerment, see Ibid, 177, 213, 256–8, 295–6.

49 Joseph Campbell, *Myths to Live By* (New York: Bantam Books, 1973), 98.

50 Maimonides, *The Guide for the Perplexed*, 366.

51 Turner, *Faith, Reason and the Existence of God*, 114–15. Turner calls music "the most 'natural' of natural theologies." Ibid, 115.

52 James, *The Varieties of Religious Experience*, 330.

53 Confucius, *The Analects*, translated by D.C. Lau (London: Penguin Books, 1979), 8.8, 93.

54 Ari L. Goldman, *Being Jewish: The Spiritual and Cultural Practice of Judaism Today* (New York: Simon and Schuster, 2000), 112.

55 Thomas Aquinas, *Compendium Theologiae*, 47, in St Thomas Aquinas, *Theological Texts*, selected and translated by Thomas Gilby (London: Oxford University Press, 1954), 46–7.

56 Rudolf Otto, *The Idea of the Holy* (Oxford: Oxford University Press, 1958, 1973), 36.

57 Pagels, *Beyond Belief*, 14. On this "latent Protestantism in Western Christian culture," see Wright, *Surprised by Hope*, 258–60; *After You Believe*, 279.

58 George Eliot, *Adam Bede* (London: Penguin Classics, 1985), 359.

59 Confucius said that simply aiming for the highest good without "regulating" it by ritual "will not in fact work." Confucius, *The Analects*, 1.12, 61.

CHAPTER SEVEN

1 John 14:6.

2 See, for example, *The Koran* 72:14–16, translated by N.J. Dawood (London: Penguin Books, 2003), 408. Also 104, 250, 270, 308, 325, 334, 346–7, 354, 356, 358, 401.

3 *The Baghavad Gita*, translated and with a preface by Eknath Easwaran (New York: Vintage Books, 2000), 66–8.

4 Ibid., 33.

5 Reza Aslan, *No god but God: The Origins, Evolution and Future of Islam* (New York: Random House, 2005), 206.

6 *Buddhist Scriptures*, selected and edited by Edward Conze (Harmondsworth: Penguin Books, 1959 1969), 112–15.

7 Joseph Campbell, *The Masks of God: Oriental Mythology* (Harmondsworth: Penguin Books, 1976), 236, 282, 310–20.

8 Bernard McGinn, ed., *The Essential Writings of Christian Mysticism* (New York: Modern Library, 2006), 149–71, 460, 451; Denys Turner, *The Darkness of God: Negativity in Christian Mysticism* (Cambridge: Cambridge University Press, 1995), 102–17; Diarmaid MacCulloch, *Christianity: The First Three Thousand Years* (New York: Viking, 2010), 439.

9 Aslan, *No god but God*, 206–16.

10 John S. Dunne, *The City of the Gods: A Study in Myth and Morality* (New York: Macmillan, 1965), 174.

11 Joel L. Kraemer, *Maimonides: The Life and World of One of Civilization's Greatest Minds* (New York: Doubleday, 2008), 275.

12 Adin Steinsaltz, *The Essential Talmud*, thirtieth anniversary edition (New York: Basic Books, 2006), 15, 24–6, 144; Donald Harman Akenson, *Saint Saul: A Skeleton Key to the Historical Jesus* (Montreal and Kingston: McGill-Queen's University Press, 2000), 265–6, n44.

13 Thomas Aquinas, *Compendium Theologiae*, 248, in St Thomas Aquinas, *Theological Texts*, selected and translated by Thomas Gilby (London: Oxford University Press, 1954), 243.

14 *The Koran* 4:43, translated by Dawood, 75.

15 Lionel Trilling, *Sincerity and Authenticity* (Cambridge, Mass.: Harvard University Press, 1972)

16 Charles Taylor, *The Malaise of Modernity* (Toronto: Anansi, 1991), 17; Charles Taylor, *A Secular Age* (Cambridge and London: The Belknap Press of Harvard University Press, 2007), Chapter 13.

17 Luke 18:9–14.

18 David Adams Richards, *God Is: My Search for Faith in a Secular World* (Toronto: Doubleday Canada, 2009), 103, 28, 41–2.

19 N.T. Wright suggests there is a difference between "pretending" and Paul's concept of "putting on," which is "the early stage of the habit of virtue. Pretending is a way of not working at it. And working at it is what counts." *After You Believe: Why Christian Character Matters* (New York: HarperCollins, 2010), 275.

20 Macarius (or "Pseudo-Macarius"), *Homily 10*, in McGinn, ed., *The Essential Writings of Christian Mysticism*, 431.

21 Deirdre N. McCloskey, *The Bourgeois Virtues: Ethics for an Age of Commerce* (Chicago: University of Chicago Press, 2006), 276.

22 William James, *The Varieties of Religious Experience* (New York: Collier Books, 1961), 301.

23 Alister McGrath, *Christianity's Dangerous Idea: The Protestant Revolution – A History from the Sixteenth Century to the Twenty-First* (New York: HarperCollins, 2007), 156.

24 *Buddhist Scriptures*, 143.

25 "The asking of questions is in itself the correct rite," said Confucius. *The Analects*, 3.15, translated by D.C. Lau (London: Penguin Books, 1979), 69.

26 John of the Cross, *The Dark Night of the Soul*, in McGinn, ed., *The Essential Writings of Christian Mysticism*, 384–8.

27 Aslan, *No god but God*, 207.

28 Stephen Mitchell, ed., *The Enlightened Heart: An Anthology of Sacred Poetry* (New York: Harper Perennial, 1989), 54.

29 *Buddhist Scriptures*, 144.

30 Karl Rahner, *The Practice of Faith: A Handbook of Contemporary Spirituality* (New York: Crossroad, 1983), 10, 57, 249.

31 Alasdair MacIntyre, *After Virtue*, second edition (Notre Dame: University of Notre Dame Press, 1984), 219.

32 Wilfred Cantwell Smith, *The Meaning and End of Religion* (New York: Macmillan, 1963), 331. Emphasis added.

### CHAPTER EIGHT

1 Actually, this charge goes right back to the beginning of the religious traditions. One of the recurring themes of the *Quran*, for example, is the scoffing of unbelievers that religious revelation is "nothing but fables of the ancients." *The Koran* 6:25, translated by N.J. Dawood (London: Penguin Books, 2003), 95.

2 Ludwig Feuerbach, *The Essence of Christianity*, in Patrick L. Gardiner, ed., *19th Century Philosophy* (New York: Free Press, 1969), 246, 245, 250.

3 Sigmund Freud, *The Future of an Illusion* (New York: Anchor Books, 1964), 45, 30.

4 John Stuart Mill, "Coleridge," in F.R. Leavis, ed., *Mill on Bentham and Coleridge* (Cambridge: Cambridge University Press, 1980), 99.

5 Sigmund Freud, *Civilization and its Discontents* (New York: Norton, 1962), 21.

6 Saint Augustine, *City of God*, translated by Henry Bettenson (London: Penguin Books, 2003), 377, 398.

7 Thomas Aquinas, *III Sentences*, IX, i. 3, sol iii; *Compendium Theologiae*, 248; *Summa Theologica*, 2a-2ae. lxxi. 5, in St Thomas Aquinas, *Theological Texts*, selected and translated by Thomas Gilby (London: Oxford University Press, 1954), 242–3, 388.

8 Thomas Aquinas, *Summa Theologica*, 2a-2ae. viii. 7, in *Theological Texts*, 256. Aquinas was merely echoing earlier Christian thinkers, such as the fourth-century writer Evagrius Ponticus who said: "Never give a shape to the divine as such when you pray, nor allow your mind to be imprinted by any form, but go immaterial to the Immaterial and you will understand." Quoted in Diarmaid MacCulloch, *Christianity: The First Three Thousand Years* (New York: Viking, 2010), 209.

9  Moses Maimonides, *The Guide for the Perplexed*, translated by M. Friedländer (New York: Dover Publications, 1956), 2.

10  Saint Augustine, *Confessions*, translated by R.S. Pine-Coffin (Harmondsworth: Penguin Books, 1961), 336; *City of God*, 727.

11  Augustine, *Confessions*, 304.

12  Samuel Taylor Coleridge, *Aids to Reflection* (Port Washington: Kenneket Press, 1971), 113. Maimonides' rejoinder was even sharper: "You appear to have studied the matter superficially, and nevertheless you imagine that you can understand a book which has been the guide of past and present generations, when you for a moment withdraw from your lusts and appetites, and glance over its contents as if you were reading a historical work or some poetical composition. Collect your thoughts and examine the matter carefully, for it is not to be understood as you at first sight think, but as you will find after due deliberation." *The Guide for the Perplexed*, 15.

13  Terry Eagleton, *Reason, Faith, and Revolution: Reflections on the God Debate* (New Haven: Yale University Press, 2009), 92; Marilynne Robinson, *The Death of Adam: Essays on Modern Thought* (New York: Picador, 2005), 91. Bernard Williams refers, for example, to William Godwin's "ferociously rational refusal to respect any consideration that an ordinary human being would find compelling." *Ethics and the Limits of Philosophy* (Cambridge, Mass.: Harvard University Press, 1985), 107.

14  Denys Turner, *Faith, Reason and the Existence of God* (Cambridge: Cambridge University Press, 2004), xv, 82–8.

15  Aristotle, *The Nicomachean Ethics*, Book x, Chapters 7 and 8, 1177a 10–1179a 35, translated by J.A.K. Thomson, revised by Hugh Tredennick (London: Penguin Books, 2004), 270–6.

16  Turner, *Faith, Reason and the Existence of God*, xiv-xvi, 75–88, 232–3.

17  Pascal, *Pensées* (Paris: Garnier-Flammarion, 1973), 92–3, 307–9.

18  Immanuel Kant, *Critique of Pure Reason*, translated by Norman Kemp Smith (London: Macmillan, 1929, 1968), 300–4; Samuel Taylor Coleridge, *Aids to Reflection*, 223.

19  Turner, *Faith, Reason and the Existence of God*, 121. "La dernière démarche de la raison est de reconnaître qu'il y a une infinité de choses qui la surpassent; elle n'est que faible, si elle ne va jusqu'à connaître cela." Pascal, *Pensées*, 134.

20  Stephen W. Hawking, *A Brief History of Time* (New York: Bantam, 1988), 174.

21  Bernard J.F. Lonergan, S.J., *Insight: A Study of Human Understanding* (New York and London: Philosophical Library and Dartman Longman and Todd, 1958, 1973), 653.

22 Iris Murdoch, *Metaphysics as a Guide to Morals* (London: Vintage, 1992, 2003), 511.

23 Charles Taylor, *Sources of the Self: The Making of the Modern Identity* (Cambridge, Mass.: Harvard University Press, 1989), 34.

24 Karl Jaspers, *Way to Wisdom*, translated by Ralph Manheim (New Haven: Yale University Press, 1960), 43; Karl Rahner, *The Practice of Faith: A Handbook of Contemporary Spirituality* (New York: Crossroad, 1983), 3, 6, 42, 66, 79, 134, 216, 248; Michael Frayn, *The Human Touch: Our Part in the Creation of the Universe* (London: Faber and Faber, 2006), 113. Thomas Aquinas and Pseudo-Dionysius argued that the unknowability of God arises not from his distance or obscurity but rather from his total inclusiveness, containing or being present in everything: "an excess of actuality." Turner, *Faith, Reason and the Existence of God*, 188–9. Bernard Williams argues that detaching ourselves "from our perspectives on the world to gain ... an 'absolute conception' of it" may be a "proper ambition for science" but cannot be an appropriate starting point for something like our "ethical consciousness." *Ethics and the Limits of Philosophy*, 111.

25 R.G. Collingwood, *An Essay on Metaphysics* (Oxford: Oxford University Press, 1940). Revised edition, edited with an introduction by Rex Martin (Oxford: Oxford University Press, 1998). "It is a fallacy of false enlightenment to suppose that the understanding by itself can know truth and being. The understanding is dependent on something else ... The source of these premises upon which thought must depend is ultimately unknowable. They are rooted in the Comprehensive out of which we live." Jaspers, *Way to Wisdom*, 94.

26 Hans-Georg Gadamer, *Truth and Method* (New York: Continuum, 2002), 270–6.

27 Karl Jaspers, "On My Philosophy," translated by Felix Kaufmann, in Walter Kaufmann, ed., *Existentialism from Dostoevsky to Sartre* (Cleveland: World Publishing Company, 1956), 133.

28 "[I]f you ask whence deliberation begins, you cannot always answer, why from previous deliberation. You must call a stop. There must be some outside principle prompting the reason to deliberate over what is the right course." Thomas Aquinas, *I Quodlibets*, iv. 7, *c.* and *ad* 1, 2, in *Theological Texts*, 160.

29 Thomas Aquinas, Opusc. XL, *Breve principium fratris Thomas de Aquino quando incepit Parisiis ut Magister in Theologia*, in St Thomas Aquinas, *Philosophical Texts*, selected and translated by Thomas Gilby (London: Oxford University Press, 1951, 1956), 188.

30 Thomas Aquinas, *Commentary on the Sentences of Pierre Lombard*, in Benoît Garceau, ed., *L'Expérience de Dieu avec Thomas d'Aquin* (Montreal:

Fides, 2001), 127–8. The image of the "cloud" that blocks human vision of the summit of truth was a common one in medieval Christian thought, expressed most memorably in the anonymous masterpiece, *The Cloud of Unknowing*. See Bernard McGinn, ed., *The Essential Writings of Christian Mysticism* (New York: Modern Library, 2006), 262–8.

31  Étienne Gilson, *Constantes philosophiques de l'être* (Paris: Vrin, 1983), 12. "Le progrès du métaphysicien consisterait plutôt à reconnaître que les principes, vers lesquels il remonte à partir de la science, s'enfoncent progressivement à ses yeux dans une sorte de brume comme si, au rebours de ce qui se passe dans les sciences de la nature, une sorte de non-savoir, ou de nescience, était en métaphysique le sommet du savoir. " My translation. On non-knowledge or unknowing as the summit of understanding, see also Jaspers, *Way to Wisdom*, especially 159–60; Turner, *Faith, Reason and the Existence of God*; and *The Darkness of God: Negativity in Christian Mysticism* (Cambridge: Cambridge University Press, 1995).

32  Maimonides, *The Guide for the Perplexed*, 3. Shlomo Pines, one of the leading twentieth-century scholarly authorities on Maimonides, suggested that Maimonides borrowed the lightning image from the Arab philosopher Ibn Sina, better known in the West as "Avicenna." Cited in Joel L. Kraemer, *Maimonides: The Life and World of One of Civilization's Greatest Minds* (New York: Doubleday, 2008), 572, note 80.

33  *Tao Te Ching* in *The Taoist Classics*, The Collected Translations of Thomas Cleary, Vol. 1 (Boston: Shambhala, 2003), 46. "God is found not, as Nietzsche thought, in the good order of 'grammar', but in the disordered collapse of speech into paradox, oxymoron, and the negation of the negation." Turner, *Faith, Reason and the Existence of God*, 106.

34  "All revelation is summons and sending." Martin Buber, *I and Thou*, second edition, translated by Ronald Gregor Smith (New York: Charles Scribner's Sons, 1958), 115.

35  Northrop Frye, *Words with Power* (New York: Harcourt Brace Jovanovich, 1990), 111–12.

36  Maimonides, *The Guide for the Perplexed*, 178, 43.

37  1 Corinthians 2:14.

38  Margaret Donaldson, *Human Minds: An Exploration* (New York: Allen Lane, 1993), 269.

39  Charles Taylor, *A Secular Age* (Cambridge and London: The Belknap Press of Harvard University Press, 2007), 741.

40  Thomas Aquinas, *Summa Theologica*, 2a-2ae. lxxxi. 5, *ad* 3, in *Philosophical Texts*, 349. Emphasis added.

41 Susanne K. Langer, *Mind: An Essay on Human Feeling*, Vol. 1 (Baltimore: Johns Hopkins University Press, 1967), 148.

42 Ibid, 149. Martha Nussbaum argues the reverse: that emotion is really a form – an "upheaval" – of thought. Martha C. Nussbaum, *Upheavals of Thought: The Intelligence of Emotions* (Cambridge: Cambridge University Press, 2001). While Langer's argument seems, on the whole, more plausible, there is obviously much truth in both views, and the real point is that reason and feeling are very closely related, and often simply forms of each other. The deepest thought is a very deep form of feeling, and feeling always contains elements of thought, or what will become thought. As usual, Coleridge said it best: we "seldom feel without thinking or think without feeling." And so "deep thinking is attainable only by a man of deep feeling." Letters to John Thelwall, 19 November 1796, and to Thomas Poole, 23 March 1801, in I.A. Richards, ed., *The Portable Coleridge* (New York: The Viking Press, 1950), 252, 273. Echoing Coleridge, Lionel Trilling says: "Intellectual power and emotional power go together." Lionel Trilling, *The Liberal Imagination: Essays on Literature and Society* (New York: Scribner's, 1950, 1976), 293–4.

43 Murdoch, *Metaphysics as a Guide to Morals*, 300.

44 Trilling, *The Liberal Imagination*, 298.

45 N.T. Wright, *Surprised by Hope: Rethinking Heaven, the Resurrection, and the Mission of the Church* (New York: HarperCollins, 2008), 73.

46 Deirdre N. McCloskey, *The Bourgeois Virtues: Ethics for an Age of Commerce* (Chicago: University of Chicago Press, 2006), 421.

47 "[I]t is intuition and not reason that grasps both the first and the ultimate terms." Aristotle, *The Nicomachean Ethics*, Book VI, Chapter 11, 1143a 35–1143b 1, translated by Thomson, revised by Tredennick, 161.

48 As perhaps only a gifted novelist and playwright could do, Michael Frayn makes many interesting attempts to describe the experience of thinking – its elusiveness, ambiguity, and close connection with feeling – in *The Human Touch*. For example: 7–8, 211–16, 226–32, 319–36.

49 Lonergan, *Insight*, 3–4.

50 Williams, *Ethics and the Limits of Philosophy*, 169; Frayn, *The Human Touch*, 212, 214.

51 The different hunches and conclusions of Albert Einstein and Niels Bohr on quantum mechanics are a case in point. See the exchange between Jeremy Bernstein and Lee Smolin in "Einstein: An Exchange," *New York Review of Books* 54, no. 13 (16 August 2007), 66.

52 William James, *The Varieties of Religious Experience* (New York: Collier Books, 1961), 74. Emphasis in original. See also Charles Taylor, *Varieties of Religion Today* (Cambridge, Mass.: Harvard University Press, 2002), 48–52.

53 Susanne K. Langer, *Mind*, Vol. 1, 241. Similarly, William James noted that "the recesses of feeling, the darker, blinder strata of character, are the only places in the world in which we catch real fact in the making, and directly perceive how events happen, and how work is actually done." *The Varieties of Religious Experience*, 389.

54 Lionel Trilling, *The Liberal Imagination*, 49.

55 Susanne K. Langer, *Feeling and Form* (New York: Scribner's, 1953), 405. Emphasis added.

56 Seyed Hossein Nasr, *Islam: Religion, History, Civilization* (New York: HarperSanFrancisco, 2003), 60.

57 Turner, *The Darkness of God*.

58 Dyonisius, *The Mystical Theology* in McGinn, ed., *The Essential Writings of Christian Mysticism*, 284; Nicholas of Cusa, *On the Vision of God*, ibid, 351.

59 Henry Vaughan, *The Night*, in Donald Davie, ed., *The New Oxford Book of Christian Verse* (Oxford: University of Oxford Press, 1981), 125.

60 *Tao Te Ching* in *The Taoist Classics*, 29.

61 *The Book of Chuang Tzu* in Mark Forstater, ed., *The Tao: Finding the Way of Balance and Harmony* (New York: Plume, 2003), 178.

62 Thomas Aquinas, *Summa Theologica*, 1a. ii. 2., in *Philosophical Texts*, 42. Leibniz also based faith on knowledge of God's "effects," of which the most important is being itself: that there is something rather than nothing. G.W. Leibniz, *Essais de Théodicée* (Paris: Garnier-Flammarion, 1969), 77, 228.

63 Thomas Aquinas, Commentary, VII *Metaphysics*, lect. 2, in *Philosophical Texts*, 186. Maimonides asserted that "our knowledge of God is aided by the study of Natural Science." *The Guide for the Perplexed*, 78.

64 Jaspers, *Way to Wisdom*, 77, 159–61.

65 Margaret Donaldson suggests that each of these two modes develops its own "transcendent" forms, that is to say, forms whose perspective moves outside of space-time. The "transcendent" stage in the "intellectual" way of looking at the world is mathematics: mathematics studies patterns of relationship that are not bounded by the limits of space-time but can be extended instead to infinity, or eternity. The highest "value-sensing" way of being is religious spirituality. *Human Minds*, 124–58, 245–70.

66 Wright, *Surprised by Hope*, 72–3.

67 *The Book of Chuang Tzu*, 231.

68 Plato, *Thaetetus* 155 D in *Thaetetus – Sophist*, translated by Harold North Fowler, Loeb Classsical Library, Plato VII (Cambridge, Mass.: Harvard University Press, 1921, 2006), 55; Aristotle, *Metaphysics*, Book 1, Chapter 2, 982b 10–15, translated by W.D. Ross, in Richard McKeon, ed., *The Basic Works of Aristotle* (New York: Random House, 1941, 1968), 692.

69 "The virtues in the moral universe within really do exist, as much as those starry skies above." McCloskey, *The Bourgeois Virtues*, 332.

70 In Maimonides' words, "the rule of the soul over the body." *The Guide for the Perplexed*, 262. Similarly, Christian thinkers such as John of the Cross argued that "We cannot become spiritual unless the bodily senses are restrained." John of the Cross, *The Living Flame of Love*, translated by David Lewis (London: Thomas Baker, 1912), in McGinn, ed., *The Essential Writings of Christian Mysticism*, 218.

71 Augustine, *Confessions*, 50–1, 164–5.

72 Charles Taylor, *Sources of the Self*, 138.

73 John, 3: 21. Emphasis added.

74 *Buddhist Scriptures*, selected and edited by Edward Conze (Harmondsworth: Penguin Books, 1959 1969), 114–15, 86, 152.

75 Maimonides, *The Guide for the Perplexed*, 18.

76 Murdoch, *Metaphysics as a Guide to Morals*, 511.

77 It is "through virtue," says Plotinus, that we rise "through wisdom to The One." *Enneads*, VI, 9, 11, in Elmer O'Brien, ed., *The Essential Plotinus* (New York: Mentor Books, 1964), 88.

78 Aristotle, *Nicomachean Ethics*, Book VI, Chapter 12, 1144a 30–7, translated by W.D. Ross, in McKeon, ed., *The Basic Works of Aristotle*, 1035. "Bad will makes truth unwelcome, and unwelcome truth tends to be overlooked." Lonergan, *Insight: A Study of Human Understanding*, 561.

79 A philosopher would call these "epistemological" conditions.

80 Friedrich Schleiermacher, *On Religion: Speeches to Its Cultured Despisers*, translated by John Oman (New York: Harper and Row, 1958), 130–1.

81 Étienne Gilson, *Constantes philosophiques de l'être* (Paris: Vrin, 1983), 204.

82 *The Book of Chuang Tzu*, 82.

83 *The Canadian Magazine*, 21 August 1976, 7.

84 Turner, *Faith, Reason and the Existence of God*, 82.

85 Maimonides, *The Guide for the Perplexed*, 18. Emphasis added.

86 Murdoch, *Metaphysics as a Guide to Morals*, 244–5.

87 In contrast to contemplation, which goes back at least to Aristotle, it has been suggested that the term "meditation" only emerges in Christian usage in the thirteenth century, especially to describe Christian writing like that of Anselm. MacCulloch, *Christianity*, 416.

88 K. Kavanaugh, *St. John of the Cross* (London: SPCK, 1987), cited in Donaldson, *Human Minds*, 153–4.

89 Charles Taylor points out the wonderful paradox that in many important forms of religious practice "real fullness only comes through emptiness." *A Secular Age*, 780, n8.

90  *Buddhist Scriptures*, 135.

91  Gilson, *Constantes philosophiques de l'être*, 12. "L'effort du métaphysicien ne saurait avoir pour objet premier et principal de déduire, ni même de cataloguer et de classer, mais plutôt de s'habituer à vivre dans la notion première en s'accoutumant à s'en éprouver les richesses, dont on ne peut dire qu'elle les a, mais plutôt qu'elle les est. " My translation. Emphasis added.

92  Karl Rahner, *The Practice of Faith*, 88–9. Similarly, N.T. Wright says that what the Christian understands by prayer is "the inarticulate groaning in which the pain of the world is felt most keenly at the point where it is being brought, by the Spirit, into the very presence of God the creator." *After You Believe: Why Christian Character Matters* (New York: HarperCollins, 2010), 94.

93  Thomas Aquinas, *Compendium Theologiae*, in Garceau, ed., *L'Expérience de Dieu*, 120–2.

94  W.H. Auden, *Forewords and Afterwords* (New York: Vintage Books, 1974), 469–70.

95  "[T]hrough faith ... unknowability is deepened experientially and not merely extended; for faith is the manner of our participation in the unknowability of God, so that the unknowable mystery grounds not merely our thought ... but also our personhood and identity and agency and community." Turner, *Faith, Reason and the Existence of God*, 76.

96  "You must rather have suspicion against your own reason." Maimonides, *The Guide for the Perplexed*, 195.

97  Thomas Aquinas, Disputations, xiv *de Veritate*, 1, in *Theological Texts*, 197–8. Alister MacGrath, *Doubting: Growing through the Uncertainties of Faith* (Downers Grove: InterVarsity Press, 2006).

98  In theological language these two poles of religious life are called the "cataphatic" (positive) and the "apophatic" (negative). The tension between these positive and negative "moments" structures the "inner nature" of religious life and practice, and even of "belief itself," at least in its Western version. Turner, *Faith, Reason and the Existence of God*, 51, 61, 80; *The Darkness of God: Negativity in Christian Mysticism*, 19–21.

99  Paul Tillich, *The Courage to Be* (New Haven: Yale University Press, 1952), 48.

100  Lonergan, *Insight*, 332.

101  Rahner, *The Practice of Faith*, 229–30.

102  Adin Steinsaltz, *The Essential Talmud*, thirtieth anniversary edition (New York: Basic Books, 2006), 8.

103  Augustine, *City of God*, 650.

104  Aquinas, *Summa Theologica*, 2a-2ae. xcii. 1, in *Philosophical Texts*, 351.

105  L.-B. Geiger, o.p., *Philosophie et Spiritualité* (Paris: les éditions du CERF, 1963), 237. "Il arrive ... que tel croit haïr Dieu ... qui, en réalité, ne hait et ne persécute qu'une certaine conception erronée qu'il s'en fait. Tel qui attaque Dieu au nom de la vérité ou de la justice, ne combat en vérité que l'idée d'un Dieu injuste ou ennemi de la vérité, alors qu'il sert le vrai Dieu, qui est Justice et Vérité, par le culte, même indiscret, qu'il a voué à la vérité et à la justice." My translation. See also Rahner, *The Practice of Faith*, 58, 64.

106  Alfred, Lord Tennyson, *In Memoriam*, XCV, in Donald Davie, ed., *The New Oxford Book of Christian Verse* (Oxford: University of Oxford Press, 1981), 234.

107  Mark 9:24. I believe I may owe this *bon mot* to W.H. Auden, but I have so far been unable to retrace the source.

108  The virtues of self-assertion embody, in Marcel Gauchet's words, "a confrontational posture toward things as they are," "a transformative non-acceptance of things," a "constitutive power of negation." *The Disenchantment of the World: A Political History of Religion*, translated by Oscar Bruge (Princeton: Princeton University Press, 1997), 22.

109  Martin Buber called these "the two primary metacosmical movements of the world." *I and Thou*, 116. Also: 3, 62–5, 77, 95–6, 100–1. On this "polar structure of being," see also Tillich, *The Courage to Be*, 86–90.

110  In Cusanus' words: "in unity otherness exists without otherness because it is unity." Nicholas of Cusa, *On the Vision of God*, in McGinn, ed., *The Essential Writings of Christian Mysticism*, 352. Karl Rahner calls this the "coexistence of diversity and unity in love." *The Practice of Faith*, 140.

111  G.W.F. Hegel, *The Phenomenology of Mind*, translated by J.B. Baillie (New York: Harper and Rowe, 1967), 599–610

112  Karl Jaspers, *Reason and Existenz*, translated by William Earle, in Walter Kaufman, ed., *Existentialism from Dostoevsky to Sartre* (Cleveland: Meridian Books, 1956), 196.

113  I take this to be the argument of the last chapter of Bernard Lonergan's *Insight: A Study of Human Understanding*, 687–730.

114  Tillich, *The Courage to Be*, 46–7, 86–112.

115  Susan Neiman reminds us that modern caricatures of the Enlightenment rarely do justice to its complexity and the diversity of its thinking, especially about something like reason. *Moral Clarity: A Guide for Grown-Up Idealists* (Orlando: Harcourt, 2008), 177–214.

116  Herbert A. Simon, *Reason in Human Affairs* (Palo Alto: Stanford University Press, 1983), 7, 106. Bernard Williams comes to much the same conclusion, at least as far as ethical reason is concerned, in *Ethics and the Limits of Philosophy*.

117 "The understanding can indeed clarify, purify, develop thought, but that which lends its opinions objective significance, its thought fulfilment, its action purpose, its philosophy authentic content must be given to it." Jaspers, *Way to Wisdom*, 94.

118 "That ... selfless love makes sense can only be discovered in choosing it." Rahner, *The Practice of Faith*, 42.

119 McCloskey, *The Bourgeois Virtues*, 271. Emphasis in original.

120 Romans 7:15, 24.

121 Harold C. Goddard, *The Meaning of Shakespeare*, Vol. 2 (Chicago: University of Chicago Press, 1951, 1962), 76.

122 Eagleton, *Reason, Faith, and Revolution: Reflections on the God Debate*, 90.

123 Taylor, *A Secular Age*, 638.

124 Thomas Mann, *The Confessions of Felix Krull, Confidence Man* (New York: Signet, 1957), 145.

125 Bernard Williams observes that "in ethics, *reflection can destroy knowledge*." *Ethics and the Limits of Philosophy*, 148, 154, 167–8. Emphasis in original.

126 Meister Eckhart, *Sermon 101*, in McGinn, ed., *The Essential Writings of Christian Mysticism*, 417–18.

127 Ibid. "'[U]nclarity' has an absolutely positive and irreplaceable function, and a person who does not accept this 'unclarity' as a good and a promise drifts into trivial stupidity." Rahner, *The Practice of Faith*, 3, 64–8.

128 Ernest Becker, *The Denial of Death* (New York: Free Press, 1973), 203–4.

CHAPTER NINE

1 "[L]a première question qu'on a droit de faire, sera, Pourquoi il y a plus tôt quelque chose que rien." G.W. Leibniz, *Principes de la nature et de la grâce fondés en raison – Principes de la philosophie ou Monadologie*, edited by André Robinet (Paris: Presses Universitaires de France, 1954, 1986), 45.

2 Marilynne Robinson, *Housekeeping* (Toronto: HarperCollins, 2004), 217.

3 *The Koran* 50:16–17, translated by N.J. Dawood (London: Penguin Books, 2003), 366.

4 A free rendering of "interior intimo meo" in Augustine's *Confessions*, Book 3, Chapter 6. See Denys Turner, *The Darkness of God: Negativity in Christian Mysticism* (Cambridge: Cambridge University Press, 1995), 55, 59; *Faith, Reason and the Existence of God* (Cambridge: Cambridge University Press, 2004), 214.

5 Plato, *The Republic*, Book 1, in *Great Dialogues of Plato*, translated by W.H.D. Rouse, edited by Eric H. Warmington and Philip G. Rouse (New

York: New American Library, 1956), 152; Bernard Williams, *Ethics and the Limits of Philosophy* (Cambridge, Mass.: Harvard University Press, 1985), 1, 117.

6 Susanne K. Langer, *Mind: An Essay on Human Feeling*, Vol. 1 (Baltimore: Johns Hopkins University Press, 1967), 326.

7 Saint Augustine, *City of God*, translated by Henry Bettenson (London: Penguin Books, 2003), 555–7

8 Langer, *Mind*, Vol. 1, 20.

9 David Hume argued (in a related insight, from which he drew quite different conclusions) that there is no such thing as the "self" but only a "bundle or collection of different perceptions," in *A Treatise of Human Nature*, edited by L.A. Selby-Bigge (Oxford: Oxford University Press, 1888, 1968), 252.

10 Thomas Aquinas, *Summa Theologica*, 1a-2ae. lxxii. 1, in St Thomas Aquinas, *Theological Texts*, selected and translated by Thomas Gilby (London: Oxford University Press, 1954), 127.

11 Iris Murdoch, *Metaphysics as a Guide to Morals* (London: Vintage, 1992, 2003), 104.

12 C.G. Jung, *Memories, Dreams, Reflections* (New York: Pantheon Books, 1961, 1973), 345.

13 Epictetus, *Discourses*, 2.10. 1–2, quoted in Martha Nussbaum, *The Therapy of Desire: Theory and Practice in Hellenistic Ethics* (Princeton: Princeton University Press, 1994), 326. For Aristotle, see *The Nicomachean Ethics*, Book III, Chapter 2, 1111b 5–1112a 17; Book VI, Chapter 2, 1139a 15–1139b 15; Book X, Chapter 4, 1175a 15–20, translated by J.A.K. Thomson, revised by Hugh Tredennick (London: Penguin Books, 2004), 54–6, 146–7, 264.

14 Samuel Johnson, *The Rambler*, no. 41, 7 August 1750, in G.B. Hill, ed., *Select Essays of Dr. Johnson*, Vol. 1 (London: J.M. Dent and Co., 1889), 59.

15 S. Kierkegaard, *Either/Or* (New York: Anchor Books, 1959), Vol. II, 180, 179. As Karl Rahner puts it, human beings cannot "withdraw into a pure dialectic of being" but must instead have the "courage" to make "historical decisions that are 'one-sided.'" *The Practice of Faith: A Handbook of Contemporary Spirituality* (New York: Crossroad, 1983), 224–5.

16 Karl Jaspers call this the "apprehension of timelessness through temporality, not through universal concepts." *Reason and Existenz*, translated by William Earle, in Walter Kaufmann, ed., *Existentialism from Dostoevsky to Sartre* (Cleveland: World Publishing Company, 1956), 193.

17 Martin Heidegger, *Existence and Being* (Chicago: Henry Regnery Company, 1949), 355.

18 Ibid, 354.

19  "Actuality ... is the existence of a thing ... and the actuality is the action ...
even the word 'actuality' is derived from 'action', and points to the complete
reality." Aristotle, *Metaphysics*, Book IX, Chapters 6–8, 1048a 30–1050b 25;
Book XII, Chapter 7, 1072b 10–30, translated by W.D. Ross, in Richard
McKeon, ed., *The Basic Works of Aristotle* (New York: Random House,
1941, 1968), 880; Étienne Gilson, *L'être et l'essence*, deuxième édition, troi-
sième tirage, (Paris: Vrin, 1987), 53, 114, 328; Bernard J.F. Lonergan, S.J.,
*Insight: A Study of Human Understanding* (New York and London:
Philosophical Library and Darton Longman and Todd, 1958, 1973), 367–71;
*Verbum: Word and Idea in Aquinas*, edited by Frederick E. Crowe and
Robert M. Doran, *The Collected Works of Bernard Lonergan*, Vol. 2
(Toronto: University of Toronto Press, 1997), 37–8. Emphasis added.

20  "Dictum esse ipse actus essentiae – 'to be is the very act whereby an essence
is,'" quoted in Étienne Gilson, *God and Philosophy* (New Haven: Yale
University Press, 1941), 64. Plotinus was one of the links between Aristotle
and Aquinas: he defined being as both an act of being *and* an act of thought.
*Enneads*, V, 9, 8, in Elmer O'Brien, ed., *The Essential Plotinus* (New York:
Mentor Books, 1964), 52–3.

21  Heidegger, *Existence and Being*, 260–1, 266–7.

22  *Chandogya Upanishad*, Chapter 8, in *The Upanishads*, translated and edited
by Valerie J. Roebuck (London: Penguin Books, 2003), 176.

23  Aristotle, *Metaphysics*, Book IV, Chapter 2, 10003a 30–1003b 35; Book V,
Chapter 7, 1017a 30–5; Book XI, Chapter 3, 1061a 10–20; Chapter 8, 1065a
20–5, in *The Basic Works of Aristotle*, 732, 761, 855; Sir David Ross,
*Aristotle* (London: Methuen, 1964), 156.

24  Saint Augustine, *Confessions*, translated by R.S. Pine-Coffin (Harmondsworth:
Penguin Books, 1961), 307; Moses Maimonides, *The Guide for the Perplexed*,
translated by M. Friedländer (New York: Dover Publications, 1956), 171, 212–
13. Augustine's and Maimonides' interpretations of Genesis reflected the earlier
thought of Origen and the even earlier Alexandrian Jewish school of "allegorical" biblical interpretation. Diarmaid MacCulloch, *Christianity: The First
Three Thousand Years* (New York: Viking, 2010), 69, 151–2.

25  Thomas Aquinas, *Summa Theologica*, 1a. viii. 1, in St Thomas Aquinas,
*Philosophical Texts*, selected and translated by Thomas Gilby (London:
Oxford University Press, 1951, 1956), 81. Similarly, Leibniz argued that "la
créature dépend continuellement de l'opération divine, et ... elle n'en dépend
moins depuis qu'elle a commencé, que dans le commencement. Cette dépendance porte qu'elle ne continuerait pas d'exister, si Dieu ne continuait pas
d'agir ... Or rien n'empêche que cette action conservatrice ne soit appelée

production et même création si l'on veut. Car la dépendance étant aussi grande dans la suite que dans le commencement, la dénomination extrinsèque, d'être nouvelle ou non, n'en change point la nature." G.W. Leibniz, *Essais de Théodicée* (Paris: Garnier-Flammarion, 1969), 344.

26  *The Koran* 96:1, translated by Dawood, 429.

27  Ibid, 2:28–30, 13.

28  Ibid, 40:66–70, 333. Emphasis added. See also 21, 47, 99, 190, 216, 312.

29  Exodus 3:14.

30  Murdoch, *Metaphysics as a Guide to Morals*, 508.

31  Karl Rahner, *The Practice of Faith*, 5–6. Pseudo-Dionysius' famous formula was: "There is no kind of a thing which God is and there is no kind of thing which God is not." *Divine Names* in *Pseudo-Dionysius: The Complete Works*, translated by Colm Luibheid and Paul Rorem (New Jersey: Paulist Press, 1987), 98, quoted in Turner, *Faith, Reason and the Existence of God*, 157, 188.

32  Gilson, *God and Philosophy*, 103. "The Word of revelation is *I am that I am*. That which reveals is that which reveals. That which is *is*, and nothing more." Martin Buber, *I and Thou*, second edition, translated by Ronald Gregor Smith (New York: Charles Scribner's Sons, 1958), 112.

33  Deuteronomy 30:15–19. Emphasis added.

34  In explaining the "figurative" meaning of this famous passage from Deuteronomy (and of other similar passages in scripture), Maimonides says: "true principles are called life, and corrupt principles death ... 'life' and 'good,' 'death' and 'evil,' are identical." Maimonides, *The Guide for the Perplexed*, 57.

35  1 Timothy 6:19

36  Romans 8:13.

37  Augustine, *City of God*, 904; N.T. Wright, *Surprised by Hope: Rethinking Heaven, the Resurrection and the Mission of the Church* (New York: HarperCollins, 2008), 191, 197–8, 200, 249; *After You Believe: Why Christian Character Matters* (New York: HarperCollins, 2010), 89.

38  2 Corinthians 4: 10–11. Karl Rahner calls this "dying in installments." *The Practice of Faith*, 151, 215–16, 295.

39  Northrop Frye, *The Great Code: The Bible and Literature* (Toronto: Academic Press, 1982), 72, 139.

40  Augustine, *City of God*, 461.

41  Samuel Taylor Coleridge, *Coleridge's Notebooks*, edited by Seamus Perry (Oxford: Oxford University Press, 2002), 123.

42  Augustine, *City of God*, 881. Even Voltaire thought that the human need for hope was a reasonable ground for believing in some kind of rational deity.

*Philosophical Dictionary*, translated by Abner Kneeland, in Lewis White Beck, ed., *18th Century Philosophy* (New York: The Free Press, 1966), 187–8.

43  Kathryn Tanner, *Jesus, Humanity and the Trinity* in Alister E. McGrath, ed., *Theology: The Basic Readings* (Oxford: Blackwell Publishing, 2008), 185.

44  Samuel Johnson, *The Rambler*, no. 69, 13 November 1750, in *Select Essays of Dr. Johnson*, Vol. 1, 122.

45  Those who find Johnson's description of old age exaggerated may wish to consult Philip Roth's later novels with their "one unifying preoccupation: death. In novel after novel Roth … leads his aging and diminished protagonists to the very edge of non-existence, only to leave them suspended, waiting, in a fury of metaphysical incomprehension and mourning. They mourn not only those they knew who have died but their own lost vitality, the reality of which they can never escape, assaulted as they are daily by the indignities of old age: impotence, incontinence, failing memory, bodily pain." Jason Crowley, "Outrage Felt from beyond the Grave," *The Guardian Weekly*, 26 September – 2 October 2008, 35.

46  *The Book of Chuang Tzu* in Mark Forstater, ed., *The Tao: Finding the Way of Balance and Harmony* (New York: Plume, 2003), 163–4.

47  Maimonides, *The Guide for the Perplexed*, 390.

48  J.S. Mill, *On Liberty* (Harmondsworth: Penguin Books, 1974), 68.

49  Samuel Johnson in *A Shorter Boswell*, edited by John Bailey (London and Edinburgh: Thomas Nelson and Sons, 1942), 112.

50  Murdoch, *Metaphysics as a Guide to Morals*, 94. Emphasis in original.

51  Even Voltaire thought the reality of evil and the human need for ultimate justice was another good reason to believe in a rational deity "creating, governing, rewarding and punishing." *Philosophical Dictionary*, in Beck, ed., *18th Century Philosophy*, 189.

52  *The Koran* 2:110, 284, translated by Dawood, 21, 42.

53  Augustine, *City of God*, 897–8.

54  "In a world of systematic injustice, bullying, violence, arrogance, and oppression, the thought that there might come a day when the wicked are firmly put in their place and the poor and the weak are given their due is the best news there can be. Faced with a world in rebellion, a world full of exploitation and wickedness, a good God *must* be a God of judgment." Wright, *Surprised by Hope*, 137. Also: 178–9. Emphasis in original.

55  Romans 14:12.

56  *The Order for the Burial of the Dead* in *The Book of Common Prayer* (Toronto: Macmillan of Canada, 1959), 599–600.

57 Augustine, *City of God*, 881. Also Rahner, *The Practice of Faith*, 310; Wright, *Surprised by Hope*.

58 Romans 8:25.

59 *The Order for the Administration of the Lord's Supper or Holy Communion* in *The Book of Common Prayer*, 85. See also Titus 3:7.

60 1 John 3:2. Emphasis added.

61 Rahner, *The Practice of Faith*, 150, 310.

62 Augustine, *Confessions*, 197, 253.

63 Karl Jaspers, *Way to Wisdom*, translated by Ralph Manheim (New Haven: Yale University Press, 1960), 58.

64 *The Koran* 30:56, translated by Dawood, 288. Emphasis added.

65 "If by eternity is understood not infinite temporal duration but non-temporality, then it can be said that a man lives eternally if he lives in the present." Ludwig Wittgenstein, *Notebooks 1914–1916*, translated by G.E.M. Anscombe (New York: Harper and Row, 1969), 75e.

66 Rahner, *The Practice of Faith*, 307–9. Charles Taylor calls this view of time "gathered time" and attributes it to Augustine, especially chapter 11 of the *Confessions*. But despite repeated re-readings of that famous chapter, I have so far been unable to discover it there. *A Secular Age* (Cambridge and London: The Belknap Press of Harvard University Press, 2007), 56–9, 714, 720, 750.

67 Maimonides, *The Guide for the Perplexed*, 313. "[W]henever life is lived in faith, hope, and love, eternity truly occurs." Rahner, *The Practice of Faith*, 311.

68 Ibid, 272.

69 Ibid, 21–8.

70 John 3:3. Emphasis added.

71 It's important to emphasize that the pursuit of final causes or of a higher reality doesn't necessarily imply an "ontological dualism" in which matter is somehow equated with "bad" and non-matter with "good." As N.T. Wright points out, that's not what the Christian scriptures mean at all. (*After You Believe*, 141–3.) John of Damascus (John Damascene) said: "I salute all ... matter *with reverence*, because God has filled it with His grace and power." Quoted in MacCulloch, *Christianity*, 447. Emphasis added. Charles Taylor suggests the Christian view involves yet another paradox. On the one hand, the material world (as God's creation) is "good." But, on the other hand, it must also be, in some sense, "renounced." This "seems to require something paradoxical: living in all the practices and institutions of human flourishing, but at the same time not fully in them. Being in them but not of them; being in them, but yet at a distance, ready to lose them." *A Secular Age*, 80–1.

CHAPTER TEN

1 Wilfred Cantwell Smith, *The Faith of Other Men* (New York, Mentor Books, 1965), 59.

2 Karl Rahner suggests that the "apparent disappearance of faith today" is just a "critical adolescent stage in the faith of mankind." *The Practice of Faith: A Handbook of Contemporary Spirituality* (New York: Crossroad, 1983), 35. Perhaps this is one of the things Charles Taylor means when he suggests that modern unbelief is "providential." *A Secular Age* (Cambridge and London: The Belknap Press of Harvard University Press, 2007), 637.

3 Aristotle said that those who deny an ultimate "final" cause "eliminate the Good without knowing it." *Metaphysics*, Book II, Chapter 2, 994b 10–15, translated by W. D. Ross, in Richard McKeon, ed., *The Basic Works of Aristotle* (New York: Random House, 1941), 714.

4 Jean-Paul Sartre, *La Nausée* (Paris: Gallimard, 1938).

5 Susan Neiman, *Evil in Modern History: An Alternative History of Philosophy* (Princeton: Princeton University Press, 2002), 321.

6 "Un jour, c'est inévitable, vous en aurez assez ... Le tourbillon des derniers jours, semaines, mois – des dernières *années*, même, peut-être – vous aura laissé confus et désorienté, habité par un malaise perpétuel, le sentiment que tout ça – votre quotidien, votre mode de vie jeune et dynamique et tellement moderne, tout ce bruit autour de vous, partout, toujours, cette interactivité constant avec l'humanité toute entière et personne en particulier, tout cet argent qui entre dans votre vie et en ressort aussitôt, toutes ces ondes traversant les murs et vos organes, toutes ces lumières brillantes, ces appâts réfléchissant, ces impulsions électriques dans vos gadgets, vos neurones, vos paupières fermées – le senti-ment que tout ça, donc, ne mène à rien, sinon à des endroits où vous ne voulez pas aller, n'avez jamais eu envie d'aller. Et vous serez fatigué, vraiment fatigué." Nicolas Langelier, *Réussir son hypermodernité et sauver le reste de sa vie en 25 étapes faciles* (Montréal: Les Éditions du Boréal, 2010), 17; Chantal Guy, "Nicolas Langelier: Le blues du *hipster*," *La Presse*, 11 September 2010.

7 Taylor, *A Secular Age*, 6, 16–21. "Flourishing" is now the accepted modern translation for the Aristotelian concept of *eudaimonia*, traditionally translat-ed as "happiness." Martha Nussbaum, *Upheavals of Thought: The Intelligence of the Emotions* (Cambridge: Cambridge University Press, 2001), 32. In juxtaposing "flourishing" with "fullness," Taylor implicitly contrasts two key terms of Aristotle and Paul, respectively, for the goal of human life.

8 Martin Buber, *I and Thou*, second edition, translated by Ronald Gregor Smith (New York: Charles Scribner's Sons, 1958), 63.

9   Saint Augustine, *Confessions*, translated by R.S. Pine-Coffin (Harmondsworth: Penguin Books, 1961), 316.

10  Leszek Kolakowski, *Religion* (New York: Oxford University Press, 1983), 198–200. Emphasis in original. "The choice is between faith or nothing … [M]ost of us do not think of these things at all, until we are faced with a di-lemma, the nature of which is on many levels twofold – personal abandon-ment and private degradation, of one form or another, by a world we had relied on. Then we seek what has always been there for us." David Adams Richards, *God Is* (Toronto: Doubleday Canada, 2009), 159.

11  "Il vous apparaîtra alors très clairement, sans doute pour la première fois … que la grande erreur de votre époque aura été de croire que la réponse à ce malaise devait être individuelle, d'où ces nombreuses panacées – des cours de yoga aux psychothérapies, en passant par les pilules colorées et les livres de croissance personnelle – qui ont toutes comme prémisse que la solution se trouve dans l'amélioration de soi et dans la négation de ses vulnérabilités … Même si la publicité et les politiciens au grand complet se sont entêtés à vous en convaincre, vous n'êtes pas le centre du monde. L'univers n'est pas une gi-gantesque mise en scène pour le spectacle de votre vie. La terre n'est pas as-servie à votre plaisir, à l'assouvissement de vos besoins, désirs, envies les plus diverses." Langelier, *Réussir son hypermodernité*, 215–16.

12  Rahner, *The Practice of Faith*, 57–64, 80–4, 128, 263, 293, 311.

13  Thomas Aquinas, *Summa Theologica*, 1a. xii. 3, *ad* 3, in St Thomas Aquinas, *Philosophical Texts*, selected and translated by Thomas Gilby (London: Oxford University Press, 1951, 1956), 86.

14  Susan Neiman, *Moral Clarity: A Guide for Grown-Up Idealists* (Orlando: Harcourt, 2008), 121.

15  As Origen, the first great Christian theologian, put it, philosophers cook fancy meals for the select few, but "we cook for the masses." Or, as another early Christian father, Clement of Alexandria, said, a religious life is a way to "phil-osophize without education." Elaine Pagels, *Adam and Eve and the Serpent* (New York: Random House, 1988), 85, 51. Indeed one of the things that most impressed the people of the late Roman Empire – including the early opponents of Christianity – was how adoption of a Christian way of living could trans-form ordinary people, even the uneducated poor and slaves, in a way years of study of the Stoic philosophers had barely or rarely been able to do, even for highly educated people. The emperor's own physician, Galen, was impressed that ordinary, uneducated Christians "in self-discipline … and in their keen pur-suit of justice, have attained a level not inferior to that of genuine philosophers." Elaine Pagels, *Beyond Belief* (New York: Random House, 2005), 8–9.

16 Augustine, *Confessions*, 60.

17 Sigmund Freud, *The Future of an Illusion* (New York: Anchor Books, 1964), 45.

18 Augustine, *Confessions*, 340, 336; Moses Maimonides, *The Guide for the Perplexed* (New York: Dover Publications, 1956), 5.

19 Maimonides, *The Guide for the Perplexed*, 181. On the spiritual and figurative interpretation of Creation and of Genesis, more generally, see Part 2, Chapters 13 to 31, 171–218. Also, Augustine, *Confessions*, Book XII, 281–309. Origen said the whole Gospel According to St John should be interpreted "spiritually" rather than literally. Pagels, *Beyond Belief*, 36–7, 118.

20 Augustine, *Confessions*, 306. See also *City of God*, translated by Henry Bettenson (London: Penguin Books, 2003), 466–7; Maimonides, *The Guide for the Perplexed*, 171, 212–13.

21 *Buddhist Scriptures*, selected and edited by Edward Conze (Harmondsworth: Penguin Books, 1959 1969), 121.

22 Augustine, *Confessions*, 309, 335–6.

23 John Macquarrie, *20th Century Religious Thought* (London: SCM Press, 1971), 362–4; John A.T. Robinson, *Honest to God* (London: SCM Press, 1963).

24 Maimonides, *The Guide for the Perplexed*, 4, 46.

25 Neiman, *Moral Clarity*, 422.

26 Denys Turner identifies the same kind of "continuum of forms of rationality," with "purely stipulative technical discourse" at one end and forms of communication like music at the other. *Faith, Reason and the Existence of God* (Cambridge: Cambridge University Press, 2004), 114.

27 Aristotle noted that words such as "malice," "shamelessness," "envy," "adultery," "theft," and "murder" are "names that directly connote depravity," just as words like "temperance" or "courage" directly express the opposite. *The Nicomachean Ethics*, Book II, Chapter 6, 1107a 10–15, translated by J.A.K. Thomson, revised by Hugh Tredennick (London: Penguin Books, 2004), 42. See also Bernard Williams, *Ethics and the Limits of Philosophy* (Cambridge, Mass.: Harvard University Press, 1985), 129–30. Also: 143, 145, 147, 152, 154, 163, 200.

28 Iris Murdoch, *Metaphysics as a Guide to Morals* (London: Vintage, 1992, 2003), 155, 315. Emphasis added.

29 Samuel Taylor Coleridge, *The Statesman's Manual* in *Lay Sermons*, R.J. White, ed., *Collected Works of Samuel Taylor Coleridge*, Vol. 6 (London and Princeton: Routledge and Kegan Paul and Princeton University Press, 1972), 30; Walter Jackson Bate, *Coleridge* (New York: Macmillan, 1968), 157.

30 Kolakowski, *Religion*, 166. Emphasis in original.

31 Ibid., 165. Like religious language, music also "collapses the signified whole and entire into the signifier," as Denys Turner points out, which is why (as noted in chapter 6) it has a "natural capacity for the transcendent." *Faith, Reason and the Existence of God*, 114–15.

32 Coleridge, *The Statesman's Manual*, 29. Emphasis in original.

33 Wilfred Cantwell Smith, *The Meaning and End of Religion* (New York: Macmillan, 1963), 325.

34 Williams, *Ethics and the Limits of Philosophy*, 117.

35 Charlie Mingus, quoted in N.T. Wright, *Paul* (Minneapolis: Fortress Press, 2009), 173.

36 Aristotle, *The Nicomachean Ethics*, Book VII, 1145a 15–1154b 35, translated by Thomson, revised by Tredennick, 167–99; G.W. Mortimore, ed., *Weakness of the Will* (London: Macmillan, 1971).

37 Romans 7: 15, 24.

38 Karen Armstrong, *The Great Transformation: The Beginning of Our Religious Traditions* (New York: Alfred A. Knopf, 2006), 283–4.

39 *Buddhist Scriptures*, 227.

40 *The Baghavad Gita*, 2:30, 2:24, translated and with a preface by Eknath Easwaran (New York: Vintage Books, 2000), 11. See also 13, 20, 24.

41 *The Book of Chuang Tzu* in Mark Forstater, ed., *The Tao: Finding the Way of Balance and Harmony* (New York: Plume, 2003), 192.

42 I think the remark may have been made by Johnson's great modern biographer, W. Jackson Bate. But I have so far been unable to retrace the reference.

43 "While the ancient world valued the individual not as an individual but as a representative of something universal, e.g. a virtue, the rebirth of antiquity [after the Renaissance] saw in the individual as an individual a unique expression of the universe, incomparable, irreplaceable, and of infinite significance." Paul Tillich, *The Courage to Be* (New Haven: Yale University Press, 1952), 19. "Previously, it had been important to establish … the impersonal universality of the subject's conduct. Now it became important to understand the special reasons determining the subject's behaviour and causing each individual's action to be attributed only to that individual, with the tacit understanding that all harbour in their concrete individuality the motives capable of driving them, which can only be explained from within their personal traits." Marcel Gauchet, *The Disenchantment of the World: A Political History of Religion*, translated by Oscar Burge (Princeton: Princeton University Press, 1997), 170.

44 Murdoch, *Metaphysics as a Guide to Morals*, 492.

45  Lionel Trilling, *Sincerity and Authenticity* (Cambridge, Mass.: Harvard University Press, 1972), 44–7, 76–80. "In one respect the self vanished with the restricting bond to both God and the other." Gauchet, *The Disenchantment of the World*, 171.

46  G.W.F. Hegel, *The Phenomenology of Mind*, translated by J.B. Baillie (New York: Harper and Rowe, 1967), 543.

47  Karl Jaspers, *Way to Wisdom*, translated by Ralph Manheim (New Haven: Yale University Press, 1960), 113. See also John of the Cross on the same theme, in Denys Turner, *The Darkness of God: Negativity in Christian Mysticism* (Cambridge: Cambridge University Press, 1995), 237–8.

48  "The authenticity that really matters is living in accordance with the genuine human being God is calling you to become." N.T. Wright, *After You Believe: Why Christian Character Matters* (New York: HarperCollins, 2010), 108. Karl Jaspers calls this "the command of my authentic self to my mere empirical existence. I become aware of myself as that which I myself am, because it is what I ought to be." *Way to Wisdom*, 55. Martin Buber's names for the two selves – the particular and eternal selves – are "individuality" and the "person": "The one is the spiritual form of natural detachment, the other the spiritual form of natural solidarity of connexion." *I and Thou*, 62–5.

49  Alasdair MacIntyre, *After Virtue*, second edition (Notre Dame: University of Notre Dame Press, 1984), 224.

50  Susanne K. Langer, *Mind: An Essay on Human Feeling*, Vol. 3 (Baltimore: Johns Hopkins University Press, 1982), 194.

51  Martha Nussbaum, *The Fragility of Goodness: Luck and Ethics in Greek Tragedy and Philosophy* (Cambridge: Cambridge University Press, 1986), 49.

52  *Buddhist Scriptures*, 152–3.

53  Bonaventure, *The Mind's Journey into God*, in Bernard McGinn, ed., *The Essential Writings of Christian Mysticism* (New York: Modern Library, 2006), 166.

54  John of Damascus (John Damascene) distinguished between two types or levels of reverence: *latreia*, the reverence given to God, and *proskynesis*, the reverence appropriate for everything else. *On the Divine Images. Three Apologies against Those Who Attack the Divine Images*, translated by D. Anderson (New York, 1980) 23, 82–8, cited in Diarmaid MacCulloch, *Christianity: The First Three Thousand Years* (New York: Viking, 2010), 448.

55  Thomas Aquinas, *Compendium Theologiae*, 248, in St Thomas Aquinas, *Theological Texts*, selected and translated by Thomas Gilby (London: Oxford University Press, 1954), 243.

56 Samuel Taylor Coleridge, *Coleridge's Notebooks*, ed. Seamus Perry (Oxford: Oxford University Press, 2002), 121. Emphasis in original. I have substituted "and" for "&".

57 G.W. Leibniz, *Essais de Théodicée* (Paris: Garnier-Flammarion, 1969), 108. "[C]omme un moindre mal est une espèce de bien, de même un moindre bien est une espèce de mal, s'il fait obstacle à un bien plus grand." My translation.

58 Thomas Aquinas, *Compendium Theologiae*, 47, in *Theological Texts*, 46–7.

59 "He who is dominated by the idol that he wishes to win, to hold, and to keep – possessed by a desire for possession – has no way to God but that of *turning*, which is a change not only of goal but also of the nature of his movement. [He] is saved by being wakened and educated to solidarity of relation, not by being led in his state of possession towards God." Buber, *I and Thou*, 105. Emphasis added.

60 Philippians 4:9.

## CHAPTER ELEVEN

1 Stephen L. Carter, *The Emperor of Ocean Park* (New York: Vintage, 203), 653.

2 I recognize this may put me at least partially in the camp of Bishop Wright's delicious caricature, Jeremy Smoothtongue, though I hope without the same intellectual obscurantism! (N.T. Wright, *Surprised by Hope: Rethinking Heaven, the Resurrection, and the Mission of the Church* (New York: HarperCollins, 2008), 292.) But fully acknowledging the validity of the various religious traditions seems to me the only place where truth and love, justice and mercy can meet.

3 Susan Neiman, *Moral Clarity: A Guide for Grown-Up Idealists* (Orlando: Harcourt, 2008), 92.

4 Mircea Eliade, *A History of Religious Ideas*, Vol. 1: *From the Stone Age to the Eleusinian Mysteries* (Chicago: University of Chicago Press, 1978), xiii. Emphasis added.

5 William James, *The Varieties of Religious Experience* (New York: Collier Books, 1961), 57–8, 390.

6 John L. Esposito, *The Future of Islam* (New York: Oxford University Press, 2010), 71–3.

7 Charles Taylor, *A Secular Age* (Cambridge and London: The Belknap Press of Harvard University Press, 2007), 646–75, 688–9. Maimonides comments perceptively on how the Axial religions grew out of their pre-Axial predecessors, preserving the forms while reversing the message: *The Guide for the*

*Perplexed*, translated by M. Friedländer (New York: Dover Publications, 1956), 323.

8  Diarmaid MacCulloch explains the religious paradox (in a Christian context) in a similar way: "[Q]uite apart from the propensity of human beings to become irrationally tribal about the most obscure matters, we need to remember that ordinary Christians experienced their God through the Church's liturgy and in a devotional intensity which seized them in holy places. Once they had experienced the divine in such particular settings, having absorbed one set of explanations about what the divine was, anything from outside which disrupted these explanation threatened their access to divine power. That would provide ample reason for the stirring of rage and fear." *Chritianity: The First Three Thousand Years* (New York: Viking, 2010), 222. Even someone as learned and wise as Maimonides could assert that the difference between Judaism and other religious traditions was like the difference between a "living, rational human being and a statue resembling a human being." However he also implicitly acknowledged that the spiritual insights of the three Western traditions are very similar, suggesting that, as imitators, Christianity and Islam had helped spread the message of Judaism to the ends of the earth. *Letter to Yemen*, cited in Joel L. Kraemer, *Maimonides: The Life and World of One of Civilization's Greatest Minds* (New York: Doubleday, 2008), 238–40.

9  John Stuart Mill, "Coleridge," in F.R. Leavis, ed., *Mill on Bentham and Coleridge* (Cambridge: Cambridge University Press, 1980), 105.

10  Robert Conquest, *Reflections on a Ravaged Century* (London: John Murray, 1999). "Is it not obvious that our century has been an almost unrelieved horror?" Neil Postman, *Building a Bridge to the Eighteenth Century: How the Past Can Improve Our Future* (New York: Alfred A. Knopf, 1999), 14. On the extent of the slaughter in eastern Europe, see Timothy Snyder, *Bloodlands: Europe between Hitler and Stalin* (New York: Basic Books, 2010); "Hitler vs. Stalin: Who Killed More?" *New York Review of Books* 58, no. 4 (10 March 2011), 35–6. On China, see Perry Link, "China: From Famine to Oslo," *New York Review of Books* 58, no. 1 (13 January 2011), 52–7; Roderick MacFarquhar, "The Worst Man-Made Catastrophe, Ever," *New York Review of Books* 58, no. 2 (10 February 2011), 26–8.

11  *Brhadāranyaka Upanishad*, Book v, Chapter 2, in *The Upanishads*, translated and edited by Valerie J. Roebuck (London: Penguin Books, 2003), 82.

12  *The Baghavad Gita*, 3, translated and with a preface by Eknath Easwaran (New York: Vintage Books, 2000), 17–22.

13  *The Koran* 4:114, translated by N.J. Dawood (London: Penguin Books, 2003), 73.

14  *The Book of Chuang Tzu* in Mark Forstater, ed., *The Tao: Finding the Way of Balance and Harmony* (New York: Plume, 2003), 123.

15  Saint Augustine, *City of God*, translated by Henry Bettenson (London: Penguin Books, 2003), 873; Edward Conze, *Buddhism: A Short History* (Oxford: Oneworld Publications, 1993, 2008), 26.

16  *Buddhist Scriptures*, selected and edited by Edward Conze (Harmondsworth: Penguin Books, 1959, 1969), 55.

17  Karen Armstrong, *The Great Transformation: The Beginnings of Our Religious Traditions* (New York: Alfred A. Knopf, 2006), 390.

18  Friedrich Schleiermacher, *On Religion: Speeches to Its Cultured Despisers*, translated by John Oman (New York: Harper and Row, 1958), 163.

19  James, *The Varieties of Religious Experience*, 390.

20  Karl Rahner, *The Practice of Faith: A Handbook of Contemporary Spirituality* (New York: Crossroad, 1983), 219.

21  Saint Augustine, *City of God*, 547.

22  Ibid, 842.

23  Deirdre N. McCloskey, *The Bourgeois Virtues: Ethics for an Age of Commerce* (Chicago: University of Chicago Press, 2006), 193.

24  In early 2011, Rabbi Richard Marker, chairman of the International Jewish Committee for Interreligious Consultation, told a Paris conference marking forty years of dialogue between Jews and Roman Catholics that the dialogue should be extended to Muslims: "The focus of the world is no longer specifically on Jewish-Christian amity. We must, for so many reasons, involve the third of our Abrahamic siblings ... Islam." Tom Heneghan, "Extend RC-Jewish amity to Islam, conference told," *Ottawa Citizen*, 6 March 2011, A8.

25  A great many mainstream Islamic leaders have condemned the outlook and violence of Islamic extremists and fundamentalists, but have received little recognition and support in the West for doing so. See Esposito, *The Future of Islam*, 29–33, 99–105.

26  *The Koran* 2:189–92, 50:45, 2:255–7, 16:123–27, 42:15, translated by Dawood, 29, 367, 38, 196, 340.

27  Esposito, *The Future of Islam*, 55, 105–111.

28  On the highly sexualized and even pornographic media culture in which children of Western countries are now immersed, see the *Avis* of Quebec's Conseil du statut de la femme, *Le sexe dans les médias: obstacle aux rapports égalitaires*, May 2008. http://www.csf.gouv.qc.ca/relechargement_publication/index.php?id=429

29  Timothy Garton Ash, "All of Us, in a Mirror, Darkly," *The Globe and Mail*, Thursday, 10 August 2006, A15.

30  Terry Eagleton, *Reason, Faith, and Revolution: Reflections on the God Debate* (New Haven: Yale University Press, 2009), 154.

31  Neiman, *Moral Clarity*, 241.

32  "[D]espite, no, because of his absoluteness God is no impersonal It, no un-moved receptacle of the transcendence and love of the spiritual person; he is the living God." Rahner, *The Practice of Faith*, 134.

33  Martha Nussbaum, *The Therapy of Desire: Theory and Practice in Hellenistic Ethics* (Princeton: Princeton University Press, 1994), 201.

34  Charles Norris Cochrane, *Christianity and Classical Culture* (New York: Oxford University Press, 1976); Martha Nussbaum, *The Fragility of Goodness: Luck and Ethics in Greek Tragedy and Philosophy* (Cambridge: Cambridge University Press, 1986); *The Therapy of Desire*. On the re-emergence of "fate" in the modern culture of self-assertion, see Martin Buber, *I and Thou*, second edition, translated by Ronald Gregor Smith (New York: Charles Scribner's Sons, 1958), 56–8.

35  Paul Tillich, *The Courage to Be* (New Haven: Yale University Press, 1952), 166.

36  Iris Murdoch, *Metaphysics as a Guide to Morals* (London: Vintage, 1992, 2003), 83.

37  Augustine, *City of God*, 870. René Descartes, *Discourse on Method* in Elizabeth S. Haldane and G.R.T. Ross, eds., *The Philosophical Works of René Descartes*, Vol. 1 (Cambridge: Cambridge University Press, 1969), 106–8; Michael Frayn, *The Human Touch: Our Part in the Creation of the Universe* (London: Faber and Faber, 2006), 55.

38  Marcel Gauchet, *The Disenchantment of the World: A Political History of Religion*, translated by Oscar Bruge (Princeton: Princeton University Press, 1997), 45.

39  C.G. Jung, "The Difference between Eastern and Western Thinking," translated by R.F.C. Hull, in Joseph Campbell, ed. *The Portable Jung*, (New York: Viking Press, 1971), 494.

40  *Buddhist Scriptures*, selected and edited by Edward Conze (Harmondsworth: Penguin Books, 1959, 1969), 92.

41  Acaranga Sutra, 1.4.1.1–2, in Paul Dundas, *The Jains*, second edition. (London and New York, 2002), 41–2, cited in Armstrong, *The Great Transformation*, 242.

42  Arthur Waley, *The Way and Its Power*, quoted in Joseph Campbell, *The Masks of God: Oriental Mythology* (Harmondsworth: Penguin Books, 1976), 427.

43  Wilfred Cantwell Smith, *The Faith of Other Men* (New York: Mentor Books, 1965), 70; David Bohm, *Wholeness and the Implicate Order* (London: Routledge, 1980), 9–11.

CHAPTER TWELVE

1  Intergovernmental Panel on Climate Change (IPCC), Fourth Assessment
   Report, *Climate Change 2007: Synthesis Report*, Summary for Policymakers,
   17 November 2007, 1–5.
2  Jim Hansen, "The Threat to the Planet," *The New York Review of Books*
   (13 July 2006), 13. In the shorter term, a 2009 study forecast a potential sea
   level rise of 0.5 metres by 2050, already putting at risk between $25–28 bil-
   lion in global assets. Tim Lenton, Anthony Footitt, and Andrew Dlugolecki,
   *Major Tipping Points in the Earth's Climate System and Consequences for
   the Insurance Sector* (Gland, Switzerland and Munich: World Wide Fund
   for Nature (WWF) and Allianz SE, November 2009), 26–36.
3  Briefing document on the expected impacts of global climate change, prepared by the European Union's foreign policy chief, Javier Solana, and
   Europe's commissioner for external relations, Benita Ferrero-Waldner, for a
   summit of twenty-seven European heads of government, March 2008. *The
   Guardian Weekly*, 14–20 March 2008, 2. The following year, a planning document for the Canadian Armed Forces echoed many of the same security
   concerns and predicted the need for military interventions in international
   and intra-national conflicts caused by climate change. *The future security
   environment, 2008–2030/L'environnement de la sécurité future 2008–2030*
   (Ottawa: National Defence, 27 January 2009). http://www.ledevoir.com/
   documents/pdf/canada_securite.pdf
4  Elizabeth Kolbert, *Field Notes from a Catastrophe: Man, Nature, and
   Climate Change* (New York: Bloomsbury, 2006), 187.
5  Tim Flannery, *The Weather Makers: How We are Changing the Climate and
   What It Means for Life on Earth* (Toronto: HarperCollins, 2006), 209.
6  IPCC, *Climate Change 2007*, 22–3.
7  "God having become Other to the world, the world now became Other to
   humans, in two ways: by its objectivity at the level of representation, and
   by its ability to be transformed at the level of action." Marcel Gauchet, *The
   Disenchantment of the World: A Political History of Religion*, translated
   by Oscar Bruge (Princeton: Princeton University Press, 1997), 95.
8  "The ideas of this oration proved to be enormously influential in the late
   Renaissance, and in the longer term they can be seen as setting the scene for
   the Enlightenment assertion of human autonomy in the eighteenth century."
   Alister McGrath, *Christianity's Dangerous Idea: The Protestant Revolution
   – A History from the Sixteenth Century to the Twenty-First* (New York:
   HarperCollins, 2007), 34.

9 Pico della Mirandola, *Oration on the Dignity of Man*, in E. Cassirer, P.O. Kristeller, and J.H. Randall, eds., *The Renaissance Philosophy of Man* (Chicago: University of Chicago Press, 1948), pp. 224–5, quoted in Charles Taylor, *Sources of the Self: The Making of the Modern Identity* (Cambridge, Mass.: Harvard University Press, 1989), 199–200. Emphasis added.

10 Quoted in R.G. Collingwood, *The Idea of History* (New York: Oxford University Press, 1956), 269. Deirdre McCloskey (citing Macaulay) notes that, as Lord Chancellor (the rough equivalent of the modern prime minister), Bacon was the last man in England to use the torture rack for official purposes. Deirdre N. McCloskey, *The Bourgeois Virtues: Ethics for an Age of Commerce* (Chicago: University of Chicago Press, 2006), 369.

11 Francis Bacon, *The New Organon*, in *The Complete Essays of Francis Bacon* (New York: Washington Square Press, 1963), 250.

12 Ibid., 262–3.

13 René Descartes, *Discourse on Method* in Elizabeth S. Haldane and G.R.T. Ross, eds., *The Philosophical Works of René Descartes*, Vol. 1 (Cambridge: Cambridge University Press, 1969), 119.

14 Taylor, *Sources of the Self*, 101, 384, 413, 503.

15 Victor Hugo, "Author's Preface to the First Edition of *Hernani*, 1830," in *The Works of Victor Hugo*, Vol. 9 (Boston and New York: The Jefferson Press, n.d.), 3.

16 Taylor, *Sources of the Self*, 375, 390.

17 Lionel Trilling, *Sincerity and Authenticity* (Cambridge, Mass.: Harvard University Press, 1972), 122.

18 Walter Pater, *The Renaissance* (1873), quoted in Iris Murdoch, *Metaphysics as a Guide to Morals* (London: Vintage, 1992, 2003), 217–18.

19 Friedrich Nietzsche, "The Beginning of 'The Will to Power,'" in Walter Kaufmann, ed., *Existentialism from Dostoevsky to Sartre* (Cleveland: World Publishing Company, 1956), 109–11.

20 Tim Flannery, *The Weather Makers*, 17.

21 Stephen L. Carter, *The Culture of Disbelief: How American Law and Politics Trivialize Religious Devotion* (New York: Anchor Books, 1993, 1994), 23–43.

22 Moses Luzatto, *Mesillat Yesharim*, Chapter 1, in Arthur Hertzberg, ed., *Judaism* (New York: Washington Square Press, 1963), 191. Emphasis added.

23 Genesis 1:26, 28.

24 John Locke, *The Second Treatise on Civil Government* in John Locke, *On Politics and Education* (Roslyn, NY: Walter J. Black, 1947), Chapter 5, 87–99.

25 Bacon, Descartes, Newton, and Locke were the heroes of Voltaire's *Lettres philosophiques*. Voltaire said that Bacon's thought was the "scaffolding"

within which the "new philosophy" of the Enlightenment was built. *Lettres philosophiques* (Paris: Garnier-Flammarion, 1964), 77.

26 William Barrett, *The Illusion of Technique* (New York: Anchor Press/ Doubleday, 1978), 335.

27 John C. Weaver, *The Great Land Rush and the Making of the Modern World* (Montreal and Kingston: McGill-Queen's University Press, 2003), 348.

28 Flannery, *The Weather Makers*, 160, 17.

29 Gregory Bateson, *Mind and Nature: A Necessary Unity* (New York: Bantam Books, 1980), 21, 19. Emphasis added.

30 Karl Jaspers, *Way to Wisdom*, translated by Ralph Manheim (New Haven: Yale University Press, 1960), 160.

31 In philosophical language, this might be called "the transcendental necessity of holism." Charles Taylor, *A Secular Age* (Cambridge and London: The Belknap Press of Harvard University Press, 2007), 157. Martin Buber calls it "the *a priori* of relation." *I and Thou*, second edition, translated by Ronald Gregor Smith (New York: Charles Scribner's Sons, 1958), 69.

32 Neil Postman, *Building a Bridge to the Eighteenth Century: How the Past Can Improve Our Future* (New York: Alfred A. Knopf, 1999).

33 Margaret Donaldson, *Human Minds: An Exploration* (New York: Allen Lane, 1993), 264.

34 Susan Neiman, *Moral Clarity: A Guide for Grown-Up Idealists* (Orlando: Harcourt, 2008), 215–85. See also David Sorkin, *The Religious Enlightenment: Protestants, Jews, and Catholics from London to Vienna* (Princeton: Princeton University Press, 2008).

35 James Lovelock, *Gaia: A New Look at Life on Earth* (Oxford: Oxford University Press, 1979).

36 Thomas McFarland, *Coleridge and the Pantheist Tradition* (London: Oxford University Press, 1969), Chapter 2, 53–106.

37 On the "juridical/penal" bias of Western Christian spirituality, see Taylor, *A Secular Age*, 78–9, 233, 262–3, 318–19, 649, 651–6, 670.

38 W.H. Auden, *A Certain World: A Commonplace Book* (London: Faber and Faber, 1971), 181.

39 "[T]hat which in myself is not only myself." Jaspers, *Way to Wisdom*, 55.

### CHAPTER THIRTEEN

1 Steve Bruce, ed., *Religion and Modernization* (Oxford: Oxford University Press, 1992), 6, quoted in Charles Taylor, *A Secular Age* (Cambridge and London: The Belknap Press of Harvard University Press, 2007), 430.

2  Taylor, *A Secular Age*, 430–1.

3  Ibid, 435.

4  Max Weber, *The Theory of Social and Economic Organization*, translated by A.M. Henderson and Talcott Parsons, edited with an introduction by Talcott Parsons (New York: Oxford University Press, 1947).

5  Ingrid Rowland, "The Real Caravaggio," *The New York Review of Books*, 7 October 1999, 14.

6  Stephen L. Carter, *The Culture of Disbelief: How American Law and Politics Trivialize Religious Devotion* (New York: Anchor Books, 1993, 1994).

7  Marilynne Robinson, *The Death of Adam: Essays on Modern Thought* (New York: Picador, 2005), 28–75. See Leibniz' contrast between the ancient view of the "natural" expressed by Aristotle and the modern one expressed by Hobbes. *Essais de Théodicée* (Paris: Garnier-Flammarion, 1969), 251.

8  Matthew, 22:21; Mark, 12:17; Luke, 20:25. On Pope Gelasius, see Diarmaid MacCulloch, *Christianity: The First Three Thousand Years* (New York: Viking, 2010), 323.

9  Karl Rahner, *The Practice of Faith: A Handbook of Contemporary Spirituality* (New York: Crossroad, 1983), 218.

10  Marcel Gauchet, *The Disenchantment of the World: A Political History of Religion*, translated by Oscar Bruge (Princeton: Princeton University Press, 1997), 134.

11  Thomas Aquinas, *IV Sentences*, XLIV. iii. 4, in St Thomas Aquinas, *Theological Texts*, selected and translated by Thomas Gilby (London: Oxford University Press, 1954), 399.

12  "[A] kind of theocracy where the church could simply tell everyone what to do … always led to disaster." N.T. Wright, *Surprised by Hope: Rethinking Heaven, the Resurrection, and the Mission of the Church* (New York: HarperCollins, 2008), 112.

13  Carter, *The Culture of Disbelief*, 4.

14  Robert N. Bellah, Richard Madsen, William M. Sullivan, Ann Swidler, and Steven M. Tipton, *Habits of the Heart*, updated edition with a new introduction (Berkeley and Los Angeles: University of California Press, 1985, 1996), 219.

15  Reginald Bibby, *Restless Gods: The Renaissance of Religion in Canada* (Toronto: Stoddart, 2002); Mirko Petricevic, "Encouraging Signs for Churches," *The Record* (Kitchener-Waterloo, Ont.), Monday, 8 April 2002. http://therecord.com/links/generic_020408155136.html

16  World Values Survey, cited in Donald Savoie, *Court Government and the Collapse of Accountability* (Toronto: University of Toronto Press, 2008), 102–6.

17  Taylor, *A Secular Age*, 431.

18  Thomas Aquinas, Disputations, xiv *de Veritate*, 1, in *Theological Texts*, 196–7.

19  John Macquarrie, *20th Century Religious Thought* (London: SCM Press, 1971), 362–4.

20  Margaret Donaldson, *Human Minds: An Exploration* (New York: Allen Lane, 1993), 159.

21  Arthur Hertzberg, ed., *Judaism* (New York: Washington Square Press, 1963), 177.

22  *The Book of Chuang Tzu* in Mark Forstater, ed., *The Tao: Finding the Way of Balance and Harmony* (New York: Plume, 2003), 216.

23  *Buddhist Scriptures*, selected and edited by Edward Conze (Harmondsworth: Penguin Books, 1959 1969), 56.

24  Plotinus, *Enneads*, vi, 9, 11, in Elmer O'Brien, ed., *The Essential Plotinus* (New York: Mentor Books, 1964), 88. "He that is sent out in the strength of the revelation takes with him, in his eyes, an image of God; however far this exceeds the senses, yet he takes it with him in the eye of the spirit, in that visual power of his spirit, which is not metaphorical but wholly real." Martin Buber, *I and Thou*, second edition, translated by Ronald Gregor Smith (New York: Charles Scribner's Sons, 1958), 117–18.

25  Ephesians 1:18.

26  *Buddhist Scriptures*, 124.

27  R.G. Collingwood, *Faith and Reason: Essays in the Philosophy of Religion*, ed. Lionel Rubinoff (Chicago: Quadrangle Books, 1968), 143.

28  Owen Barfield, *What Coleridge Thought* (Middletown: Wesleyan University Press, 1971), 10–11.

29  Rahner, *The Practice of Faith*, 21, 31, 35, 61.

30  John S. Dunne, *The City of the Gods: A Study in Myth and Morality* (New York: Macmillan, 1965), 4. "[Reason] reaches its limit not in some final question-stopping answer but rather in a final answer-stopping question." Denys Turner, *Faith, Reason and the Existence of God* (Cambridge: Cambridge University Press, 2004), 232.

## CHAPTER FOURTEEN

1  "As the condition that makes knowledge and freedom in everyday life possible ... God is experienced in [his] necessity and inescapability, so that the person is faced with the question whether he will also make this inescapability the centre of his existence, in free, primal trust; or whether he will suppress it by escaping to the surveyable individual realities in his life which he

can control." Karl Rahner, *The Practice of Faith: A Handbook of Contemporary Spirituality* (New York: Crossroad, 1983), 59.

2　Taylor, *Sources of the Self: The Making of the Modern Identity* (Cambridge, Mass.: Harvard University Press, 1989), 23, 211. Denys Turner points out that the "denial of God" has become "unalarming" to the "practical mentality" of contemporary culture "for which nothing is required except that nothing is required." *Faith, Reason and the Existence of God* (Cambridge: Cambridge University Press, 2004), 153.

3　"[T]he question: what for? cannot be suppressed completely. It is silenced but always ready to come into the open." Paul Tillich, *The Courage to Be* (New Haven: Yale University Press, 1952), 111.

4　Samuel Taylor Coleridge, *Aids to Reflection* (Port Washington, New York: Kennikat Press, 1971), 118. Emphasis added. "[L]a véritable paix, " as Pascal said, "est inséparable de la vérité. " *Lettres écrites à un provincial* (Paris: Garnier-Flammarion, 1967), 287. Truth is not just a mental or abstract thing. It's also the truth about a life, or the way a life is lived, in relation to truth. "[T]he sort of life which will in fact be true to itself – though the 'self' to which it will at last be true is the redeemed self, the transformed self, not merely the 'discovered' self of popular thought." N.T. Wright, *After You Believe: Why Christian Character Matters* (New York: HarperCollins, 2010), 7. To have found truth is not necessarily a matter of agreeing to certain propositions or statements, but rather to have entered into a certain way of life. It is not so much a matter of *knowing* truth as *being* in truth. Leszek Kolakowski, *Religion* (New York: Oxford University Press, 1983), 219. Rahner, *The Practice of Faith*, 12, 65; Tillich, *The Courage to Be*, 81.

5　Karl Rahner suggests that concern for ourselves and our lives as a whole, "as one," is what Christians mean by "salvation." *The Practice of Faith*, 261. N.T. Wright puts this in a splendid, pithy formula: "We are saved not as souls but as wholes." *Surprised by Hope: Rethinking Heaven, the Resurrection, and the Mission of the Church* (New York: HarperCollins, 2008), 199.

6　Charles Taylor has suggested that those who argue for an entirely secular or non-religious approach to life are fooling themselves, because they're trying to have their cake and eat it too. They think they can jettison religious practices, but hang onto the moral and ethical reflexes that have their roots in the Western religious traditions. The language and rhetoric of secular thinkers implicitly rely on values their own explicit world view can't supply, but are simply lingering holdovers, a kind of afterglow, from the previous religious culture they oppose. The value of "universal benevolence," for example, continues to play a large role in modern, public culture, at least for the time being. It provides the moral energy that fuels the impulses to improvement and reform that are such a big part of modern public life, and are among the things we can be most proud of, in our modern world. But "universal benevolence" is just a secularized form of the religious value of "charity." Why should it be expected to survive in a world where its religious root, and even the memory of it, have withered? *Sources of the Self*, 319, 367, 448, 455, 517. N.T. Wright emphasizes the importance of Christian "eschatology," the "future-oriented" outlook of the Christian New Testament, one that looks forward not so much to life in a future heaven as to the future "transformation" of our own "earth." *Surprised by Hope*, 101.

7 *Buddhist Scriptures*, selected and edited by Edward Conze (Harmondsworth: Penguin Books, 1959 1969), 112–13, 186–7, 236.

8 *The Koran* 29:40, 31:21, translated by N.J. Dawood (London: Penguin Books, 2003), 281, 289.

9 Matthew 7:26; 6:19; John 6:27; Luke 12:33.

10 Québécois film director Bernard Émond says: "Pendant toute ma vie de cinéaste j'ai eu la conviction qu'on devait faire des films 'pour' quelque chose, quelque chose qui serait comme au-dessus des films, qui les justifierait, et sans quoi le cinéma ne serait qu'une technique perfectionnée du mensonge." Cited in Louis Cornellier, "Bernard Émond ou le droit à la tragédie," *Le Devoir*, 29 January 2011, F6.

11 Charles Taylor, *A Secular Age* (Cambridge and London: The Belknap Press of Harvard University Press, 2007), 430–1; Thomas Aquinas, Commentary, 2 *Corinthians*, ii, lect. 3, in St Thomas Aquinas, *Theological Texts*, selected and translated by Thomas Gilby (London: Oxford University Press, 1954), 184.

12 Christopher Lasch, *The Culture of Narcissism: American Life in an Age of Diminishing Expectations* (New York: W.W. Norton, 1978).

13 Pascal, *Pensées et Opuscules* (Paris: Larousse, 1934, 1961), 63–4. "Les preuves ne convainquent que l'esprit. La coutume fait nos preuves les plus fortes et les plus crues; elle incline l'automate, qui entraine l'esprit sans qu'il y pense ... en avoir toujours les preuves présentes, c'est trop d'affaire. Il faut acquérir une créance plus facile, qui est celle de l'habitude, qui, sans violence, sans art, sans argument, nous fait croire les choses, et incline toutes les puissances à cette croyance, en sorte que notre âme y tombe naturellement. "

14 Pascal, *Pensées* (Paris: Garnier-Flammarion, 1973), 129. Emphasis added. "Vous voulez aller à la foi, et vous n'en savez le chemin ... apprenez de ceux qui ont été liés comme vous et qui parient maintenant tout leur bien: ce sont gens qui savent ce chemin que vous voudrez suivre, et guérir d'un mal dont

vous voulez guérir. Suivez la manière par où ils ont commencé: c'est en faisant tout comme s'ils croyaient." My translation.

15 Plato, *Phaedo*, in *Great Dialogues of Plato*, translated by W.H.D. Rouse, edited by Eric H. Warmington and Philip G. Rouse (New York: New American Library, 1956), 518.

16 Arthur Hertzberg, editor, *Judaism* (New York: Washington Square Press, 1963), 59.

17 Confucius, *The Analects*, 12.1, translated by D.C. Lau (London: Penguin Books, 1979), 112.

18 Bruno Bettelheim, *The Informed Heart* (Harmondsworth: Penguin Books, 1986), 16, cited in Margaret Donaldson, *Human Minds: An Exploration* (New York: Allen Lane, 1993), 197–8. Emphasis added.

19 Rahner, *The Practice of Faith*, 45.

20 Edward Conze, *Buddhism: A Short History* (Oxford: Oneworld Publications, 1993, 2008), xi.

21 Psalm 34:8

22 Taylor, *A Secular Age*, 833, n17. "In the realm of existence there are realities which can be discovered to be real, 'true' and 'certain' only in being chosen." Rahner, *The Practice of Faith*, 42.

23 "[T]he premises of faith have their source in historical tradition." Karl Jaspers, *Way to Wisdom*, translated by Ralph Manheim (New Haven: Yale University Press, 1960), 94.

24 Stephen L. Carter, *The Culture of Disbelief: How American Law and Politics Trivialize Religious Devotion* (New York: Anchor Books, 1993, 1994), 231.

25 Samuel Johnson, *Preface to Shakespeare* in *Lives of the Most Eminent English Poets* (London: Frederick Warne and Co., n.d.), 507.

26 "[T]he virtues of faith, hope, and love, as expressed in worship, are to be worked at, thought through, figured out, and then planned, prepared and celebrated with a new depth that will stir passions which the 'matches' of quick romantic attraction could not reach … [T]he church that cherishes a mature, deep, and long-lasting love for God will want to think carefully about how to worship him – not because that worship isn't 'coming naturally' but because what they're interested in is the '*second* nature,' the developed and sustained virtues, of a love that has thought through why it is worshipping this God and has figured out ways of doing so which express that deeply and richly." Wright, *After You Believe*, 221.

27 Attributed to a "one-time Dean of the School of Theology of the University of the South in Sewanee, Tennessee" (perhaps William Porcher DuBose?),

cited in Robert J. Moore and Gerald T. Rayner, *Audacious Anglicans: Heroes of the Anglican Communion* (Picton: Blue Jay Publishing, 2008), 216.

28 Martin Buber calls these primal encounters the "original relational incident." *I and Thou*, second edition, translated by Ronald Gregor Smith (New York: Charles Scribner's Sons, 1958), 54.

29 Hertzberg, ed., *Judaism*, 64.

30 On the two kinds of spiritual community, see Thomas Aquinas, *Summa Theologica*, 3a. viii. 3, in *Theological Texts*, 338.

31 Carter, *The Culture of Disbelief*, 142, 271; Rahner, *The Practice of Faith*, 167.

32 "Man knows himself in the intersubjective community of which he is just a part, in the support and opposition the community finds in its enveloping world of sense, in the tools of its making, in the rites and ceremonies that at once occupy its leisure, vent its psychic awareness of cosmic significance, express its incipient grasp of universal order and its standards of praise and blame." Bernard J.F. Lonergan, S.J., *Insight : A Study of Human Understanding* (New York and London: Philosophical Library and Dartman Longman and Todd, 1958, 1973), 536.

33 Robert N. Bellah, Richard Madsen, William M. Sullivan, Ann Swidler, and Steven M. Tipton, *Habits of the Heart*, updated edition with a new introduction (Berkeley and Los Angeles: University of California Press, 1985, 1996), 219–49, 275–96.

34 Alasdair MacIntyre, *After Virtue*, second edition (Notre Dame: University of Notre Dame Press, 1984), 223.

35 Iris Murdoch, *Metaphysics as a Guide to Morals* (London: Vintage, 1992, 2003), 433. Emphasis added.

36 Joseph Veroff, Elizabeth Douvan, and Richard A. Koulka, *The Inner American: A Self-Portrait from 1957 to 1976* (New York: Basic Books, 1981), 19–25, 115–22, cited in Bellah et al., *Habits of the Heart*, 319. On anxiety, see Tillich, *The Courage to Be*, 32–85.

37 Taylor, *A Secular Age*, 680.

38 Ibid, 719.

39 Rahner, *The Practice of Faith*, 37–41, 265.

40 Eagleton, *Reason, Faith and Revolution*, 111.

41 Taylor, *A Secular Age*, 173.

42 "Modern market societies tend to be secular, relativist, pragmatic and materialistic. They are this by virtue of what they do, not just of what they believe. As far as these attitudes go, they do not have much of a choice." Eagleton, *Reason, Faith and Revolution*, 143. Marcel Gauchet lists some of the

"practices" of the modern culture of self-assertion that "carry" the beliefs of unbelief: "taking hold of human bodies to inform them of the full potential of the powers and pleasures they are capable of ... the refusal to suffer one's bequeathed lot, the concern to control its mysteries and functions, and the attempt to maximize its capabilities and resources. To understand, to master, and to increase ... to embrace our own flesh ... an endless reworking of the entire terrestrial condition ... the uncontrollable necessity to innovate ... an imperative to create a new maximizing transformative relation to the given." *The Disenchantment of the World: A Political History of Religion*, translated by Oscar Burge (Princeton: Princeton University Press, 1997), 96–7, 179.

43 Robert Bellah and his colleagues make a similar point in observing that the "practices of separation" (or, in my language, self-assertion) establish a "first language" for modern Americans, so the "practices of commitment" (or reverence) can generate no more than a "second language." Bellah et al., *Habits of the Heart*, 154–5, 210, 334–5.

44 Charles Taylor, *Hegel* (Cambridge: Cambridge University Press, 1975), 382; *Sources of the Self*, 91–2; Bernard Williams, *Ethics and the Limits of Philosophy* (Cambridge, Mass.: Harvard University Press, 1985), 114, 146–8, 152–4; Wright, *Surprised by Hope*, 263.

45 Rahner, *The Practice of Faith*, 59–65

46 Bernard Lonergan, *Verbum: Word and Idea in Aquinas*, edited by Frederick E. Crowe and Robert M. Doran, *The Collected Works of Bernard Lonergan*, Vol. 2 (Toronto: University of Toronto Press, 1997), 10.

47 Bellah et al., *Habits of the Heart*, 137. Confucius agreed. *The Analects*, 1.12, translated by Lau, 61.

48 Friedrich Schleiermacher, *On Religion: Speeches to Its Cultured Despisers*, translated by John Oman (New York: Harper and Row, 1958), 207. Similarly, Karl Rahner suggests doctrine and dogma can turn into "a secret idol" in which "once again man replaces God with self." *The Practice of Faith*, 68.

49 Kolakowski, *Religion*, 219.

50 Thomas Aquinas, *Summa Theologica*, 2a-2ae. xci. 1, in St Thomas Aquinas, *Philosophical Texts*, selected and translated by Thomas Gilby (London: Oxford University Press, 1951, 1956), 350.

51 Vida Dutton Scudder, *On Journey* in Richard H. Schmidt, ed., *Glorious Companions: Five Centuries of Anglican Spirituality* (Grand Rapids: Wm. B. Eerdmans, 2002), 228.

52 1 Corinthians 4:20. "Man receives ... not a specific 'content' but a Presence, a Presence as power." Buber, *I and Thou*, 110.

53 *The Baghavad Gita*, 3:8, translated and with a preface by Eknath Easwaran (New York: Vintage Books, 2000), 18. See also 25, 90, 94.

54 Jaspers, *Way to Wisdom*, 19.

55 "It is not the *I*, then that is given up, but that false self-asserting instinct." Buber, *I and Thou*, 78.

56 *The Bhagavad Gita*, 5:5, quoted in Joseph Campbell, *Myths to Live By* (New York: Bantam Books, 1973), 126.

57 *The Book of Chuang Tzu* in Mark Forstater, ed., *The Tao: Finding the Way of Balance and Harmony* (New York: Plume, 2003), 93, 60–1.

58 Martin Buber contrasts "self-will" with the "grand will" that is its opposite. *I and Thou*, 59–60, 83.

59 Seyed Hossein Nasr, *Islam: Religion, History, Civilization* (New York: HarperSanFrancisco, 2003), 57.

60 "That which from the point of view of the finite world appears as self-negation is from the point of view of ultimate being the most perfect self-affirmation, the most radical form of courage." Tillich, *The Courage to Be*, 158. Karl Rahner calls this highest form of self-assertion "a radical self-positing of the subject in an unconditional surrender." *The Practice of Faith*, 77.

61 Thomas Aquinas, *Summa Theologica*, 1a-2ae. lxiv. 4, in *Theological Texts*, 182.

62 Ari L. Goldman, *Being Jewish: The Spiritual and Cultural Practice of Judaism Today* (New York: Simon and Schuster, 2000), 263.

63 Saint Augustine, *City of God*, translated by Henry Bettenson (London: Penguin Books, 2003), Book v, Chapters 18–21, 207–16.

64 Taylor, *A Secular Age*, 430. N.T. Wright uses almost the same language in saying that the religious "vision of a genuinely human existence goes *way beyond* Aristotle's 'happiness' and into a different sphere altogether." *After You Believe*, 89. Emphasis added.

65 Vicki Hearne, *Adam's Task: Calling Animals by Name* (New York: Knopf, 1987), 154.

66 G.W.F. Hegel, *The Phenomenology of Mind*, translated by J.B. Baillie (New York: Harper and Rowe, 1967), 607–10; *Philosophy of Right*, §5, §135, in *Hegel's Philosophy of Right* translated with notes by T.M. Knox (Oxford: Oxford University Press, 1952, 1967), 21–2, 89–90.

67 Murdoch, *Metaphysics as a Guide to Morals*, 507.

68 "[E]vil ... has its source in self-will." Plotinus, *Enneads*, v, 1, 1, in Elmer O'Brien, ed., *The Essential Plotinus* (New York: Mentor Books, 1964), 91.

69 *Tao Te Ching* in *The Taoist Classics, The Collected Translations of Thomas Cleary*, Vol. 1 (Boston: Shambhala, 2003), 15.

70 G.W.F Hegel, *Philosophy of Right*, §148, in *Hegel's Philosophy of Right*, 106–7; Williams, *Ethics and the Limits of Philosophy*, 12, 117–18. Value can only come from "the working of the human spirit in the morass of existence in which it always at every moment finds itself immersed." Murdoch, *Metaphysics as a Guide to Morals*, 507. From some broader "horizon" or objective – the ultimate form of which is what some religious traditions call "God." Rahner, *The Practice of Faith*, 146, 212–14.

71 Wright, *Surprised by Hope*, 102.

72 Samuel Johnson, "Sermon 14" in *Sermons*, edited by Jean Hagstrum and James Gray, The Yale Edition of the Works of Samuel Johnson, Vol. 14 (New Haven and London: Yale University Press, 1978), 158. Similarly, from a psychological perspective, William James noted that religious practice "freshens our vital powers ... and imparts endurance to the Subject, or a zest, or a meaning, or an enchantment and glory to the common objects of life." William James, *The Varieties of Religious Experience* (New York: Collier Books, 1961), 391. N.T. Wright suggests why this may occur: "we rise from prayer with the heart formed that bit more securely in its settled second nature of trust and obedience." *After You Believe*, 282.

73 Tillich, *The Courage to Be*, 34.

74 *The Book of Chuang Tzu* in Forstater, ed., *The Tao*, 178; *The Baghavad Gita*, 2:49, translated by Easwaran, 14. In the Western spiritual traditions, Meister Eckhart's teaching of "detachment" comes very close to the Eastern mode of pure reverence from which all self-assertion has been removed. Indeed it was partly for that reason that he was accused of heresy, thus illustrating the difference between Eastern and Western spiritual emphases. But Denys Turner points out that, for Eckhart, the "practice of detachment" is not "the severing of desire's relation with its object but the restoration of desire to a proper relation of objectivity; as we might say, of *reverence* for its object." *The Darkness of God: Negativity in Christian Mysticism* (Cambridge: Cambridge University Press, 1995), Chapter 7, 168–85. Emphasis added.

75 Romans 8:28.

76 Ludwig Feuerbach, *The Essence of Christianity*, in Patrick L. Gardiner, ed., *19th Century Philosophy* (New York: Free Press, 1969), 246.

77 Coleridge, *Aids to Reflection*, 70.

78 In Karl Rahner's words, the human spirit is "sustained by the direction in which it tends" and "supported by what it reaches for." *The Practice of Faith*, 57, 249.

79 Northrop Frye, *Words with Power* (New York: Harcourt Brace Janovich, 1990), 118.

80  A saintly Indian guru once set Joseph Campbell to contemplate on a standard
    question from the *jnana* or "knowledge" yoga: "Where are you between two
    thoughts?" (Joseph Campbell, *Myths to Live By* (New York: Bantam Books,
    1973), 132) Undoubtedly one of the things the guru hoped the exercise would
    demonstrate was that reality is always something beyond language, even be-
    yond thought, and that words are only tools for expressing that reality and
    making it come to consciousness, and are relatively weak tools at best. The
    depths of the spirit often speak to us with sighs and groanings "too deep for
    words." (Romans 8:26) Clearly Frye uses the term "verbal" in harmony with
    the Christian concept of the Word, the Second Person of the Trinity. But wheth-
    er in its Christian or any imaginative context, as Frye himself remarks, there
    seems to be an inevitable point "where a change of element from 'words' to
    'Word' takes place." (*Words with Power*, 132) The Word, in the Christian
    sense, certainly means far more than words in our everyday sense. Like the
    French word "Verbe," by which it is translated in that language, it has more
    the sense of action, motion, and creative power. It expresses something about
    the creative, active force at the heart of life and of reality. As the author of
    *Hebrews* puts it, "the word of God is living and active." (Hebrews 4:12)
81  N.T. Wright, *Paul* (Minneapolis: Fortress Press, 2009), 173.
82  N.T. Wright, *Surprised by Hope: Rethinking Heaven, the Resurrection and
    the Mission of the Church* (New York: HarperCollins, 2008), 239.
83  Charles Taylor, *A Secular Age*, 702. (Emphasis added.) In this kind of deep
    but everyday experience, "object, ground and horizon, and all that we see in
    these, merge – so to speak – into one another." Karl Rahner, *The Practice of
    Faith*, 64; Paul Tillich, *The Courage to Be*, 25, 124–5; Martin Buber, *I and
    Thou*, 33.
84  Karl Rahner, *The Practice of Faith*, 64; Northrop Frye, *Spiritus Mundi:
    Essays on Literature, Myth, and Society* (Bloomington and London: Indiana
    University Press, 1976), *xiii.*
85  Nasr, *Islam*, 87–89.
86  Rahner, *The Practice of Faith*, 10.
87  C.G. Jung, *Memories, Dreams, Reflections* (New York: Pantheon Books,
    1961, 1973), 354.
88  Frye, *Words with Power*, 135. "'Peace which surpasses all understanding'
    is what faith actually is. It is nothing less than a complete transcending of
    earth, of geopolitical concerns … It is a transcendence of what is not living
    or life-affirming toward what is. That is all." David Adams Richards, *God Is*
    (Toronto: Doubleday Canada, 2009), 154.

89 Rahner, *The Practice of Faith*, 275. "If only we love the real world ... if only we venture to surround it with the arms of our spirit, our hands will meet hands that grip them." Buber, *I and Thou*, 94–5.

90 Soren Kierkegaard, *Concluding Unscientific Postscript* in Robert Bretall, ed., *A Kierkegaard Anthology* (New York: Modern Library, 1946), 229.

91 Marilynne Robinson, *Gilead* (Toronto: HarperCollins, 2004), 245.

92 John of the Cross, *The Ascent of Mount Carmel*, 11.3.1, quoted in Turner, *The Darkness of God*, 245.

93 Ari L. Goldman, *Being Jewish: The Spiritual and Cultural Practice of Judaism Today* (New York: Simon and Schuster, 2000), 207–8. Karl Rahner makes a similar comparison with piano practice. *The Practice of Faith*, 56, 256. Aristotle had already made the connection between "moral states" and "exercise": "people develop qualities corresponding to the activities that they pursue. This is evident from the example of people training for any competition or undertaking: they spend all their time in exercising." *The Nicomachean Ethics*, Book 111, Chapter 5, 1114a 5–10, translated by J. A.K. Thomson, revised by Hugh Tredennick (London: Penguin Books, 2004), 63.

94 N.T. Wright describes a "virtuous circle" with five mutually reinforcing elements: scripture, stories, examples, community, and practices – all of which have been discussed in this book. *After You Believe*, 260.

95 The anonymous author of *The Cloud of Unknowing* said that practices of reading, meditation, and prayer are the ladder of "menes" by which the soul makes progress toward the goal of contemplative union with God. Turner, *The Darkness of God*, 197.

96 Wilfred Cantwell Smith, *The Meaning and End of Religion* (New York: Macmillan, 1963), 321. Some passages where the Authorized Version of the Christian Bible used the verb "believe" are now translated in the New Revised Standard Version as "trust." See, for example, 2 Timothy 1:12.

97 Rahner, *The Practice of Faith*, 5–9, 42–3, 59, 61.

98 "[T]he Jewish tradition ... asks first that we pray and later that we feel. Going through the motions of prayer helps lead the worshiper to emotional engagement." Goldman, *Being Jewish*, 209.

99 Thomas Aquinas, *Summa Theologica*, I-II, q. 62, a. 4, in Anton C. Pegis, ed., *Introduction to St. Thomas Aquinas* (New York: Modern Library, 1945, 1948), 595; Wright, *Surprised by Hope*, 72; *After You Believe*, 108.

100 The attempt can be and is made, but it will always feel like an *a posteriori* rationalization of a truth that has already been encountered in quite another way. See, for example, Lonergan, *Insight*, 698–702.

101 Thomas Aquinas, *Summa Theologica*, 1-11, q. 62, in Pegis, ed., *Introduction to St Thomas Aquinas*, 590–6; Thomas Aquinas, *Summa Theologica*, 3a. vii. 2 *ad* 2, in *Philosophical Texts*, 319.

102 Taylor, *Sources of the Self*, 246–7.

103 William Barrett, *The Illusion of Technique* (New York: Anchor Press/ Doubleday, 1978), 231–2.

104 Susan Neiman, *Evil in Modern History: An Alternative History of Philosophy* (Princeton: Princeton University Press, 2002), 317.

105 Isaiah 43:2, 5; Psalm 91:15.

106 Psalm 46. Maimonides pointed out that this and similar passages in scripture can be interpreted as figurative images for the rise and fall of nations. But they surely also have another spiritual meaning closely related to the literal image. Moses Maimonides, *The Guide for the Perplexed*, translated from Arabic by M. Friedländer (New York: Dover Publications, 1956), 209.

107 Samuel Johnson, "Sermon 14" in *Sermons*, 156–8.

108 Dietrich Bonhoeffer echoed Samuel Johnson in asserting that "faith only becomes faith in the act of obedience." *The Cost of Discipleship*, quoted in Marilynne Robinson, *The Death of Adam: Essays on Modern Thought* (New York: Picador, 2005), 119.

109 Psalm 145:18; James 4:8; Psalm 84:6; Psalm 65:9; Jeremiah 17:7–8; Matthew 10:22; Psalm 125:1.

# Index

Abelard, Peter, 222n5

Abraham, 50–1, 65, 77, 150, 213n5, 254n24

absence, 62–5, 67. *See also* presence

act(s), 35–6, 51–2, 55, 79, 92–4, 97–101, 106–7, 110–19, 201–5, 225n45; and reverence, 26, 52, 54, 56, 70, 73, 197, 199–201; and self-assertion, 20, 41, 92, 111, 133, 199–201. *See also* behaviour, deeds, exercise, practice(s), religious life, religious practice

*ahimsá* (Sanskrit,"do no harm"), 143

*Analects* (Confucius), 23–4

*anatta* (Sanskrit "no self"), 132. *See also* Buddha(s)

Anselm, 238n87

apophatic (negative pole of religious life), 239n98. *See also* cataphatic

Aquinas, Thomas, 49, 51, 55–6, 66–7, 78, 86, 88, 90, 92, 95, 101, 103, 115, 117, 137, 151, 162, 177, 180–2, 184, 188, 192, 198, 200, 206, 212n14, 217n20, 225n45, 234n24, 234n28, 243n20, 264n30

Aristotle, 23, 28–9, 40, 49, 73, 84, 88, 96, 98, 106, 113, 115–16, 121–2, 181, 211n14, 213n1, 215n1, 224n30, 236n47, 242n13, 243n19, 247n3, 247n7, 249n27, 259n7, 266n64, 269n93

Armstrong, Karen, 143, 223n17

Arndt, Johann, 225n46

art, 30–1, 35–6, 59–60, 74–5, 90–2, 94, 107–8, 125, 127–9, 187–8, 191, 195–6, 222n6

Ash, Timothy Garton, 147–8

Aslan, Reza, 75

assumption(s), 6, 13, 38, 41–2, 46–9, 51–2, 72–3, 83–6, 89–90, 92–3, 96, 102, 106, 110, 124, 126–8, 129, 139, 141, 145–7, 160–1, 174–9, 184, 188–9, 196, 198–9, 202, 221n1, 223n17, 234n25, 263n23. *See also* presupposition(s)

atheism/atheist, 1, 41, 48, 117, 122–3, 125, 145

attachment, 16–18, 24, 36–7, 202. *See also* connectedness, detachment, holism, oneness, reverence; reverence, virtues of; union, wholeness